THE LIFE OF OLAUDAH EQUIANO
OR GUSTAVUS VASSA, THE AFRICAN

DOVER THRIFT EDITIONS

Olaudah Equiano

DOVER PUBLICATIONS, INC.
MINEOLA, NEW YORK

DOVER THRIFT EDITIONS

GENERAL EDITOR: PAUL NEGRI
EDITOR OF THIS VOLUME: JOSLYN T. PINE

Copyright

Bibliographical Note

This Dover edition, first published in 1999, is an unabridged and slightly corrected republication of the work originally published in 1814 by James Nichols, Leeds (England). A new introductory Note has been specially prepared for this edition.

Library of Congress Cataloging-in-Publication Data

Equiano, Olaudah, b. 1745.
 [Interesting narrative of the life of Olaudah Equiano]
 The life of Olaudah Equiano, or Gustavus Vassa, the African / Olaudah Equiano.
 p. cm. — (Dover thrift editions)
 Originally published: The interesting narrative of the life of Olaudah Equiano, or Gustavus Vassa, the African. A new ed., corr. Leeds : Printed for James Nichols, 1814. With new introductory note.
 ISBN-13: 978-0-486-40661-9 (pbk.)
 ISBN-10: 0-486-40661-X (pbk.)
 1. Equiano, Olaudah, b. 1745. 2. Slaves—Biography. I. Title.
II. Series.
HT869.E6A3 1999
305.5'67'092—dc21
[B]
 98–48384
 CIP

Manufactured in the United States by LSC Communications
40661X13 2018
www.doverpublications.com

Note

I have no hesitation in saying that three-fourths of the slaves *sent abroad* from Africa are the fruit of wars fomented by the avarice of our own race. We stimulate the negro's passions by the introduction of wants and fancies never dreamed of by the simple native, while slavery [in Africa] was an institution of domestic need and custom alone. But what was once a luxury has now ripened into an absolute necessity; so that *man*, in truth has become the coin of Africa.
— Capt. Theodore Canot, *Adventures of an African Slaver* (1854)

ONE VICTIM of the evil compellingly described above was Olaudah Equiano (c. 1745–c. 1797[1]), also known as Gustavus Vassa, an Ibo from northeast Nigeria, West Africa, kidnapped at age eleven, and sold into slavery. He experienced the tortures often associated with the horrendous "middle passage" while being shipped to Barbados by British slavers. Traditionally, the slave ships set out first from a home port bound for the Atlantic coast of Africa. After exchanging their cargoes of various goods for slaves, they departed Africa for the West Indies or another destination on the American continents—the so-called middle passage, or second leg of the voyage—where the human cargo was stored onboard in the most inhumane conditions imaginable.[2] Finally, the ships would head homeward, laden with products from the

[1] Most major dates in Olaudah Equiano's life should be considered approximate; they vary from source to source, as do the more general time frames of some of the factual information.

[2] To again quote Captain Canot: "As I crawled between decks, I could not imagine how this little army was to be packed or draw breath in a hold but twenty-two inches high! . . . we made them lie down in each other's laps, like sardines in a can, and in this way obtained space for the entire cargo." And again, regarding a smallpox epidemic aboard another slave ship: "At length death was satisfied, but not until the 800 beings we had shipped in high health had dwindled to 497 skeletons."

American plantations. Molasses was one of the most highly valued of the commodities obtained from the slave trade, since it was used to make rum—which, in turn, served as currency to buy more slaves for the next voyage.

British slavers later brought Olaudah Equiano to Virginia where he was sold to a British naval officer. Traveling widely with his master, he became a worthy seaman in his own right, participating in major naval battles during the French and Indian wars, as well as in the search for a northwest passage led by the Phipps expedition of 1772–1773. And finally, after more than a decade of enslavement, Equiano earned enough money to buy his freedom, and settled in England. There he became a central figure in the British abolitionist movement, initiated by the Quakers[3] whose stand against the slave trade dated back to 1671, when their founder George Fox expressed strong anti-slavery sentiments. In addition to Equiano's role as a forceful lecturer intent upon exposing the barbarism and cruelties of slavery, he was appointed in 1786 to serve as commissary for the ship that was to carry over 500 of London's freed slaves to establish a settlement in Freetown, Sierra Leone (at that time a British colony on the west coast of Africa), a voyage laudable in intention but a failure in the event.

Olaudah Equiano's most valuable and enduring achievement, however, is contained in the present volume—his autobiography—written and published in London in 1789 when he was forty-four years old. In his own time, the work was a best-seller and published in nine different editions, including an American edition (1791), and German and Dutch editions (1790 and 1791, respectively). Eventually, by 1837, nine more editions were published. It remained in print well into the mid-19th century, and helped spur the American abolitionist movement. In our own time, the book is regarded by scholars as the prototypical slave narrative, one of a handful of documents which form the genesis of the black literary tradition. It is also regarded as an outgrowth of the genre of spiritual autobiography (generally marked by three phases: the life of sin, conversion, and rebirth), exhibiting the classic three-part structure of slave narrative literature: slavery, escape, and freedom.

Equiano's story is unique in its inclusion of vivid descriptions of African culture and society before the wrenching onslaught of the white man and the slave trade. At the same time, Equiano does not blind himself to the corruption of those of his countrymen who were lured by the promise of riches from the trafficking in slaves. It is important to

[3] More active even than their British brethren were the American Quakers, who in 1696 advised their members in various states to take a stand against the slave trade and participate in pro-abolition propagandizing.

emphasize here, underscoring what has already been expressed in the opening quote above, that slavery in Africa before the advent of the slave trade, was altogether more benign than its non-native form. In fact, among certain ethnic groups in African society, there is no distinction between the words "prisoner" and "slave," a fact that goes far in articulating the sheer punitive value embodied by slavery in Africa where it was an integral part of the economic and justice systems. Slaves were often prisoners of war or individuals who had committed crimes like adultery; by consistent good conduct in their masters' households, they could rise through the ranks to become leaders or marry their master's daughters. In total opposition to this native form of slavery was the white man's complete subjugation and isolation of the African slave on the basis of race alone.

In conclusion, *The Life of Olaudah Equiano, or Gustavus Vassa, the African,* is a stunning testament to the power of the human spirit to transcend seemingly insurmountable obstacles in the struggle for survival and the quest for freedom.

Behold, God is my salvation; I will trust, and not be afraid: for the Lord Jehovah is my strength and my song; he also is become my salvation.

And in that day shall ye say, Praise the Lord, call upon his name, declare his doings among the people.

Isa. xii. 2. 4.

DEDICATION

Preface

WHEN THIS "Interesting Narrative" was first given to the world, some of the most public-spirited gentlemen and eminent philanthropists in Great Britain had begun to exert themselves, and to interest the public, in favor of the degraded sons of Africa. The subscription list of the first edition could boast, that it was graced with the names of a greater number of worthy characters than had before adorned the pages of any small book published in this country. Their Royal Highnesses the Prince of Wales, the Dukes of York and Cumberland; the Dukes of Marlborough, Bedford, Northumberland, &c.; the Earls of Aylesbury, Dartmouth, Stanhope, &c.; the Duchess of Buccleugh, &c.; Lady Ann Erskine, the Countess of Huntingdon, &c.; Miss Hannah Moore, Miss J. Baillie, &c.; Samuel Whitbread, the Hon. Wm. Wyndham, George Rose, Henry Thornton, Tho. Steel, &c.; Esqrs. M P.; the Rev. Doctors Baker, Jowett, Kippis, Peckard, Adam Clarke, &c.; the Rev. Tho. Clarkson, Rowland Hill, John Wesley, Miles Atkinson, &c.; Sir Sidney Smith, Sir Richard Hill, Dr. Hey, Granville Sharp, Esq. Lindley Murray, Esq. Pim Nevins, Esq. Wm. Tuke, Esq. are a small part of the bright constellation of worthies who patronized the author and this his production. The notice of such men confers honour on a humble individual, and their approbation is the highest praise.

His *round unvarnished tale* was of great service in the noble cause which they had undertaken. Being a true relation of occurrences which had taken place, and of sufferings which he had endured, it produced a degree of humane feeling in men's minds, to excite which the most animated addresses and the most convincing abstract reasoning would have laboured in vain.

Some judgment may be formed of the popularity of this narrative, and of the ability with which it is written, from the circumstance of its having raised the indignation, and engendered the hatred of many persons interested in the prosperity of the slave-trade. In various ways the author was persecuted: They tried to asperse his character, by representing him as an impostor; and to invalidate his testimony, by accusing him of wilful falsehoods. They carried the violence of their passions to such a height as to assert that he was not a native of Afric., but that he was born in the Danish Island of Santa Cruz, in the West Indies. His dismissal, by government, from his situation of *Commissary to the black poor going to Africa,** furnished these inveterate adversaries with another opportunity of pouring contumely on an innocent man, and of insinuating crimes against him of which he was never guilty. But they failed in this, as in their former attacks. For it appeared in explanation, that the only circumstance which bore the colour of a charge against him in this affair, was his determination not *silently* to sit and connive at the frauds which were committed by others.

Whenever he defended himself, FACTS were the foundation of his assertions; and no statement was made by him, for which he had not some voucher or authority. He appealed to these, and to persons that had known him in early life; and the envious shafts of his opposers fell pointless. If his enemies possessed arrogance and industry, his favourers in a righteous cause were courageous and indefatigable. They traced several injurious reports to their polluted sources; and compelled the editor of one paper, in which his character had been traduced, to make a suitable apology for his conduct, though he was not himself the author of the offensive paragraph.

The Editor of another paper, in which the same calumny was copied, in making his apology, says, *After examining the paragraph which immediately follows the one in question, I am inclined to believe that the one respecting Gustavus Vassa may have been fabricated by some of the advocates for continuing the slave-trade, for the purpose of weakening the force of the evidence brought against that trade; for I believe, if they could, they would stifle the evidence altogether.*

An objection, but a very unreasonable one, has been raised against the author, for the account which he gives of his native country; his own noble extraction; and the manners, customs, and religion of his countrymen. To many people it has seemed too circumstantial to be recollected by a youth, who was but eleven years of age when he was forced to visit foreign lands. But whoever will give himself the trouble

*See Page 175.

of reflecting on what passed during his own infancy, in the neighbour-
hood which he has not since visited, will believe that, if questioned on
the customs, &c. of the villagers, he could himself give a very accurate
detail of their sports and usages. Had he, moreover, been torn from the
land of his birth at as early a period as Gustavus was, he will readily con-
ceive that the people among whom he sojourned would soon hear from
him a succinct account of his extraction; and that he would not be
backward at informing them of his being the son of an Esquire. On this
account he would naturally think himself entitled to greater commiser-
ation, than would be claimed by a youth whose father had been a poor
chimney-sweeper. There is a mournful pleasure enjoyed by unwilling
exiles, in frequently stirring up "busy-meddling memory," and dwelling
with rapture on those scenes and events which were enchanting in
childhood and youth. Such images are the most pleasing that can be
afforded to them by reflection on the past; and the greatest wonder is,
that there is not more of this extatic feeling discovered in the follow-
ing narrative.

But the Calvinism of the author has also excited the spleen of some
people. A late editor of this work has been pleased to say, in his preface
to it, that *It is true, that here and there a tincture of superstition seems to
have spread over the author's mind. But this appears to be the natural
effect of the false idea of christianity, and of the Great Author of it, which
had taken possession of his mind. In common with many (in other
respects) enlightened Europeans, he seems to consider the benevolent
Author of our existence, as an arbitrary tyrant or partial parent; dooming,
by an arbitrary, eternal decree, some of his creatures to a state of impos-
sibility of obtaining his favor or their own future happiness; while at the
same time, others are as arbitrarily elected to be his distinguished
favourites! The rational and thinking of our race, when they discover the
traces of such a system,—a system so dishonorable to God, and so dis-
graceful to man, in the narrative before us, will do well to remember, that
it is the production of the "untutored mind" of an African. Candour will
suggest to them, that he might have formed his notions of the Christian
God, from the conduct of those, who unworthily take upon them the chris-
tian name. Nurtured at the icy bosom of slavery, accustomed to the whip
and the rack, why should it appear strange, that he should coincide in
opinion with the free-born Briton, who while he possesses the light of phi-
losophy and revelation, yet views the God of Nature, as the unfeeling
despot, and the cruel task-master? But reason blushes at such a charge,
and true piety droops her head at the supposition.* This is exceedingly
illiberal. Every man has a right to form his religious opinions according
to the oracles of truth; and if he imitate Gustavus, in searching the
scriptures and embracing the way which he thinks they point out as the

most excellent, he will act properly, and will not wander far astray. Professors of religion are greatly influenced, in their views of the doctrines of the gospel, by the views of those among whom they have been educated. The peculiar doctrines of their system are constantly inculcated on them, "grow with their growth, and strengthen with their strength." The same observations apply partially to those, who, like the subject of this narrative, know little of their natural state and less of God, their Creator and Redeemer, till they are advanced in years. It seems natural that such persons should be gratefully attached to the congregation of believers among whom they found rest to their souls; and should esteem that company of people, however despised by others, as the excellent of the earth, and their doctrines and discipline as salutary and scriptural.

On this subject the Monthly Reviewers, who were never yet suspected of religious enthusiasm, have said,

We entertain no doubt of the general authenticity of this very intelligent African's story, though it is not improbable that some English writer has assisted him in the compilement, or at least the correction of his book, for it is sufficiently well-written. The narrative wears an honest face; and we have conceived a good opinion of the man, from the artless manner in which he has detailed the variety of adventures and vicissitudes which have fallen to his lot. His publication appears very seasonably, at a time when negro-slavery is the subject of public investigation; and it seems calculated to increase the odium that has been excited against the West India planters, on account of the cruelties that some are said to have exercised on their slaves, many instances of which are here detailed.

The sable author of this volume appears to be a very sensible man; and he is, surely, not the less worthy of credit from being a convert to Christianity. He is a Methodist, and has filled many pages, towards the end of his work, with accounts of his dreams, visions, and divine influences; but all this, supposing him to have been under any delusive influence, only serves to convince us that he is guided by principle, and that he is not one of these poor converts, who, having undergone the ceremony of baptism, have remained content with that portion, only, of the christian religion; instances of which are said to be almost innumerable in America and the West Indies.*

Gustavus Vassa appears a very different character; and, therefore, we heartily wish success to his publication, which we are glad to see has been encouraged by a very respectable subscription.

The writer of this preface has not been able to collect any particulars concerning Gustavus Vassa beyond what he gives of himself in the

*To whom or to what will the Reviewer attribute any inclination to good, but to a *Divine Influence?*

following narrative, except that he died a few years ago at some place in the South of England. How highly gratified would this good man have been, had he lived to peruse the Bill for the Abolition of the Slave-trade!* To the accomplishment of this desirable object obstacles almost innumerable were opposed when this narrative was first published. Yet the author of it formed great hopes that the cause of the oppressed would prevail. And so it has proved; every difficulty has been sur-mounted by the activity, firmness, and perseverance of the real friends of God's universal family. The men who were at the time Ministers of State, threw all their influence into the scale of humanity and justice. Their short-lived administration did not allow them time for attempting much; yet had they no other achievements of which to boast, this deed of mercy will, in retirement, afford them a divine satisfaction; and their names will be venerated as long as religion, virtue, and legitimate free-dom are esteemed by men. When the greatest glory of the warrior and the political sagacity of the statesman are forgotten, — no longer exciting interest in others, or yielding delight to themselves, — this durable mon-ument of god-like benevolence to the oppressed Children of Africa will remain, to give the most refined pleasure to those who raised it. This, one of the glories peculiar to England, will, it is hoped, never suffer from the negligence of those who are its appointed guardians. May other European nations be induced, by the excellence and success of our example, to erect similar trophies of humanity and true greatness! And may universal kindness find an asylum in every breast; and all men "own its pleasing sway!"

Leeds, 25th August, 1814.

*It was passed in March, 1807.

Contents

CHAPTER		PAGE
I.	The author's account of his country, their manners and customs, &c.	9
II.	The author's birth and parentage—His being kidnapped with his sister—Horrors of a slave ship	23
III.	The author is carried to Virginia—Arrives in England—His wonder at a fall of snow, &c.	37
IV.	A particular account of the celebrated engagement between Admiral Boscawen and Monsieur le Clue	50
V.	Various interesting instances of oppression, cruelty, and extortion	66
VI.	Favourable change in the author's situation—Surprised by two earthquakes—He commences merchant with three-pence	82
VII.	The author's disgust at the West Indies—Forms schemes to obtain his freedom, &c.	97
VIII.	Three remarkable dreams—The author is shipwrecked on the Bahama-bank, &c.	108
IX.	The author arrives at Martinico—Meets with new difficulties, and sails for England, &c.	120
X.	Some account of the manner of the author's conversion to the faith of Jesus Christ	134
XI.	Picks up eleven miserable men at sea in returning to England from Spain, &c.	151
XII.	Different transactions of the author's life—Petition to the Queen—The author's marriage—Conclusion	169
Appendix		181

CHAPTER I

The Author's account of his country. — The manners and customs of the Inhabitants — Administration of justice — Embrenche — Marriage ceremony, and public entertainments — Mode of living — Dress — Manufactures — Buildings — Commerce — Agriculture — War and religion — Superstition of the natives — Funeral ceremonies of the Priests or Magicians — Curious mode of discovering Poison — Some hints concerning the origin of the author's countrymen, with the opinions of different writers on that subject.

I.

I BELIEVE it is difficult for those who publish their own memoirs to escape the imputation of vanity. Nor is this the only disadvantage under which they labour: it is also their misfortune, that whatever is uncommon is rarely, if ever, believed, and from what is obvious we are apt to turn with disgust, and to charge the writer of it with impertinence. People generally think those memoirs only worthy to be read or remembered which abound in great or striking events; those in short, which, in a high degree, excite either admiration or pity: all others they consign to contempt and oblivion. It is therefore, I confess, not a little hazardous in a private and obscure individual, and a stranger too, thus to solicit the indulgent attention of the public; especially when I own I offer here the history of neither a saint, a hero, nor a tyrant. I believe there are a few events in my life which have not happened to many. It is true the incidents of it are numerous; and did I consider myself an European, I might say my sufferings were great: but when I compare my lot with that of most of my countrymen, I regard myself as a *particular*

favourite of Heaven, and acknowledge the mercies of Providence in every occurrence of my life. If, then, the following narrative does not appear sufficiently interesting to engage general attention, let my motive be some excuse for its publication. I am not so foolishly vain as to expect from it either immortality or literary reputation. If it affords any satisfaction to my numerous friends, at whose request it has been written, or in the smallest degree promotes the interests of humanity, the ends for which it was undertaken will be fully attained, and every wish of my heart gratified. Let it therefore be remembered that, in wishing to avoid censure, I do not aspire to praise.

II.

That part of Africa, known by the name of Guinea, to which the trade of slaves is carried on, extends along the coast above 3,400 miles, from Senegal to Angola, and includes a variety of kingdoms. Of these the most considerable is the kingdom of Benin, both as to extent and wealth, the richness and culture of the soil, the power of its king, and the number and warlike disposition of its inhabitants. It is situated nearly under the line, and extends along the coast about 170 miles, but runs back into the interior of Africa to a distance hitherto, I believe, unexplored by any traveller; and seems only terminated at length by the empire of Abyssinia, near 1,500 miles from its beginning. This kingdom is divided into many provinces or districts; in one of the most remote and fertile of which, named Essaka, situated in a charming fruitful vale, I was born, in the year 1745. The distance of this province from the capital of Benin and the sea coast must be very considerable: for I had never heard of white men or Europeans, nor of the sea; and our subjection to the king of Benin was little more than nominal. Every transaction of the government, as far as my slender observation extended, was conducted by the chiefs or elders of the place. The manners and government of a people who have little commerce with other countries, are generally very simple; and the history of what passes in one family or village, may serve as a specimen of the whole nation. My father was one of those elders or chiefs of whom I have spoken, and was stiled Embrenche; a term, as I remember, importing the highest distinction, and signifying in our language "a mark of grandeur." This mark is conferred on the person entitled to it by cutting the skin across at the top of the forehead, and drawing it down to the eyebrows; and applying a warm hand to it, while in this situation, and rubbing it until it shrinks up into a thick wale across the lower part of the forehead. Most of the

judges and senators were thus marked; my father had long borne this badge: I had seen it conferred on one of my brothers, and I also was destined to receive it by my parents. Those Embrenche, or chief men, decided disputes, and punished crimes; for which purpose they always assembled together. The proceedings were generally short; and in most cases the law of retaliation prevailed. I remember a man was brought before my father, and the other judges, for kidnapping a boy; and, although he was the son of a chief, or senator, he was condemned to make recompense by a man or woman slave. Adultery, however, was sometimes punished by slavery or death; a punishment which, I believe, is inflicted on it throughout most of the nations of Africa;* so sacred among them is the honour of the marriage bed, and so jealous are they of the fidelity of their wives. Of this I recollect an instance;— A woman was convicted, before the judges, of adultery, and delivered over, as the custom was, to her husband to be punished. Accordingly he determined to put her to death; but it being found, just before the execution, that she had an infant at her breast; and no woman being prevailed on to perform the part of a nurse, she was spared on account of the child. The men, however, do not preserve the same constancy to their wives, which they expect from them; for they indulge in a plurality, though seldom in more than two. Their mode of marriage is this:— Both parties are usually betrothed when young by their parents, though I have known the males betroth themselves. On this occasion a feast is prepared, and the bride and bridegroom stand up in the midst of all their friends, who are assembled for the purpose, while he declares she is henceforth to be looked upon as his wife, and that no person is to pay any addresses to her. This is also immediately proclaimed in the vicinity, on which the bride retires from the assembly. Some time after she is brought home to her husband, and then another feast is made, to which the relations of both parties are invited. Her parents then deliver her to the bridegroom, accompanied with a number of blessings, and at the same time they tie round her waist a cotton string of the thickness of a goose-quill, which none but married women are permitted to wear. She is now considered as completely his wife; and at this time the dowry is given to the new-married pair, which generally consists of *portions of land, slaves and cattle, household goods, and implements of husbandry.* These are offered by the friends of both parties: besides which the parents of the bridegroom present gifts to those of the bride, whose property she is looked upon before marriage; but after it she is esteemed the sole

*See Anthony Benezet's "Some Account of Guinea, with an Inquiry into the Slave Trade" (1771) throughout.

property of the husband. The ceremony being now ended, the festival begins, which is celebrated with bonfires, and loud acclamations of joy, accompanied with music and dancing.

III.

We are almost a nation of dancers, musicians, and poets. Every great event, such as a triumphant return from battle, or other cause of public rejoicing, is celebrated in public dances, which are accompanied with songs and music suited to the occasion. The assembly is separated into four divisions, which dance either apart or in succession, and each with a character peculiar to itself. The first division contains the married men, who in their dances frequently exhibit feats of arms, and the representation of a battle. To these succeed the married women, who dance in the second division. The young men occupy the third; and the maidens the fourth. Each represents some interesting scene of real life, such as a great achievement, domestic employment, a pathetic story, or some rural sport. And as the subject is generally founded on some recent event, it is therefore ever new. This gives our dances a spirit and variety which I have scarcely seen elsewhere.* We have many musical instruments, particularly drums of different kinds, a piece of music which resembles a guitar, and another much like a sticcado. These last are chiefly used by betrothed virgins, who play on them on all grand festivals.

As our manners are simple, our luxuries are few. The dress of both sexes is nearly the same. It generally consists of a long piece of calico or muslin, wrapped loosely round the body, somewhat in the form of a Highland plaid. This is usually dyed blue, which is our favorite colour. It is extracted from a berry, and is brighter and richer than any I have seen in Europe. Besides this, our women of distinction wear golden ornaments, which they dispose with some profusion on their arms and legs. When our women are not employed with the men in tillage, their usual occupation is spinning and weaving cotton, which they afterward dye, and make into garments. They also manufacture earthen vessels, of which we have many kinds; among the rest, tobacco pipes, made after the same fashion, and used in the same manner, as those in Turkey.†

Our manner of living is entirely plain; for as yet the natives are

*When I was in Smyrna I frequently saw the Greeks dance after this manner.

†The bowl is earthen, curiously figured, to which a long reed is fixed as a tube. This tube is sometimes so long as to be borne by one, and frequently, out of grandeur, by two boys.

unacquainted with those refinements in cookery which debauch the taste. Bullocks, goats, and poultry, supply the greatest part of their food. These constitute likewise the principal wealth of the country, and the chief articles of its commerce. The flesh is usually stewed in a pan; to make it savory we sometimes use also pepper, and other spices, and we have salt made of wood ashes. Our vegetables are mostly plantains, eadas, yams, beans, and Indian corn. The head of the family usually eats alone; his wives and slaves have also their separate tables. Before we taste food we always wash our hands: indeed our cleanliness on all occasions is extreme; but on this it is an indispensable ceremony. After washing, libation is made, by pouring out a small portion of the drink on the floor, and by tossing a small quantity of the food in a certain place, for the spirits of departed relations, which the natives suppose to preside over their conduct, and to guard them from evil. They are totally unacquainted with strong or spirituous liquors; and their principal beverage is palm wine. This is got from a tree of that name, by tapping it at the top, and fastening a large gourd to it; and sometimes one tree will yield three or four gallons in a night. When just drawn it is of a delicious sweetness; but in a few days it acquires a spirituous flavour: though I never saw any one intoxicated by it. The same tree also produces nuts and oil. Our principal luxury is in perfumes; one sort of these is an odoriferous wood of delicious fragrance: the other a kind of earth, a small portion of which thrown into the fire diffuses a most powerful odour.* We beat this wood into powder, and mix it with palm oil; with which both men and women perfume themselves.

IV.

In our buildings we study convenience rather than ornament. Each master of a family has a large square piece of ground, surrounded with a moat or fence, or enclosed with a wall, made of red earth tempered: which, when dry, is as hard as brick. Within this are his houses to accommodate his family and slaves; which, if numerous, frequently cause these tenements to present the appearance of a village. In the middle stands the principal building, appropriated to the sole use of the master, and consisting of two apartments; in one of which he sits in

*When I was in Smyrna I saw the same kind of earth, and brought some of it with me to England; it resembles musk in strength, but is more delicious in scent, and is not unlike the smell of a rose.

the day with his family, the other is left apart for the reception of his friends. He has besides these a distinct apartment in which he sleeps, together with his male children. On each side are the apartments of his wives, who have also their separate day and night houses. The habitations of the slaves and their families are distributed throughout the rest of the enclosure. These houses never exceed one story in height: they are always built of wood, or stakes driven into the ground, crossed with wattles, and neatly plastered within and without. The roof is thatched with reeds. Our day houses are left open at the sides; but those in which we sleep are always covered, and plastered in the inside with a composition mixed with cow dung, to keep off the different insects, which annoy us during the night. The walls and floors also of these are generally covered with mats. Our beds consist of a platform, raised three or four feet from the ground, on which are laid skins, and different parts of a spungy tree called plantain. Our covering is calico, or muslin, the same as our dress. The usual seats are a few logs of wood; but we have benches, which are generally perfumed, to accommodate strangers: these compose the greater part of our household furniture. Houses so constructed and furnished require but little skill to erect them. Every man is a sufficient architect for the purpose. The whole neighbourhood afford their unanimous assistance in building them, and in return receive, and expect no other recompense than a feast.

As we live in a country where nature is prodigal of her favours, our wants are few, and easily supplied; of course we have few manufactures. They consist, for the most part, of calicoes, earthenware, ornaments, and instruments of war and husbandry. But these make no part of our commerce, the principal articles of which, as I have observed, are provisions. In such a state money is of little use; however we have some small pieces of coin, if I may call them such. They are made something like an anchor; but I do not remember either their value or denomination. We have also markets, at which I have been frequently with my mother. These are sometimes visited by stout mahogany-coloured men from the south-west of us. We call them Oye-Eboe, which term signifies "red men living at a distance." They generally bring us fire-arms, gunpowder, hats, beads, and dried fish. The last we esteemed a great rarity, as our waters were only brooks and springs. These articles they barter with us for odoriferous woods and earth, and our salt of wood ashes. They always carry slaves through our land; but the strictest account is exacted of their manner of procuring them, before they are suffered to pass. Sometimes, indeed, we sold slaves to them, but they were only prisoners of war, or such among us as had been convicted of kidnapping, or adultery, and some other crimes, which we esteemed heinous. This practice of kidnapping induces me to think, that, notwithstanding all our strictness,

their principal business among us was to trepan our people. I remember, too, they carried great sacks along with them, which not long after, I had an opportunity of fatally seeing applied to that infamous purpose.

V.

Our land is uncommonly rich and fruitful, and produces all kinds of vegetables in great abundance. We have plenty of Indian corn, and vast quantities of cotton and tobacco. Pineapples grow without culture; they are about the size of the largest sugar loaf, and finely flavoured. We have also spices of different kinds, particularly pepper; and a variety of delicious fruits which I have never seen in Europe; together with gums of various kinds, and honey in abundance. All our industry is exerted to improve those blessings of nature. Agriculture is our chief employment; and every one, even to children and women, is engaged in it. Thus we are habituated to labour from our earliest years. Every one contributes something to the common stock: and as we are unacquainted with idleness, we have no beggars. The benefits of such a mode of living are obvious. — The West India planters prefer the slaves of Benin or Eboe, to those of any part of Guinea, for their hardiness, intelligence, integrity and zeal. — Those benefits are felt by us in the general healthiness of the people, and in their vigour and activity; I might have added, too, to their comeliness. Deformity is indeed unknown amongst us. I mean that of shape. Numbers of the natives of Eboe, now in London, might be brought in support of this assertion: for, in regard to complexion, ideas of beauty are wholly relative. I remember while in Africa to have seen three negro children, who were tawny, and another quite white, who were universally regarded as deformed by myself and the natives in general, as far as related to their complexions. Our women too, were, in my eyes at least, uncommonly graceful, alert, and modest to a degree of bashfulness; nor do I remember to have ever heard of an instance of incontinence amongst them before marriage. They are also remarkably cheerful. Indeed cheerfulness and affability are two of the leading characteristics of our nation.

Out tillage is exercised in a large plain or common, some hours' walk from our dwellings, and all the neighbours resort thither in a body. They use no beasts of husbandry; and their only instruments are hoes, axes, shovels, and beaks, or pointed iron to dig with. Sometimes we are visited by locusts, which come in large clouds, so as to darken the air, and destroy our harvest. This, however, happens rarely, but when it does, a famine is produced by it. I remember an instance or two of this

happening. This common is often the theatre of war; and therefore, when our people go out to till their land, they not only go in a body, but generally take their arms with them for fear of a surprise: and when they apprehend an invasion, they guard the avenues to their dwellings by striking sticks into the ground, which are so sharp at one end as to pierce the foot, and are generally dipped in poison. From what I can recollect of these battles, they appear to have been irruptions of one little state or district into another, to obtain prisoners or booty. Perhaps they were incited to this by those traders, who brought amongst us the European goods which I mentioned. Such a mode of obtaining slaves in Africa is common; and I believe more are procured in this way, and by kidnapping, than in any other.* When a trader wants slaves, he applies to a chief for them, and tempts him with his wares. It is not extraordinary, if on this occasion he yields to the temptation with as little firmness, and accepts the price of his fellow-creature's liberty with as little reluctance as the enlightened merchant. Accordingly he falls on his neighbours, and a desperate battle ensues. If he prevails and takes prisoners, he gratifies his avarice by selling them; but if his party be vanquished, and he falls into the hands of the enemy, he is put to death: for, as he has been known to foment their quarrels, it is thought dangerous to let him survive, and no ransom can save him, though all other prisoners may be redeemed. We have fire-arms, bows and arrows, broad two-edged swords, and javelins, also shields which will cover a man from head to foot. All are taught the use of these weapons; even our women are warriors, and march boldly out to fight along with the men. Our whole district is a kind of militia: on a certain signal given, such as the firing of a gun at night, they all rise in arms and rush upon their enemy. It is, perhaps, sometimes remarkable, that when our people march to the field, a red flag or banner is borne before them. I was once a witness to a battle on our common. We had all been at work in it one day, as usual, when our people were suddenly attacked. I climbed a tree at some distance, from which I beheld the fight. There were many women, as well as men, on both sides; among others my mother was there, and armed with a broad sword. After fighting for a considerable time with great fury, when many had been killed, our people obtained the victory, and took their enemy's chief prisoner. He was carried off in great triumph, and though he offered a large ransom for his life, he was put to death. A virgin of note among our enemies had been slain in the battle, and her arm was exposed in our marketplace, where our trophies

*See Anthony Benezet's "Account of that Part of Africa inhabited by the Negroes" (1762) throughout.

were always exhibited. The spoils were divided according to the merit of the warriors. Those prisoners which were not sold or redeemed we kept as slaves: but how different was their condition from that of the slaves in the West Indies! With us they do no more work than other members of the community, than even their master; their food, clothing, and lodging, were nearly the same as theirs, except that they were not permitted to eat with those who were free-born; and there was scarcely any other difference between them than a superior degree of importance, which the head of a family possesses in our state, and that authority which, as such, he exercises over every part of his household. Some of these slaves have even slaves under them, as their own property, and for their own use.

VI.

As to religion, the natives believe that there is one Creator of all things, and that he lives in the sun, and is girded round with a belt that he may never eat or drink; but, according to some, he smokes a pipe, which is our own favourite luxury. They believe he governs events, especially our deaths or captivity; but as for the doctrine of eternity, I don't remember to have ever heard of it: some, however, believe in the transmigration of souls in a certain degree.—Those spirits, which are not transmigrated, such as their dear friends or relations, they believe always attend them, and guard them from the bad spirits, or their foes. For this reason they always before eating, as I have observed, put some small portion of the meat, and pour some of the drink, on the ground for them; and they often make oblations of the blood of beasts, or of fowls at their graves. I was very fond of my mother, and was almost constantly with her. When she went to make these oblations at her mother's tomb, which was a kind of small solitary thatched house, I sometimes attended her. There she made her libations, and spent most of the night in cries and lamentations. I have been often extremely terrified on these occasions. The loneliness of the place, the darkness of the night, and ceremony of libation, naturally awful and gloomy, were heightened by my mother's lamentations; and these concurring with the doleful cries of birds, by which these places were frequented, gave an inexpressible terror to the scene.

We compute the year from the day on which the sun crosses the line, and, on its setting that evening, there is a general shout throughout the land; at least I can speak from my own knowledge, throughout our vicinity. The people, at the same time, make a great noise with rattles, not

unlike the basket rattles used by children here, though much larger, and hold up their hands to heaven for a blessing. It is then the greatest offerings are made, and those children who, our wise men foretel, will be fortunate, are then presented to different people. I remember many used to come to see me, and I was carried about to others for that purpose. They have many offerings, particularly at full moons; generally two at harvest, before the fruits are taken out of the ground: and when any young animals are killed, they sometimes offer up a part of them as a sacrifice. These offerings, when made by one of the heads of a family, serve for the whole. I remember we often had them at my father's and my uncle's, and their families have been present. Some of our offerings are eaten with bitter herbs. We had a saying among us to any one of a cross temper, "that if they were to be eaten, they should be eaten with bitter herbs."

We practised circumcision like the Jews, and made offerings and feasts on that occasion in the same manner as they did. Like them also, our children were named from some event, some circumstance, or fancied foreboding at the time of their birth. I was named Olaudah, which, in our language, signifies "vicissitude or fortunate," also, "one favoured, and having a loud voice and well spoken." I remember we never polluted the name of the object of our adoration; on the contrary, it was always mentioned with the greatest reverence; and we are totally unacquainted with swearing, and all those terms of abuse and reproach which find their way so readily and copiously into the language of more civilized people. The only expressions of that kind I remember were, "May you rot!" or "may you swell!" or "may a beast take you!"

I have before remarked that the natives of this part of Africa are extremely cleanly. This necessary habit of decency was with us a part of religion, and therefore we had many purifications and washings; indeed almost as many, and used on the same occasions, if my recollection does not fail me, as the Jews. Those that touched the dead, at anytime, were obliged to wash and purify themselves before they could enter a dwelling-house, or touch any person or any thing we eat. I was so fond of my mother I could not keep from her, or avoid touching her at some of those periods, in consequence of which I was obliged to be kept out with her, in a little house made for that purpose, till offering was made, and then we were purified.

Though we had no places of public worship, we had priests and magicians, or wise men. I do not remember whether they had different offices, or whether they were united in the same persons, but they were held in great reverence by the people. They calculated our time, and foretold events, as their name imported, for we called them Ah-affoe-way-cah, which signifies "calculators or yearly men," our year being called Ah-affoe. They wore their beards; and when they died they were succeeded by

their sons. Most of their implements and things of value were interred
with them. Pipes and tobacco were also put into the graves with the
corpse, which was always perfumed and ornamented, and animals were
offered in sacrifice to them. None accompanied their funerals but those
of the same profession or tribe. These buried them after sunset, and
always returned from the grave by a different way from that by which
they went.

These magicians were also our doctors or physicians. They practised
bleeding by cupping: and were very successful in healing wounds and
expelling poisons. They had likewise some extraordinary method of dis-
covering jealousy, theft, and poisoning; the success of which, no doubt,
they derived from their unbounded influence over the credulity and
superstition of the people. I do not remember what those methods
were, except that, as to poisoning, I recollect an instance or two, which
I hope it will not be deemed impertinent here to insert, as it may serve
as a kind of specimen of the rest, and is still used by the negroes in the
West Indies. A young woman had been poisoned, but it was not known
by whom. The doctors ordered the corpse to be taken up by some per-
sons and carried to the grave. As soon as the bearers had raised it on
their shoulders, they seemed seized with some* sudden impulse, and
ran to and fro unable to stop themselves. At last, after having passed
through a number of thorns and prickly bushes unhurt, the corpse fell
from them close to a house, and defaced it in the fall; and the owner
being taken up, he immediately confessed to the poisoning.†

The natives are extremely cautious about poison. When they buy any
eatable, the seller kisses it all round before the buyer, to shew him it is
not poisoned; and the same is done when meat and drink are presented,
particularly to a stranger. We have serpents of different kinds, some of
which are esteemed ominous when they appear in our houses, and these

*See also Lieutenant Matthew's "Voyage," p. 123 [of that volume].

†An instance of this kind happened at Montserrat in the West Indies, in the year 1763.
I then belonged to the Charming Sally, Capt. Doran.—The chief mate, Mr. Mansfield,
and some of the crew being one day on shore, were present at the burying of a poisoned
negro girl. Though they had often heard of the circumstance of the running in such
cases, and had even seen it, they imagined it to be a trick of the corpse bearers. The
mate therefore desired two of the sailors to take up the coffin, and carry it to the grave.
The sailors, who were all of the same opinion, readily obeyed; but they had scarcely
raised it to their shoulders, before they began to run furiously about, quite unable to
direct themselves, till, at last, without intention, they came to the hut of him who had
poisoned the girl. The coffin then immediately fell from their shoulders against the
hut, and damaged part of the wall. The owner of the hut was taken into custody on
this, and confessed the poisoning. I give this story as it was related by the mate and
crew on their return to the ship. The credit which is due to it, I leave with the reader.

we never molest. I remember two of those ominous snakes, each of which was as thick as the calf of a man's leg, and in colour resembling a dolphin in the water, crept into my mother's night house, where I always lay with her, and coiled themselves into folds, and each time they crowed like a cock. I was desired by some of our wise men to touch these, that I might be interested in the good omens, which I did, for they were quite harmless, and would tamely suffer themselves to be handled; and then were put into a large open earthen pan, and set on one side of the highway. Some of our snakes, however, were poisonous: one of them crossed the road one day, as I was standing on it, and passed between my feet without offering to touch me, to the great surprise of many who saw it; and these incidents were accounted by the wise men, and likewise by my mother and the rest of the people, as remarkable omens in my favour.

VII.

Such is the imperfect sketch, with which my memory has furnished me, of the manners and customs of a people among whom I first drew my breath. And here I cannot forbear suggesting what has long struck me very forcibly, namely, the strong analogy, which, even by this sketch, imperfect as it is, appears to prevail in the manners and customs of my countrymen and those of the Jews, before they reached the Land of Promise, and particularly the Patriarchs, while they were yet in that pastoral state which is described in Genesis—an analogy which alone would induce me to think that the one people had sprung from the other. Indeed this is the opinion of Dr. Gill, who, in his commentary on Genesis, very ably deduces the pedigree of the Africans from Afer and Afra, the descendants of Abraham by Keturah his wife and concubine (for both these titles are applied to her). It is also comformable to the sentiments of Dr. John Clarke, formerly Dean of Sarum, in his "Truth of the Christian Religion." Both these authors concur in ascribing to us this original. The reasonings of those gentlemen are still further confirmed by the scripture chronology of the Rev. Arthur Bedford; and if any further corroboration were required, this resemblance in so many respects is a strong evidence in support of the opinion.—Like the Israelites in their primitive state, our government was conducted by our chiefs or judges, our wisemen, and elders; and the head of a family, with us, enjoyed a similar authority over his household with that which is ascribed to Abraham and the other Patriarchs. The law of retaliation prevailed almost universally with us as with them: and even their religion appeared to have

shed upon us a ray of its glory, though broken and spent in its passage, or eclipsed by the cloud with which time, tradition, and ignorance might have enveloped it. For we had our circumcision (a rite, I believe, peculiar to that people): we had also our sacrifices and burnt-offerings, our washings and purifications, on the same occasions as they had.

As to the difference of colour between the Eboan Africans and the modern Jews, I shall not presume to account for it. It is a subject which has engaged the pens of men both of genius and learning, and is far above my strength. The most able and Rev. Mr. T. Clarkson, however, in his much admired "Essay on the Slavery and Commerce of the Human Species" has ascertained the cause in a manner that at once solves every objection on that account, and, on my mind at least, has produced the fullest conviction. I shall therefore refer to that performance for the theory,* contenting myself with extracting a fact as related by Dr. Mitchell.† "The Spaniards, who have inhabited America under the torrid zone, for any time, are become as dark coloured as our native Indians of Virginia; of which I myself have been a witness." There is also another instance‡ of a Portuguese settlement at Mitomba, a river in Sierra Leona, where the inhabitants are bred from a mixture of the first Portuguese discoverers with the natives, and are now become in their complexion, and in the woolly quality for their hair, perfect negroes, retaining, however, a smattering of the Portuguese language.

These instances, and a great many more which might be adduced, while they shew how the complexions of the same persons vary in different climates, it is hoped may tend also to remove the prejudice that some conceive against the natives of Africa on account of their colour. Surely the minds of the Spaniards did not change with their complexions! Are there not causes enough to which the apparent inferiority of an African may be ascribed, without limiting the goodness of God, and supposing He forebore to stamp understanding on what is certainly his own image, because "carved in ebony?" Might it not naturally be ascribed to their situation? When they come among Europeans, they are ignorant of their language, religion, manners, and customs. Are any pains taken to teach them these? Are they treated as men? Does not slavery itself depress the mind, and extinguish all its fire, and every noble sentiment? But above all, what advantages do not a refined people possess over those who are rude and uncultivated! Let the polished and haughty European recollect that his ancestors were once like the Africans, uncivilized and even barbarous. Did Nature make them inferior to their sons? And should they too have

*Page 178 to 216 [of Clarkson's "Essay" cited above].
†Philos. Trans. No. 476, Sect. 4, cited by the Rev. Mr. Clarkson, p. 205.
‡Same page.

been made slaves? Every rational mind answers, "No." Let such reflections as these melt the pride of their superiority into sympathy for the wants and miseries of their sable brethren, and compel them to acknowledge, that understanding is not confined to feature or colour. If, when they look round the world, they feel exultation, let it be tempered with benevolence to others and gratitude to God, "who hath made of one blood all nations of men for to dwell on all the face of the earth;" (Acts xvii. 26.) and whose wisdom is not our wisdom, neither are our ways his ways.

CHAPTER II

The author's birth and parentage—His being kidnapped with his sister—
Their separation—Surprise at meeting again—Are finally separated—
Account of the different places and incidents the author met with till
his arrival on the coast—The effect the sight of a slave ship had on
him—He sails for the West Indies—Horrors of a slave ship—Arrives at
Barbadoes, where the cargo is sold and dispersed.

I.

I HOPE the reader will not think I have trespassed on his patience, in
introducing myself to him with some account of the manners and cus-
toms of my country. They had been implanted in me with great care,
and made an impression on my mind, which time could not erase, and
which all the adversity and variety of fortune I have since experienced,
served only to rivet and record; for, whether the love of one's country
be real or imaginary, a lesson of reason or an instinct of nature, I still
look back with pleasure on the first scenes of my life, though that plea-
sure has been for the most part mingled with sorrow.

I have already acquainted the reader with the time and place of my
birth. My father, besides many slaves, had a numerous family, of which
seven lived to grow up, including myself and a sister, who was the only
daughter. As I was the youngest of the sons, I became, of course, the
greatest favourite with my mother, and was always with her, and she
used to take particular pains to form my mind. I was trained up from
my earliest years in the art of war: my daily exercise was shooting and
throwing javelins; and my mother adorned me with emblems, after the
manner of our greatest warriors. In this way I grew up till I was turned
the age of eleven, when an end was put to my happiness in the following

manner:—When the grown people in the neighbourhood were gone far in the fields to labour, the children generally assembled together in some of the neighbours' premises to play; and some of us often used to get up into a tree to look out for any assailant, or kidnapper, that might come upon us. For they sometimes took those opportunities of our parents' absence, to attack and carry off as many as they could seize. One day, as I was watching at the top of a tree in our yard, I saw one of those people come into the yard of our next neighbour but one, to kidnap, there being many stout young people in it. Immediately on this I gave the alarm of the rogue, and he was surrounded by the stoutest of them, who entangled him with cords, so that he could not escape till some of the grown people came and secured him.

II.

But alas! ere long it was my fate to be thus attacked, and to be carried off, when none of the grown people were nigh. One day, when all our people were gone out to their work as usual, and only I and my sister were left to mind the house, two men and a woman got over our walls, and in a moment seized us both; and without giving us time to cry out, or to make any resistance, they stopped our mouths and ran off with us into the nearest wood. Here they tied our hands, and continued to carry us as far as they could, till night came on, when we reached a small house, where the robbers halted for refreshment and spent the night. We were then unbound, but were unable to take any food; and being quite overpowered by fatigue and grief, our only relief was some sleep, which allayed our misfortune for a short time. The next morning we left the house, and continued travelling all the day. For a long time we had kept the woods, but at last we came into a road which I believed I knew. I had now some hopes of being delivered; for we had advanced but a little way before I discovered some people at a distance, on which I began to cry out for their assistance; but my cries had no other effect than to make them tie me faster and stop my mouth; they then put me into a large sack. They also stopped my sister's mouth, and tied her hands; and in this manner we proceeded till we were out of sight of these people.

When we went to rest the following night, they offered us some victuals; but we refused it; and the only comfort we had was in being in one another's arms all that night, and bathing each other with tears. But alas! we were soon deprived of even the small comfort of weeping together. The next day proved one of greater sorrow than I had yet experienced; for my sister and I were then separated, while we lay clasped

in each other's arms. It was in vain that we besought them not to part
us; she was torn from me, and immediately carried away, while I was left
in a state of distraction not to be described. I cried and grieved continually;
and for several days did not eat any thing but what they forced into my
mouth. At length, after many days' travelling, during which I had often
changed masters, I got into the hands of a chieftain, in a pleasant country.
This man had two wives and some children, and they all used me
extremely well, and did all they could to comfort me; particularly the
first wife, who was something like my mother. Although I was a great
many days' journey from my father's house, yet these people spoke
exactly the same language with us. This first master of mine, as I may
call him, was a smith, and my principal employment was working his
bellows, which were the same kind as I had seen in my vicinity. They
were in some respects not unlike the stoves here in gentlemen's kitchens;
and were covered over with leather, and in the middle of that leather a
stick was fixed, and a person stood up and worked it, in the same man-
ner as is done to pump water out of a cask with a hand pump. I believe
it was gold he worked, for it was of a lovely bright yellow colour, and
was worn by the women on their wrists and ankles.

I was there, I suppose, about a month, and they at length used to trust
me some little distance from the house. I employed this liberty in
embracing every opportunity to inquire the way to my own home: and
I also sometimes, for the same purpose, went with the maidens, in the
cool of the evenings, to bring pitchers of water from the springs for the
use of the house. I had also remarked where the sun rose in the morn-
ing, and set in the evening, as I had travelled along: and had observed
that my father's house was towards the rising of the sun. I therefore
determined to seize the first opportunity of making my escape, and to
shape my course for that quarter; for I was quite oppressed and weighed
down by grief after my mother and friends; and my love of liberty, ever
great, was strengthened by the mortifying circumstance of not daring to
eat with the free-born children, although I was mostly their companion.

III.

While I was projecting my escape, one day an unlucky event hap-
pened, which quite disconcerted my plan, and put an end to my hopes.
I used to be sometimes employed in assisting an elderly woman slave to
cook and take care of the poultry: and one morning, while I was feed-
ing some chickens, I happened to toss a small pebble at one of them,
which hit it on the middle, and directly killed it. The old slave having

soon after missed the chicken, inquired after it; and on my relating the accident (for I told her the truth, because my mother would never suffer me to tell a lie) she flew into a violent passion, threatened that I should suffer for it; and, my master being out, she immediately went and told her mistress what I had done. This alarmed me very much, and I expected an instant flogging, which to me was uncommonly dreadful; for I had seldom been beaten at home. I therefore resolved to fly; and accordingly I ran into a thicket that was hard by, and hid myself in the bushes. Soon afterwards my mistress and the slave returned, and, not seeing me, they searched all the house, but not finding me, and I not making answer when they called me, they thought I had run away, and the whole neighbourhood was raised in the pursuit of me.

In that part of the country, as well as in ours, the houses and villages were skirted with woods, or shrubberies, and the bushes were so thick that a man could readily conceal himself in them, so as to elude the strictest search. The neighbours continued the whole day looking for me, and several times many of them came within a few yards of the place where I lay hid. I expected every moment, when I heard a rustling among the trees, to be found out, and punished by my master. But they never discovered me, though they often were so near that I even heard their conjectures, as they were looking about for me; and I now learned from them, that any attempt to return home would be hopeless. Most of them supposed I had fled towards home; but the distance was so great, and the way so intricate, that they thought I could never reach it, and that I should be lost in the woods. When I heard this I was seized with a violent panic, and abandoned myself to despair. Night too began to approach, and aggravated all my fears. I had before entertained hopes of getting home and had determined when it should be dark to make the attempt; but I was now convinced it was fruitless, and began to consider that, if possibly I could escape all other animals, I could not those of the human kind; and that, not knowing the way, I must perish in the woods. Thus was I like the hunted deer:

> Ev'ry leaf, and ev'ry whisp'ring breath
> Convey'd a foe, and ev'ry foe a death.

I heard frequent rustlings among the leaves, and being pretty sure they were snakes, I expected every instant to be stung by them. This increased my anguish, and the horror of my situation became now quite insupportable. I at length quitted the thicket, very faint and hungry, for I had not eaten nor drunk any thing all the day. I crept to my master's kitchen, from whence I set out at first, which was an open shed, and laid myself down in the ashes with an anxious wish for death

to relieve me from all my pains. I was scarcely awake in the morning, when the old woman slave, who was the first up, came to light the fire, and saw me in the fire place. She was very much surprised to see me, and could scarcely believe her own eyes. She now promised to intercede for me, and went for her master, who soon after came, and, having slightly reprimanded me, ordered me to be taken care of, and not ill treated.

IV.

Soon after this my master's only daughter and child by his first wife, sickened and died, which affected him so much that for some time he was almost frantic, and really would have killed himself, had he not been watched and prevented. However, in a small time afterwards he recovered, and I was again sold. I was now carried to the left of the sun's rising, through many dreary wastes and dismal woods, amidst the hideous roaring of wild beasts. The people I was sold to used to carry me very often, when I was tired, either on their shoulders or on their backs. I saw many convenient well-built sheds along the road, at proper distances, to accommodate the merchants and travellers. They lie in those buildings along with their wives, who often accompany them: and they always go well armed.

From the time I left my own nation I always found somebody that understood me till I came to the sea coast. The languages of different nations did not totally differ, nor were they so copious as those of the Europeans, particularly the English. They were therefore easily learned; and, while I was journeying thus through Africa, I acquired two or three different tongues. In this manner I had been travelling for a considerable time, when one evening, to my great surprise, whom should I see brought to the house where I was, but my dear sister? As soon as she saw me she gave a loud shriek, and ran into my arms. I was quite overpowered: neither of us could speak; but for a considerable time, clung to each other in mutual embraces, unable to do any thing but weep. Our meeting affected all who saw us; and indeed I must acknowledge, in honour of those sable destroyers of human rights, that I never met with any ill treatment, or saw any offered to their slaves, except tying them, when necessary, to keep them running away.

When these people knew we were brother and sister, they indulged us to be together; and the man, to whom I supposed we belonged, lay with us, he in the middle, while she and I held one another by the hands across his breast all night; and thus for a while we forgot our misfortunes in the joy of being together. But even this small comfort

was soon to have an end, for scarcely had the fatal morning appeared, when she was again torn from me for ever! I was now more miserable, if possible, than before. The small relief which her presence gave me from pain was gone, and the wretchedness of my situation was redoubled by my anxiety after her fate, and my apprehensions lest her sufferings should be greater than mine, when I could not be with her to alleviate them.

Yes, dear partner of all my childish sports! Sharer of my joys and sorrows; happy should I have ever esteemed myself to encounter every misery for you, and to procure your freedom by the sacrifice of my own! Though you were early forced from my arms, your image has been always rivetted in my heart, from which neither time nor fortune has been able to remove it: so that, while the thoughts of your sufferings have damped my prosperity, they have mingled with adversity and increased its bitterness. To that Heaven, which protects the weak from the strong, I commit the care of your innocence and virtues, if they have not already received their full reward, and if your youth and delicacy have not long since fallen victims to the violence of the African trader, the pestilential stench of a Guinea ship, the seasoning in the European colonies, or the lash and lust of a brutal and unrelenting overseer.

I did not long remain after my sister. I was again sold, and carried through a number of places, till, after travelling a considerable time, I came to a town called Tinmah, in the most beautiful country I had yet seen in Africa. It was extremely rich, and there were many rivulets which flowed through it, and supplied a large pond in the centre of the town, where the people washed. Here I first saw and tasted cocoa nuts, which I thought superior to any nuts I had ever tasted before; and the trees which were loaded, were also interspersed among the houses, which had commodious shades adjoining, and were in the same manner as ours, the insides being neatly plastered and whitewashed. Here I also saw and tasted, for the first time, sugar-cane. Their money consisted of little white shells, the size of the fingernail. I was sold for one hundred and seventy-two of these, by a merchant who lived at this place. I had been about two or three days at his house, when a wealthy widow, a neighbour of his came there one evening, and brought with her an only son, a young gentleman about my own age and size. Here they saw me; and, having taken a fancy to me, I was bought of the merchant, and went home with them. Her house and premises were situated close to one of those rivulets I have mentioned, and were the finest I ever saw in Africa: they were very extensive, and she had a number of slaves to attend her. The next day I was washed and perfumed, and when mealtime came, I was led into the presence of my mistress, and ate and drank before her with her son. This filled me with astonishment; and I

could scarcely avoid expressing my surprise that the young gentleman should suffer me, who was bound, to eat with him who was free; and not only so, but that he would not at any time either eat or drink till I had taken first, because I was the eldest, which was agreeable to our custom. Indeed every thing here, and their treatment of me, made me forget that I was a slave. The language of these people resembled ours so nearly, that we understood each other perfectly. They had also the very same customs as we. There were likewise slaves daily to attend us, while my young master and I, with other boys, sported with our darts, and bows and arrows, as I had been used to do at home. In this resemblance to my former happy state, I passed about two months; and now I began to think I was to be adopted into the family, and was beginning to be reconciled to my situation, and to forget by degrees my misfortunes, when all at once the delusion vanished; for, without the least previous knowledge, one morning, early, while my dear master and companion was still asleep, I was awakened out of my reverie to fresh sorrow, and hurried away even amongst the uncircumcised.

Thus, at the very moment I dreamed of the greatest happiness, I found myself most miserable; and it seemed as if fortune* wished to give me this taste of joy, only to render the reverse more poignant. The change I now experienced was as painful as it was sudden and unexpected.

*This indiscreet mode of calling the providence of God, in his particular dealings with the children of men, by the name of fortune is exceedingly blameworthy. It is a conformity to the expressions of a vain world not to be expected from Gustavus, who generally manifests a becoming sense of the benefits which he received, and a knowledge of the Blessed Fountain from whence they issued. After censuring it as a slip of his pen, let none venture to attribute it to atheistical motives. The tenor of his conduct and of his words belies such an insinuation. He had heard the term thus misapplied by others, and from an imitative habit, he thoughtlessly gave it the same appellation.

What can be thought by short sighted mortals, to have been the designs of a gracious God in permitting such complicated evils to hover around and to oppress this youthful African? The purposes of Him, who afflicts not willingly any of the children of men, cannot but be merciful. Every stripe which He suffers to be inflicted, will hereafter be interpreted into so many varied tokens of His paternal affection towards his redeemed creatures; for "whom He loveth He chasteneth, and scourgeth every son whom He receiveth." While there is an aptitude in human nature to call Divine good "evil," a righteous man is greatly benefited by the cure of this propensity; and in committing all things to the complete disposal of "One supremely good and wise," he has the best possible security and assurance of all things working together for his good. Let the pious reader say, after rising up from the perusal of this narrative, if it is not his firm persuasion, that in all these "hidden dangers, toils, and deaths," is evinced the intention of Divine Wisdom to bring the man, who was exercised with them, to partake of the purchased blessings of salvation. Who, that knows the value of it, would desist from praising God "for his unspeakable gift," or would slightingly speak of the almost imperceptible means by which he was led to the enjoyment of religion?

It was a change indeed from a state of bliss to a scene which is inexpressible by me, as it discovered to me an element I had never before beheld, and of which till then had no idea; and wherein such instances of hardship and cruelty continually occurred, as I can never reflect on but with horror.

V.

All the nations and people I had hitherto passed through resembled our own in their manners, customs, and language: but I came at length to a country, the inhabitants of which differed from us in all these particulars. I was very much struck with this difference, especially when I came among a people who did not circumcise, and who ate without washing their hands. They cooked their provisions also in iron pots, and had European cutlasses and cross bows, which were unknown to us; and fought with their fists among themselves. Their women were not so modest as ours, for they ate, drank, and slept with their men. But, above all, I was amazed to see no sacrifices or offerings among them. In some of those places the people ornamented themselves with scars, and likewise filed their teeth very sharp. They sometimes wanted to ornament me in the same manner, but I would not suffer them; hoping that I might sometime be among a people who did not thus disfigure themselves, as I thought they did. At last I came to the banks of a large river, covered with canoes, in which the people appeared to live, with their household utensils, and provisions of all kinds. I was beyond measure astonished at this, as I had never before seen any water larger than a pond or a rivulet: and my surprise was mingled with no small fear when I was put into one of these canoes, and we began to paddle and move along the river. We continued going on thus till night; and when we came to land, and made fires on the banks, each family by themselves, some dragged their canoes on shore, others cooked in theirs, and laid in them all night. Those on the land had mats, of which they made tents, some in the shape of little houses: in these we slept: and after the morning meal, we embarked again, and proceeded as before. I was often very much astonished to see some of the women as well as the men, jump into the water, dive to the bottom, come up again, and swim about. Thus I continued to travel, both by land and by water, through different countries and various nations, till at the end of six or seven months after I had been kidnapped, I arrived at the sea coast.

It would be tedious and uninteresting to relate all the incidents which befell me during this journey, and which I have not yet forgotten,

or to mention the various lands I passed through, and the manners and customs of the different people among whom I lived: I shall therefore only observe, that in all the places where I was, the soil was exceedingly rich; the pomkins, aedas, plantains, yams, &c. &c. were in great abundance, and of incredible size. There were also large quantities of different gums, though not used for any purpose; and every where a great deal of tobacco. The cotton even grew quite wild; and there was plenty of red wood. I saw no mechanics whatever in all the way, except such as I have mentioned. The chief employment in all these countries was agriculture, and both the males and females, as with us, were brought up to it, and trained in the arts of war.

The first object that saluted my eyes when I arrived on the coast was the sea, and a slave ship, which was then riding at anchor, and waiting for its cargo. These filled me with astonishment, that was soon converted into terror, which I am yet at a loss to describe, and much more the then feelings of my mind when I was carried on board. I was immediately handled and tossed up to see if I was sound, by some of the crew; and I was now persuaded that I had got into a world of bad spirits, and that they were going to kill me. Their complexions too, differing so much from ours, their long hair, and the language they spoke, which was very different from any I had ever heard, united to confirm me in this belief. Indeed such were the horrors of my views and fears at the moment, that if ten thousand worlds had been my own, I would have freely parted with them all to have exchanged my condition with the meanest slave in my own country. When I looked round the ship too, and saw a large furnace or copper boiling and a multitude of black people, of every description, chained together, every one of their countenances expressing dejection and sorrow, I no longer doubted of my fate; and, quite overpowered with horror and anguish, I fell motionless on the deck, and fainted. When I recovered a little, I found some black people about me, who I believed were some of those who brought me on board, and had been receiving their pay: they talked to me in order to cheer me, but all in vain. I asked them if we were not to be eaten by those white men with horrible looks, red faces, and long hair. They told me I was not: and one of the crew brought me a small portion of spirituous liquor in a wine glass; but, being afraid of him, I would not take it out of his hand. One of the blacks therefore took it from him and gave it to me, and I took a little down my palate, which, instead of reviving me, as they thought it would, threw me into the greatest consternation at the strange feeling it produced, having never tasted any such liquor before.

Soon after this the blacks who brought me on board went off, and left me abandoned to despair. I now saw myself deprived of all chance of returning to my native country, or even the least glimpse of gaining the

shore, which I now considered as friendly; and I even wished for my former slavery, in preference to my present situation, which was filled with horrors of every kind, still heightened by my ignorance of what I was to undergo. I was not long suffered to indulge my grief. I was soon put down under the decks, and there I received such a salutation in my nostrils as I had never experienced in my life: so that, with the loathsomeness of the stench, and with my crying together, I became so sick and low that I was not able to eat, nor had I the least desire to taste any thing. I now wished for the last friend, death, to relieve me; but soon, to my grief, two of the white men offered me eatables; and, on my refusing to eat, one of them held me fast by the hands, and laid me across, I think, the windlass, and tied my feet, while the other flogged me severely. I had never experienced any thing of this kind before, and although, not being used to the water, I naturally feared that element the first time I saw it, yet nevertheless, could I have got over the nettings, I would have jumped over the side, but I could not; and besides the crew used to watch us very closely, who were not chained down to the decks, lest we should leap into the water. I have seen some of these poor African prisoners most severely cut for attempting to do so, and hourly whipped for not eating. This indeed was often the case with myself. In a little time after, amongst the poor chained men, I found some of my own nation, which in a small degree gave ease to my mind. I inquired of these what was to be done with us. They gave me to understand we were to be carried to these white people's country to work for them. I was then a little revived, and thought if it were no worse than working, my situation was not so desperate. But still I feared I should be put to death, the white people looked and acted, as I thought, in so savage a manner; for I had never seen among any people such instances of brutal cruelty: and this is not only shewn towards us blacks, but also to some of the whites themselves. One white man in particular I saw, when we were permitted to be on deck, flogged so unmercifully with a large rope near the foremast, that he died in consequence of it; and they tossed him over the side as they would have done a brute. This made me fear these people the more; and I expected nothing less than to be treated in the same manner. I could not help expressing my fearful apprehensions to some of my countrymen; I asked them if these people had no country, but lived in this hollow place, the ship. They told me they did not, but came from a distant one. 'Then,' said I, 'how comes it, that in all our country we never heard of them?' They told me, because they lived so very far off. I then asked, where their women were: had they any like themselves. I was told they had. 'And why,' said I, 'do we not see them?' They answered, because they were left behind. I asked how the vessel could go. They told me they could not tell; but that there was

cloth put upon the masts by the help of the ropes I saw, and then the vessel went on; and the white men had some spell or magic they put in the water, when they liked, in order to stop the vessel. I was exceedingly amazed at this account, and really thought they were spirits. I therefore wished much to be from amongst them, for I expected they would sacrifice me; but my wishes were in vain, for we were so quartered that it was impossible for any of us to make our escape.

VI.

While we stayed on the coast I was mostly on deck; and one day, to my great astonishment, I saw one of these vessels coming in with the sails up. As soon as the whites saw it, they gave a great shout, at which we were amazed; and the more so as the vessel appeared larger by approaching nearer. At last she came to an anchor in my sight, and when the anchor was let go, I and my countrymen who saw it, were lost in astonishment to observe the vessel stop, and were now convinced it was done by magic. Soon after this the other ship got her boats out, and they came on board of us, and the people of both ships seemed very glad to see each other. Several of the strangers also shook hands with us black people, and made motions with their hands, signifying, I suppose, we were to go to their country; but we did not understand them. At last, when the ship, in which we were, had got in all her cargo, they made ready with many fearful noises, and we were all put under deck, so that we could not see how they managed the vessel.

But this disappointment was the least of my grief. The stench of the hold, while we were on the coast, was so intolerably loathsome, that it was dangerous to remain there for any time, and some of us had been permitted to stay on the deck for the fresh air; but now that the whole ship's cargo were confined together, it became absolutely pestilential. The closeness of the place, and the heat of the climate, added to the number in the ship, being so crowded that each had scarcely room to turn himself, almost suffocated us. This produced copious perspirations, so that the air soon became unfit for respiration, from a variety of loathsome smells, and brought on a sickness among the slaves, of which many died, thus falling victims to the improvident avarice, as I may call it, of their purchasers. This deplorable situation was again aggravated by the galling of the chains, now become insupportable; and the filth of necessary tubs, into which the children often fell, and were almost suffocated. The shrieks of the women, and the groans of the dying, rendered it a scene of horror almost inconceivable. Happily, perhaps,

for myself, I was soon reduced so low here that it was thought necessary to keep me almost continually on deck; and from my extreme youth, I was not put in fetters. In this situation I expected every hour to share the fate of my companions, some of whom were almost daily brought upon deck at the point of death, and I began to hope that death would soon put an end to my miseries. Often did I think many of the inhabitants of the deep much more happy than myself; I envied them the freedom they enjoyed, and as often wished I could change my condition for theirs. Every circumstance I met with served only to render my state more painful, and heighten my apprehensions and my opinion of the cruelty of the whites. One day they had taken a number of fishes; and when they had killed and satisfied themselves with as many as they thought fit, to our astonishment who were on the deck, rather than give any of them to us to eat, as we expected, they tossed the remaining fish into the sea again, although we begged and prayed for some as well as we could, but in vain; and some of my countrymen, being pressed by hunger, took an opportunity, when they thought no one saw them, of trying to get a little privately; but were discovered, and the attempt procured for them some very severe floggings.

One day, when we had a smooth sea and moderate wind, two of my wearied countrymen, who were chained together (I was near them at the time), preferring death to such a life of misery, somehow made through the nettings and jumped into the sea: immediately another quite dejected fellow, who on account of his illness was suffered to be out of irons also followed their example; and I believe many more would very soon have done the same, if they had not been prevented by the ship's crew, who were instantly alarmed. Those of us who were the most active were in a moment put down under the deck; and there was such a noise and confusion amongst the people of the ship as I never heard before, to stop her and get the boat out to go after the slaves. However, two of the wretches were drowned; but they got the other, and afterward flogged him unmercifully, for thus attempting to prefer death to slavery. In this manner we continued to undergo more hardships than I can now relate, hardships which are inseparable from this accursed trade. Many a time we were near suffocation from the want of fresh air, being deprived thereof for days together. This, and the stench of the necessary tubs, carried off many.

VII.

During our passage I first saw flying fishes, which surprised me very much: they used frequently to fly across the ship, and many of them fell on deck. I also now first saw the use of the quadrant. I had often with

astonishment seen the mariners make observations with it, and I could not think what it meant. They at last took notice of my surprise: and one of them, willing to increase it, as well as to gratify my curiosity, made me one day look through it. The clouds appeared to me to be land, which disappeared as they passed along. This heightened my wonder; and I was now more persuaded than ever that I was in another world, and that every thing about me was magic At last we came in sight of the island of Barbadoes, at which the whites on board gave a great shout, and made many signs of joy to us. We did not know what to think of this, but as the vessel drew nearer we plainly saw the harbour, and other ships of different kinds and sizes; and we soon anchored amongst them off Bridge Town. Many merchants and planters now came on board, though it was in the evening. They put us in separate parcels, and examined us attentively. They also made us jump, and pointed to the land, signifying we were to go there. We thought by this we should be beaten by these ugly men, as they appeared to us; and, when soon after we were all put down under the deck again, there was much dread and trembling among us, and nothing but bitter cries to be heard all the night from these apprehensions, insomuch that at last the white people got some old slaves from the land to pacify us. They told us we were not to be eaten, but to work, and were soon to go on land, where we should see many of our country people. This report eased us much; and, sure enough, soon after we landed, there came to us Africans of all languages.

We were conducted immediately to the merchant's yard, where we were all pent up together like so many sheep in a fold, without regard to sex or age. As every object was new to me, every thing I saw filled me with surprise. What struck me first was that the houses were built with bricks in stories, and were in every other respect different from those I had seen in Africa; but I was still more astonished at seeing people on horseback. I did not know what this could mean; and indeed I thought these people full of nothing but magical arts. While I was in this astonishment one of my fellow prisoners spoke to a countryman of his about the horses, who said they were the same kind they had in their country. I understood them, though they were from a distant part of Africa, and I thought it odd I had not seen any horses there; but afterwards, when I came to converse with different Africans, I found they had many horses amongst them, and much larger than those I then saw.

We were not many days in the merchants' custody before we were sold after the usual manner, which is this:—On a signal given, such as the beat of a drum, the buyers rush at once into the yard where the slaves are confined, and make choice of that parcel they like best. The noise and clamour with which this is attended, and the eagerness visible in the countenances of the buyers, serve not a little to increase the

apprehensions of the terrified Africans, who may well be supposed to consider them the ministers of that destruction to which they think themselves devoted. In this manner, without scruple, are relations and friends separated, most of them never to see each other again. I remember in the vessel in which I was brought over in, in the man's apartment, there were several brothers, who, in the sale, were sold in different lots; and it was very moving on this occasion to see their distress and hear their cries at parting. O, ye nominal Christians! might not an African ask you, "learned you this from your God, who says unto you, Do unto all men as you would men should do unto you? Is it not enough that we are torn from our country and friends, to toil for your luxury and lust of gain? Must every tender feeling be likewise sacrificed to your avarice? Are the dearest friends and relations now rendered more dear by their separation from the rest of their kindred, still to be parted from each other, and thus prevented from cheering the gloom of slavery, with the small comfort of being together, and mingling their sufferings and sorrows? Why are parents to lose their children, brothers their sisters, or husbands their wives? Surely this is a new refinement in cruelty, which, while it has no advantage to atone for it, thus aggravates distress, and adds fresh horrors even to the wretchedness of slavery."

CHAPTER III

*The author is carried to Virginia—His distress—Surprise at seeing a
picture and a watch—Is bought by Captain Pascal, and sets out for
England—His terror during the voyage—Arrives in England—His
wonder at a fall of snow—Is sent to Guernsey, and in some time goes
on board a ship of war with his master—Some account of the expedi-
tion against Louisbourg, under the command of Admiral Boscawen,
in 1758.*

I.

I NOW totally lost the small remains of comfort I had enjoyed in con-
versing with my countrymen; the women, too, who used to wash and
take care of me, were all gone different ways, and I never saw one of
them afterwards.

I stayed in this island for a few days; I believe it could not be above
a fortnight; when I and some few more slaves, who from very much fret-
ting were not saleable among the rest, were shipped off in a sloop for
North America. On the passage we were better treated than when
coming from Africa, and we had plenty of rice and fat pork. We were
landed up a river a good way from the sea, about Virginia county,
where we saw few of our native Africans, and not one soul who could
talk to me. I was a few weeks weeding grass and gathering stones in a
plantation; and at last all my companions were distributed different
ways, and only myself was left. I was now exceedingly miserable, and
thought myself worse off than any of the rest of my companions; for
they could talk to each other, but I had no person to speak to that I
could understand. In this state I was constantly grieving and pining,

and wishing for death rather than any thing else. While I was in this plantation the gentleman to whom I supposed the estate belonged being unwell, I was one day sent for to his dwelling-house to fan him. When I came into the room where he was, I was very much affrighted at some things I saw, and the more so, as I had seen a black woman slave as I came through the house, who was cooking the dinner, and the poor creature was cruelly loaded with various kinds of iron machines; she had one particularly on her head, which locked her mouth so fast that she could scarcely speak, and could not eat or drink. I much astonished and shocked at this contrivance, which I afterwards learned was called the iron muzzle. Soon after I had a fan put into my hand, to fan the gentleman while he slept; and so I did indeed with great fear. While he was fast asleep I indulged myself a great deal in looking about the room, which to me appeared very fine and curious. The first object that engaged my attention was a watch, which hung on the chimney, and was going. I was quite surprised at the noise it made, and was afraid it would tell the gentleman any thing I might do amiss: and when I immediately after observed a picture hanging in the room, which appeared constantly to look at me, I was still more affrighted, having never seen such things as these before. At one time I thought it was something relative to magic; and not seeing it move, I thought it might be some way the whites had to keep their great men when they died, and offer them libations, as we used to do to our friendly spirits. In this state of anxiety I remained till my master awoke, when I was dismissed out of the room, to my no small satisfaction and relief; for I thought that these people were all made up of wonders. In this place I was called JACOB; but on board the African Snow* I was called MICHAEL.

II.

I had been some time in this miserable, forlorn, and much dejected state, without any one to talk to, which made my life a burden, when the kind and unknown hand of the Creator, who in every deed leads the blind in a way they know not, now began to appear to my comfort; for one day the captain of a merchant ship, called the "Industrious Bee," came on some business to my master's house. This gentleman, whose name was Michael Henry Pascal, was a lieutenant in the royal navy, but now commanded this trading ship, which was somewhere in the confines

*A large two-masted Ship.

of the county many miles off. While he was at my master's house it happened that he saw me, and liked me so well that he made a purchase of me. I think I have often heard him say he gave thirty or forty pounds sterling for me; the exact sum I do not now remember. However he meant me for a present to some of his friends in England: and I was sent accordingly from the house of my then master, one Mr. Campbell, to the place where the ship lay. I was conducted on horseback by an elderly black man, a mode of travelling which appeared very odd to me. When I arrived, I was carried on board a fine large ship, loaded with tobacco, &c. and just ready to sail for England. I now thought my condition much mended; having sails to lie on, and plenty of good victuals to eat; and every body on board used me very kindly, quite contrary to what I had seen of any white people before; I therefore began to think that they were not all of the same disposition. A few days after I was on board we sailed for England. I was still at a loss to conjecture my destiny. By this time, however I could smatter a little imperfect English, and I wanted to know as well I could where we were going. Some of the people of the ship used to tell me they were going to carry me back to my own country, and this made me very happy. I was quite rejoiced at the idea of going back; and thought if I should get home what wonders I should have to tell. But I was reserved for another fate, and was soon undeceived when we came within sight of the English coast.

While I was on board of this ship my captain and master named me GUSTAVUS VASSA. I at that time began to understand him a little, and refused to be called so, and told him, as well as I could, that I would be called JACOB; but he said I should not, and still called me Gustavus. And when I refused to answer to my new name, which at first I did, it gained me many a cuff; so at length I submitted, and by it I have been known ever since. The ship had a very long passage; and on that account we had very short allowance of provisions; having towards the last only one pound and a half of bread per week, and about the same quantity of meat, and one quart of water a-day. We spoke with only one vessel during the voyage, and but once caught a few fishes. In our extremity the captain and people told me in jest they would kill and eat me, but I thought them in earnest, and was depressed beyond measure, expecting every moment to be my last. While I was in this situation one evening they caught a large shark, and got it on board. This rejoiced my heart exceedingly, as I thought it would serve the people to eat instead of their eating me; but very soon, to my astonishment, they cut off a small part of the tail, and tossed the rest over the side. This increased my consternation; and I did not know what to think of these white people, though I very much feared they intended to kill and eat me.

III.

There was on board the ship a young lad, who had never been at sea before, about four or five years older than myself; his name was Richard Baker. He was a native of America, had received an excellent education, and was of a most amiable temper. Soon after I went on board he shewed me a great deal of partiality and attention, and in return I grew very fond of him. We at length became inseparable; and, for the space of two years, he was of great use to me, and was my constant companion and instructor. Although this dear youth had many slaves of his own, yet he and I have gone through many sufferings together on shipboard; and have many nights lain in each other's bosoms, when in great distress. Thus such a friendship was cemented between us, as we cherished till his death, which, to my very grief, happened in the year 1759, when he was up the Archipelago, on board his Majesty's ship the Preston: an event which I never ceased to regret, as I lost at once a kind interpreter, an agreeable companion, and a faithful friend; who at the age of fifteen, discovered a mind superior to prejudice, being not ashamed to notice, to associate with, and to be the friend and instructor of one who was ignorant, a stranger, and a slave! My master had lodged in his mother's house in America: he respected him very much, and made him always eat with him in the cabin. He used often to tell him jocularly that he would kill and eat me. Sometimes he used to say to me—the black people were not good to eat, and ask me if we did not eat people in my country. I said "No:" then he said he would first kill Dick, as he always called him, and afterwards me. Though this hearing relieved my mind a little as to myself, I was alarmed for Dick, and whenever he was called I used to be very much afraid he was to be killed; and I would peep and watch to see if they were going to kill him; nor was I free from this consternation till we made the land.

One night we lost a man overboard; and the cries and noise were so great and confused, in stopping the ship, that I, who did not know what was the matter, began, as usual, to be very much afraid, and to think they were going to make an offering with me, and perform some magic; in which I still believed that they dealt. As the waves were very high, I thought the Ruler of the seas was angry, and I expected to be offered up to appease him. This filled my mind with agony, and I could not any more, that night, close my eyes again to rest. However, when daylight appeared, I was a little eased in my mind; but still, when called, I thought it was that I might be killed. Some time after this we saw some very large fishes, which I afterwards found were called grampusses.

They looked to me extremely terrible, and made their appearance just at dusk. They were so near as to blow the water on the ship's deck. I believed them to be the rulers of the sea: and as the white people did not make any offerings at any time, I thought they were angry at them: and, at last, what confirmed my belief, the wind just then died away, and a calm ensued, and in consequence of it the ship ceased from going. I supposed that the fishes had performed this, and hid myself in the forepart of the ship, through fear of being offered up to appease them, every minute peeping and quaking; but my good friend Dick came shortly to me, and I took an opportunity to ask him, as well as I could, what these fishes were. Not being able to talk much English, I could but just make him understand my question; and not at all, when I asked him if any offerings were to be made to them: however he told me these fishes would devour any body, which sufficiently alarmed me. Here he was called away by the captain, who was leaning over the quarter-deck railing, and looking at the fishes; and most of the people were busied in getting a barrel of pitch to light, for them to play with. The Captain now called me, having learned some of my apprehensions from Dick; and having diverted himself and others, for some time, with my fears, which appeared ludicrous enough in my crying and trembling, he dismissed me. The barrel of pitch was then lighted and put over the side into the water: by this time it was just dark, and the fishes went after it; and to my great joy, I saw them no more.

IV.

However, all my alarms began to subside when we got sight of land; and at last the ship reached Falmouth, after a passage of thirteen weeks. Every heart on board seemed gladdened on our reaching the shore, and none more than mine. The captain immediately went on shore, and sent on board some fresh provisions, which we wanted very much: we made good use of them, and our famine was soon turned into feasting, almost without ending. It was about the beginning of spring 1757, when I arrived in England, and I was nearly twelve years of age at that time. I was very much struck with the buildings and the pavement of the streets in Falmouth; and, indeed, every object I saw filled me with fresh surprise. One morning, when I got upon deck, I perceived it covered all over with the snow that fell over-night. As I had never seen any thing of the kind before, I thought it was salt; so I immediately ran down to the mate and desired him, as well as I could, to come and see how somebody in the night had thrown salt all over the deck. He, knowing what it was,

desired me to bring some of it down to him: accordingly I took up a handful of it, which I found very cold indeed; and when I brought it to him he desired me to taste it. I did so, and was surprised above measure. I then asked him what it was; he told me it was snow; but I could not by any means understand him. He asked me if we had no such thing in our country; I told him "No." I then asked him the use of it, and who made it: he told me a great man in the heavens, called God: but here again I was to all intents and purposes at a loss to understand him; and the more so, when a little after I saw the air filled with it, in a heavy shower, which fell down on the same day.

After this I went to church; and having never been at such a place before, I was again amazed at seeing and hearing the service. I asked all I could about it; and they gave me to understand it was "worshiping God, who made us and all things." I was still at a loss, and soon got into an endless field of inquiries, as well as I was able to speak and ask about things. However, my dear little friend Dick used to be my best interpreter; for I could make free with him and he always instructed me with pleasure. And from what I could understand by him of this God, and in seeing that these white people did not sell one another as we did, I was much pleased: and in this I thought they were much happier than we Africans. I was astonished at the wisdom of the white people in all things which I beheld; but I was greatly amazed at their not sacrificing, nor making any offerings, and at their eating with unwashen hands, and touching the dead. I also could not help remarking the particular slenderness of their women, which I did not at first like, and I thought them not so modest and shamefaced as the African women.

I had often seen my master and Dick employed in reading; and I had a great curiosity to talk to the books, as I thought they did; and so to learn how all things had a beginning. For that purpose I have often taken up a book, and talked to it, and then put my ears to it, when alone, in hopes it would answer me; and I have been very much concerned when I found it remained silent.

V.

My master lodged at the house of a gentleman in Falmouth, who had a fine little daughter, about six or seven years of age, and she grew prodigiously fond of me; insomuch that we used to eat together, and had servants to wait on us. I was so much caressed by this family, that it often reminded me of the treatment I had received from my little noble

African master. After I had been here a few days, I was sent on board of the ship; but the child cried so much after me, that nothing could pacify her till I was sent for again. It is ludicrous enough, that I began to fear I should be betrothed to this young lady; and when my master asked me if I would stay there with her behind him, as he was going away with the ship, having taken in the tobacco again, I cried immediately, and said I would not leave him. At last, by stealth, one night I was sent on board the ship again; and in a little time sailed for Guernsey, where she was in part owned by a merchant, one Nicholas Doberry.

As I was now amongst a people who had not their faces scarred, like some of the African nations where I had been, I was very glad at my not having permitted them to ornament me in that manner. When we arrived at Guernsey, my master placed me to board and lodge with one of his mates, who had a wife and family there; and some months afterwards he returned to England, and left me in care of this mate, together with my friend Dick. This mate had a little daughter, aged about five or six years, with her I used to be much delighted. I had often observed that when her mother washed her face it looked very rosy; but when she washed mine it did not look so: I therefore tried oftentimes myself if I could not by washing make my face of the same colour as my little playmate, Mary, but it was all in vain; and I then began to be mortified at the difference in our complexions. This woman behaved to me with great kindness and attention. She taught me every thing in the same manner as she did her own child, and indeed in every respect treated me as such. I remained here till the summer of the year 1757; when my master, being appointed first lieutenant of his majesty's ship the Roebuck, sent for Dick and me, and his old mate: on this we all left Guernsey, and set out for England in a sloop bound for London. As we were coming up towards the Nore, where the Roebuck lay, a man of war's boat came alongside to press our people: on which each man ran to hide himself. I was very much frightened at this, though I did not understand the meaning thereof, or what to think or do. However I went and hid myself also under a hen-coop. Immediately the press-gang came on board, with their swords drawn, and searched all about, pulled the people out by force, and put them into the boat. At last I was found out also, and the man that discovered me held me up by the heels, while they all made their sport of me, I roaring and crying out all the time most lustily; but at last the mate, my conductor, seeing this, came to my assistance, and did all he could to pacify me; but all to very little purpose, till I had seen the boat go off. Soon afterwards we came to the Nore, where the Roebuck lay; and, to our great joy, my master came on board to us, and brought us to the ship.

VI.

When I got on board this large ship, I was indeed amazed to see the quantity of men and the guns. However my surprise began to diminish, as my knowledge increased; and I ceased to feel those apprehensions and alarms which took such strong possession on me when I came first among the Europeans, and for some time after. I began now to pass to an opposite extreme; and was so far from being afraid of any thing new which I saw, that after I had been some time in this ship, I even began to long for an engagement. My griefs too, which in young minds are not perpetual, were now wearing away; and I soon enjoyed myself pretty well, and felt tolerably easy in my situation. There was a number of boys on board, and this made it still more agreeable; being constantly together, and spending a great part of our time in play.

I remained in this ship a considerable time, during which we made several cruises, and visited a variety of places: among others we were twice in Holland, and brought over several persons of distinction from it, but their names have escaped my memory. On the passage one day, for the diversion of those gentlemen, all the boys were called on the quarter-deck, and were paired proportionably, and then made to fight; after which the gentlemen gave the combatants from five to nine shillings each. This was the first time I ever fought with a white boy; and I never had a bloody nose before. This made me fight most desperately; I suppose considerably more than a hour, and at last, both of us being tired, we were parted. I had a great deal of this kind of sport afterwards, in which the captain and the ship's company used very much to encourage me. Some time afterwards the ship went to Leith, in Scotland, and from thence to the Orkneys, where I was surprised at seeing scarcely any night; and from thence we sailed with a great fleet, full of soldiers, for England. All this time we had never come to an engagement, though frequently cruising off the coast of France, during which we chased many vessels, and took in all seventeen prizes. I had been learning many of the manœuvres of the ship during our cruise; and I was several times made to fire the guns.

One evening, off Havre de Grace, just as it was growing dark, we were standing off shore, and met with a fine large French-built frigate. We immediately got all things ready for fighting: and I now expected I should be gratified in seeing an engagement, which I had so long wished for in vain. But the very moment the word of command was given to fire, we heard those on board the other ship cry, 'Haul down the jib!' and in that instant she hoisted English colours. There was instantly with us an amazing cry of—'Avast!' or 'stop firing!' and I think

one or two guns had been let off, but happily they did no mischief. We had hailed them several times; but they not hearing, we received no answer, and that caused us to fire. The boat was then sent on board of her, and she proved to be the Ambuscade man of war, to my no small disappointment.

We returned to Portsmouth, without having been in any action, just at the trial of Admiral Byng, whom I saw several times during it: and my master having left the ship, and gone to London for promotion, Dick and I were put on board the Savage sloop of war, to assist in bringing off the St. George man of war, that had run ashore somewhere on the coast. After staying a few weeks on board the Savage, Dick and I were sent on shore at Deal, and remained there till my master sent for us to London, the place I had long desired exceedingly to see. We therefore both with great pleasure got into a wagon and came to London, where we were received by a Mr. Guerin, a relation of my master. This gentleman had two sisters, very amiable ladies. They took much notice and great care of me.

VII.

Though I had desired so much to see London, when I arrived in it I was unfortunately unable to gratify my curiosity; for I had at this time the chilblains to such a degree, that I could not stand for several months, and was obliged to be sent to St. George's hospital. There I grew so ill, that the doctors wanted to cut my leg off at different times, apprehending a mortification; but I always said I would rather die than suffer it: and, I thank God, I happily recovered without the operation. After being there several weeks, and just as I had recovered, the small pox broke out on me, so that I was again confined; and I thought myself now particularly unfortunate. However I soon recovered again; and by this time my master having been promoted to be first lieutenant of the Preston man of war, of fifty guns, then new at Deptford, Dick and I went on board her, and soon after sailed for Holland to bring over the late Duke of Cumberland to England.

While I was in this ship an incident happened, which, though trifling, I beg leave to relate, as I could not help taking particular notice of it, and considering it then as a judgment of God. One morning a young man was looking up to the fore-top, and in a wicked tone, common on shipboard, d——d his eyes about something. Just at the moment some small particles of dirt fell into his left eye, and by the evening it was very much inflamed. The next day it grew worse, and within six or seven

days he lost it. From this ship my master was appointed a lieutenant on board the Royal George. When he was going he wished me to stay on board the Preston, to learn the French horn; but the ship being ordered for Turkey I could not think of leaving my master, to whom I was very warmly attached; and I told him if he left me behind, it would break my heart. This prevailed with him to take me with him; but he left Dick on board: whom I embraced at parting for the last time.

The Royal George was the largest ship I had ever seen; so that when I came on board of her I was surprised at the number of people, men, women, and children, of every denomination and description, and the largeness of the guns, many of them also of brass, which I had never seen before. Here were also shops or stalls for every kind of goods, and people crying their different commodities about the ship, as in a town. To me it appeared a little world, into which I was again cast without a friend, for I had no longer my dear companion Dick.

We did not stay long here. My master was not many weeks on board before he got an appointment to be sixth lieutenant of the Namur, then at Spithead, fitting up for Vice-admiral Boscawen, who was going, with a large fleet, on an expedition against Louisbourgh. The crew of the Royal George were turned over to her, and the flag of that gallant admiral was hoisted on board, the blue at the main-top-gallant-mast head. There was a very great fleet of men of war of every description assembled together for this expedition, and I was in hopes soon to be gratified with a sea-fight. All things being now in readiness, this mighty fleet, for there was also Admiral Cormsh's fleet in company, destined for the East Indies, at last weighed anchor, and sailed. The two fleets continued in company for several days, and then parted; Admiral Cormsh, in the Lenox, having first saluted our admiral in the Namur, which he returned. We then steered for America; but, by contrary winds, were driven to Teneriffe, where I was struck with its noted peak. Its prodigious height and its form, resembling a sugar-loaf, filled me with wonder. We remained in sight of this island some days, and then proceeded for America, which we soon made, and got into a commodious harbour called St. George, in Halifax. Here we had fish in abundance, and all other fresh provisions. We were here joined by different men of war, and transport ships with soldiers; after which, our fleet being increased to a prodigious number of ships of all kinds, we sailed for Cape Breton in Nova Scotia. We had the good and gallant General Wolfe on board our ship, whose affability made him highly esteemed and beloved by all the men. He often honoured me, as well as other boys, with marks of his notice; and saved me once a flogging for fighting with a young gentleman.

VIII.

We arrived at Cape Breton in the summer of 1758: and here the soldiers were to be landed, in order to make an attack upon Louisbourgh. My master had some part in superintending the landing; and here I was in a small degree gratified in seeing an encounter between our men and the enemy. The French were posted on the shore to receive us, and disputed our landing for a long time: but at last they were driven from their trenches, and a complete landing was effected. Our troops pursued them as far as the town of Louisbourgh. In this action many were killed on both sides. One thing remarkable I saw this day:—A lieutenant of the Princess Amelia, who, as well as my master, superintended the landing, was giving the word of command, and while his mouth was open a musket ball went through it, and passed out at his cheek. I had that day in my hand the scalp of an Indian king, killed in the engagement: the scalp was taken off by an Highlander. I saw the king's ornaments too, which were very curious, and made of feathers.

Our land forces laid seige to the town of Louisbourgh, while the French men of war were blocked up in the harbour by the fleet, the batteries at the same time playing upon them from the land. This they did with such effect, that one day I saw some of the ships set on fire by the shells from the batteries, and I believe two or three of them were quite burnt. At another time, about fifty boats belonging to the English men of war, commanded by Captain George Belfour, of the Ætna fire-ship, and Mr. Laforey, another junior captain, attacked and boarded the only two remaining French men of war in the harbour. They also set fire to a seventy gun ship: but a sixty-four, called the Bienfaisant, they brought off. Whilst here I had often an opportunity of being near captain Belfour, who was pleased to notice me, and liked me so much that he often asked my master to let him have me, but he would not part with me; and no consideration could have induced me to leave him.

At last Louisbourgh was taken, and the English men of war came into the harbour before it, to my very great joy; for I had now liberty of indulging myself, and I went often on shore. When the ships were in harbour we had the most beautiful procession on the water I ever beheld. All the admirals and captains full dressed, and in their barges, ornamented with pendants, came alongside of the Namur. The vice-admiral then went on shore in his barge, followed by the other officers in order of seniority, to take possession of the town and fort. Some time after this the French governor, his lady, and other persons of note, came

on board our ship to dine. On this occasion our ships were dressed with colours of all kinds, from the top-gallant-mast head to the deck; and this, with the firing of guns, formed a most grand and magnificent spectacle.

IX.

As soon as every thing here was settled, Admiral Boscawen sailed with part of the fleet for England, leaving some ships behind with rear-Admirals Sir Charles Hardy and Durell. It was now winter; and one evening, during our passage home, about dusk, being in the channel, or near soundings, and beginning to look for land, we described seven sail of large men of war standing off shore. Several people on board of our ship said, as the two fleets were, in forty minutes from the first sight, within hail of each other, that they were English men of war; and some of our people even began to name some of the ships. By this time both fleets began to mingle, and our admiral ordered his flag to be hoisted. At that instant the other fleet, which were French, hoisted their ensigns, and gave us a broadside as they passed. Nothing could create greater surprise and confusion among us than this: the wind was high, the sea rough, and we had our lower and middle deck guns housed in, so that not a single gun on board was ready to be fired at any of the French ships. However, the Royal William and the Somerset, being our stern-most ships, became a little prepared; and each gave the French ships a broadside as they passed by.

I afterwards heard this was a French squadron, commanded by Mons. Conflans; and certainly had the Frenchmen known our condition, and had a mind to fight us, they might have done us great mischief. But we were not long before we were prepared for an engagement. Immediately many things were tossed overboard; the ships made ready for fighting, and about ten at night we had bent a new mainsail, the old one being split. We now wore ship, and stood after the French fleet, which were one or two ships more than we. However we gave them chase, and continued the pursuit all night; and at day-light we saw six of them, all large ships of the line, and an English East Indiaman, a prize they had taken. We chased them all day till between three and four o'clock in the evening, when we came up with, and passed within a musket shot of one seventy-four gun ship, and the Indiaman also, who now hoisted her colours, but immediately hauled them down again. On this we made a signal for the other ships to take possession of her; and, supposing the man of war would likewise strike, we cheered, but she did not; tho' if we had fired into her, from being so near, we must have taken her. To

my utter surprise, the Somerset, who was the next ship a-stern of the Namur, made way likewise; and, thinking they were sure of this French ship, they cheered in the same manner, but still continued to follow us. The French Commodore was about a gun-shot a-head of all, running from us with all speed; and about four o'clock he carried his fore-top-mast overboard. This caused another loud cheer with us; and a little after the top-mast came close by us; but, to our great surprise, instead of coming up with her, we found she went as fast as ever, if not faster.

The sea grew now much smoother; and the wind lulling, the seventy-four gun ship we had passed came again by us in the very same direction, and so near, that we heard the people talk as she passed by; yet not a shot was fired on either side; and about five or six o'clock, just as it grew dark, she joined her commodore. We chased all night; but the next day we were out of sight, so that we saw no more of them; and we only had the old Indiaman, called Carnarvon, I think, for our trouble. After this we stood in for the channel, and soon made the land; and, about the close of the year 1758–9, we got safe to St. Helen's. Here the Namur ran aground; and also another large ship a-stern of us; but, by starting our water, and tossing many things overboard to lighten her, we got the ships off without any damage. We stayed for a short time at Spithead, and then went into Portsmouth harbour to refit; from whence the admiral went to London, and my master and I soon followed, with a pressgang, as we wanted some hands to complete our complement.

CHAPTER IV.

The author is baptized—Narrowly escapes drowning—Goes on an expedition to the Mediterranean—Incidents he met with there—Is witness of an engagement between some English and French ships—A particular account of the celebrated Engagement between Admiral Boscawen and Mons. Le Clue, off Cape Logas, in August 1759—Dreadful explosion of a French ship—The author sails for England—His master appointed to the command of a fire ship—Meets a negro boy, from whom he experiences much benevolence—Prepares for an expedition against Belleisle—A remarkable story of a disaster which befel his ship—Arrives at Belleisle—Operations of the landing and siege—The author's danger and distress, with his manner of extricating himself—Surrender of Belleisle—Transactions afterwards on the coast of France—Remarkable instance of kidnapping—The author returns to England—Hears a talk of peace, and expects his freedom—His ship sails for Deptford to be paid off, and when he arrives there he is suddenly seized by his master, and carried forcibly on board a West-India ship, and sold.

I.

IT WAS now between two and three years since I first came to England, a great part of which I had spent at sea; so that I became mured to that service, and began to consider myself as happily situated; for my master treated me always extremely well; and my attachment and gratitude to him were very great. From the various scenes I had beheld on ship-board, I soon grew a stranger to terror of every kind, and was, in that respect at least, almost an Englishman. I have often reflected with surprise that I

never felt half the alarm, at any of the numerous dangers in which I have been, that I was filled with at the first sight of the Europeans, and at every act of theirs, even the most trifling, when I first came among them, and for some time afterwards. That fear, however, the effect of my ignorance, wore away as I began to know them.

I could now speak English tolerably well, and perfectly understood every thing that was said. I not only felt myself quite easy with these new countrymen, but relished their society and manners. I no longer looked upon them as spirits, but as men superior to us; and therefore I had the stronger desire to resemble them, to imbibe their spirit, and imitate their manners. I therefore embraced every occasion of improvement; and every new thing that I observed I treasured up in my memory. I had long wished to be able to read and write; and for this purpose I took every opportunity to gain instruction, but had made as yet but very little progress. However, when I went to London with my master, I had soon an opportunity of improving myself, which I gladly embraced. Shortly after my arrival, he sent me to wait upon the Miss Guerins, who had treated me with so much kindness when I was there before, and they sent me to school.

While I was attending these ladies, their servants told me I could not go to Heaven, unless I was baptized. This made me very uneasy; for I had now some faint idea of a future state: accordingly I communicated my anxiety to the eldest Miss Guerin, with whom I was become a favourite, and pressed her to have me baptized; when, to my great joy, she told me I should. She had formerly asked my master to let me be baptized, but he had refused; however she now insisted on it; and he, being under some obligation to her brother, complied with her request; so I was baptized at St. Margaret's church, Westminster, in February 1759, by my present name. The clergyman, at the same time, gave me a book, called "a Guide to the Indians," written by the Bishop of Sodor and Man. On this occasion, Miss Guerin did me the honour to stand as godmother, and afterwards gave me a treat.

I used to attend these ladies about the town, in which service I was extremely happy, as I had thus very many opportunities of seeing London, which I desired of all things. I was sometimes, however, with my master at his rendezvous-house, at the foot of Westminster-bridge. Here I used to enjoy myself in playing about the bridge stairs, and often in the watermen's wherries, with other boys. On one of these occasions there was another boy with me in a wherry, and we went out into the current of the river; while there, two more stout boys came to us in another wherry, and, abusing us for taking the boat, desired me to get into the other wherry-boat. Accordingly I went to get out of the wherry I was in; but just as I had got one of my feet into the other boat, the boys

shoved it off, so that I fell into the Thames, and not being able to swim, I should unavoidably have been drowned, but for the assistance of some watermen, who providentially came to my relief.

II.

The Namur being again got ready for sea, my master, with his gang, was ordered on board; and, to my no small grief, I was obliged to leave my school-master, whom I liked very much and always attended while I stayed in London, to repair on board with my master. Nor did I leave my kind patronesses, the Miss Guerins, without uneasiness and regret. They often used to teach me to read, and took great pains to instruct me in the principles of religion and the knowledge of God. I therefore parted from those amiable ladies with reluctance; after receiving from them many friendly cautions how to conduct myself, and some valuable presents.

When I came to Spithead, I found we were destined for the Mediterranean, with a large fleet ready to put to sea. We only waited for the arrival of the admiral, who soon came on board; and about the beginning of the spring, 1759, we sailed; and in eleven days from the Land's End, got to Gibraltar. While we were here I used to be often on shore, and got various fruits in great plenty, and very cheap.

I had frequently told several people, in my excursions on shore, the story of my being kidnapped with my sister, and of our being separated, as before related; and I had as often expressed my anxiety for her fate, and my sorrow at having never met her again. One day, when I was on shore, and mentioning these circumstances to some persons, one of them told me he knew where my sister was, and if I would accompany him, he would conduct me to her. Improbable as this story was, I believed it immediately, and agreed to go with him, while my heart leaped for joy; and, indeed, he conducted me to a black young woman, who was so like my sister that, at first sight, I really thought it was she; but I was quickly undeceived; and, on talking to her, I found her to be of another nation.

While laying here the Preston came in from the Levant. As soon as she arrived, my master told me I should now see my old companion Dick, who was gone in her when she sailed for Turkey. I was much rejoiced at this information, and expected every minute to embrace him; and when the captain came on board, of our ship, which he did immediately after, I ran to inquire about my friend; but with inexpressible sorrow, I learned from the boat's crew that the dear youth was dead,

and that they had brought his chest, and all his other things to my master: these he afterwards gave to me, and I regarded them as a memorial of my friend, whom I loved and grieved for as a brother.

While we were at Gibraltar I saw a soldier hanging by the heels at one of the moles:* I thought this a strange sight, as I had seen a man hanged in London by his neck. At another time I saw the master of a frigate towed to shore on a grating, by several of the men of war's boats, and discharged the fleet, which I understand was a mark of disgrace for cowardice. On board the same ship a sailor was also hung up at the yard-arm.

III.

After lying at Gibraltar for some time, we sailed up the Mediterranean, a considerable way above the Gulph of Lyons, where we were one night overtaken by a terrible gale of wind, much greater than any I had yet experienced. The sea ran so high that, though all the guns were well housed, there was great reason to fear their getting loose, the ship rolled so much; and if they had, it must have proved our destruction. After cruising here for a short time, we came to Barcelona, a Spanish sea-port, remarkable for its silk manufacturers. Here the ships were all to be watered; and my master, who spoke different languages, and used often to interpret for the admiral, superintended the watering of ours. For that purpose he, and the officers of the other ships who were on the same service, had tents pitched in the bay; and the Spanish soldiers were stationed along the shore, — I suppose to see that no depredations were committed by our men.

I constantly attended my master, and was charmed with this place. All the time of our stay it was like a fair with the natives, who brought us fruits of all kinds, and sold them to us much cheaper than I had got them in England. They used also to bring wine down to us in hog and sheep-skins, to my great diversion. The Spanish officers here treated our officers with great politeness and attention; and some of them, in particular, used to come often to my master's tent to visit him; where they did sometimes divert themselves by mounting me on the horses or mules, so that I could not fall, and setting them off at full gallop, my imperfect skill in horsemanship affording them no small entertainment. After the ships were watered, we returned to our old station of

*He had drowned himself in endeavouring to desert.

cruising off Toulon, for the purpose of intercepting a fleet of French men of war that lay there. One Sunday in our cruise, we came off a place where there were two small French frigates lying in shore; and our admiral thinking to take or destroy them, sent two ships in after them— the Culloden and the Conqueror. They soon came up to the Frenchmen; and I saw a smart fight here, both by sea and land: for the frigates were covered by batteries, and they played upon our ships most furiously, which they as furiously returned, and for a long time a constant firing was kept up, on all sides, at an amazing rate. At last one frigate sunk, but the people escaped, though not without much difficulty: and a little after some of the people left the other frigate also, which was a mere wreck. However, our ships did not venture to bring her away, they were so much annoyed from the batteries, which raked them both in going and coming; their top-masts were shot away, and they were otherwise so much shattered, that the admiral was obliged to send in many boats to tow them back to the fleet. I afterwards sailed with a man who fought in one of the French batteries during the engagement, and he told me our ships had done considerable mischief that day on shore and in the batteries.

IV.

After this we sailed for Gibraltar, and arrived there about August, 1759. We remained here with all our sails unbent, while the fleet was watering and doing other necessary things. While we were in this situation, one day the admiral, together with most of the principal officers, and many people of all stations, being on shore, about seven o'clock in the evening we were alarmed by signals from the frigates stationed for that purpose, and in an instant there was a general cry that the French fleet was out, and just passing through the streights. The admiral immediately came on board with some other officers; and it is impossible to describe the noise, hurry, and confusion, throughout the fleet, in bending their sails and slipping their cables; many people and ship's boats were left on shore in the bustle. We had two captains on board of our ship, who came away in the hurry and left their ships to follow. We shewed lights from the gunwales to the main-top-mast-head; and all our lieutenants were employed amongst the fleet to tell the ships not to wait for their captains, but to put the sails to the yards, slip their cables, and follow us; and, in this confusion of making ready for fighting, we set out for sea in the dark after the French fleet. Here I could have exclaimed with Ajax,

O Jove! O father! if it be thy will
That we must perish, we thy will obey,
But let us perish by the light of day.

They had got the start of us so far that we were not able to come up
with them that night; but at day-light we saw seven sail of the line some
miles ahead. We immediately chased them till four o'clock in the
evening, our ships then came up with them; and though we were about
fifteen large ships, our gallant admiral only fought them with his own
division, consisting of seven, so that we were just ship for ship. We
passed by the whole of the enemy's fleet in order to come at their com-
mander, Mon. Le Clue, who was in the Ocean, an eighty-four gun
ship. As we passed they all fired at us; and at one time three of them
fired together, continuing to do so for some time. Notwithstanding
which our admiral, to my astonishment, would not suffer a gun to be
fired at any of them, but made us lie on our bellies on the deck till we
came quite close to the Ocean, which was ahead of them all, when we
had orders to pour the whole three tiers into her at once.

The engagement now commenced with great fury on both sides: the
Ocean immediately returned our fire, and we continued engaged with
each other for some time; during which I was frequently stunned with
the thundering of the great guns, whose dreadful contents burned
many of my companions into eternity. At last the French line was
entirely broken, and we obtained the victory, which was immediately
proclaimed with loud huzzas and acclamations. We took three prizes,
La Modeste, of sixty-four guns, and Le Temeraire and Centaur, of seventy-
four guns each. The rest of the French ships took to flight, with all the
sail they could crowd. Our ship being very much damaged, and quite
disabled from pursuing the enemy, the admiral immediately quitted
her, and went in a broken boat, the only one we had left, on board the
Newark, with which, and some other ships, he went after the French.
The Ocean, and another large French ship, called the Redoubtable,
endeavouring to escape, ran ashore at Cape Logas, on the coast of
Portugal, and the French admiral and some of the crew got ashore; but
we, finding it impossible to get the ships off, set fire to them both. About
midnight I saw the Ocean blew up with a most dreadful explosion. I
never beheld a more awful scene. About the space of a minute, the
midnight seemed turned into day by the blaze, attended with a noise
louder and more terrible than thunder, that seemed to rend every element
around us.

My station during the engagement was on the middle deck, where I was
quartered with another boy, to bring powder to the aftermost Gun. And

here I was witness to the dreadful fate of many of my companions, who, in the twinkling of an eye, were dashed to pieces, and launched into eternity. Happily I escaped unhurt, though the shot and splinters flew thick about me during the night. Towards the latter part of it my master was wounded, and I saw him carried down to the surgeon; but though I was much alarmed for him, and longed to assist him, I durst not quit my post.

At this station my gun-mate* and I ran a very great risk, for more than half an hour, of blowing up the ship. For when we had taken the cartridges out of the boxes, the bottoms of many of them proving rotten, the powder ran all about the deck, near the match tub: we scarcely had water enough at the last to throw on it. We were also, from our employment, very much exposed to the enemy's shots; for we had to go through nearly the whole length of the ship to bring the powder. I expected therefore every minute to be my last; especially when I saw our men fall so thick about me. But, wishing to guard as much against the dangers as possible, at first I thought it would be the safest not to go for the powder till the Frenchmen had fired their broadside; and then, while they were charging, I could go and come with my powder. But immediately afterwards I thought this caution was fruitless; and, cheering myself with the reflection that there was a time allotted for me to die as well as to be born, I instantly cast off all fear or thought whatever of death, and went through the whole of my duty with alacrity; pleasing myself with the hope, if I survived the battle, of relating it and the dangers I had escaped, to the Miss Guerins, and others, when I should return to London.

V.

Our ship suffered very much in this engagement; for, besides the number of our killed and wounded, she was almost torn to pieces, and our rigging so much shattered, that our mizen-mast, main-yard, &c. hung over the side of the ship; so that we were obliged to get many carpenters and others, from some of the ships of the fleet, to assist in setting us in some tolerable order. Notwithstanding which, it took us some time before we were completely refitted; after which we left Admiral Broderick to command, and we, with the prizes, steered for England.

On the passage, and as soon as my master recovered of his wounds, the admiral appointed him captain of the Ætna fire-ship, on which he and I left the Namur, and went on board of her at sea. I liked this small

*A Partner in bringing powder to the same gun.

ship very much. I now became the captain's steward, in which situation I was very happy: for I was extremely well treated by all on board; and had leisure to improve myself in reading and writing. Of the latter I had learned a little before I left the Namur, there being a school on board. When we arrived at Spithead, the Ætna went into Portsmouth harbour to refit, which being done, we returned to Spithead, and joined a large fleet that was thought to be intended against Havannah. But about that time the king died; whether that prevented the expedition I know not; but it caused our ship to be stationed at Cowes, in the isle of Wight, till the beginning of the year 1761. Here I spent my time very pleasantly: I was much on shore all about this delightful island, and found the inhabitants very civil.

While I was here, I met with a trifling incident, which surprised me agreeably. I was one day in a field belonging to a gentleman, who had a black boy about my own size; this boy having observed me from his master's house, was transported at the sight of one of his own country-men, and ran to meet me with the utmost haste. I, not knowing what he was about, turned a little out of his way at first, but to no purpose: he soon came close to me, and caught me in his arms as if I had been his brother, though we had never seen each other before. After we had talked together for some time, he took me to his master's house, where I was treated very kindly. This benevolent boy and I were very happy in frequently seeing each other, till about the month of March 1761, when our ship had orders to fit out again for another expedition. When we got ready, we joined a very large fleet at Spithead, commanded by Commodore Keppel, destined against Belleisle; and having a number of transport ships in company, with troops on board, to make a descent on the place, we sailed once more in quest of fame. I longed to engage in new adventures, and to see fresh wonders.

I had a mind, on which every thing uncommon, and every thing which I considered marvellous, made their full impression. Every extraordinary escape, or signal deliverance, either of myself or others, I looked upon to be effected by the interposition of Providence. We had not been above ten days at sea before an incident of this kind happened, which, whatever cred-it it may obtain from the reader, made no small impression upon my mind.

VI.

We had on board a gunner, whose name was John Mondle, a man of very indifferent morals. This man's cabin was between the decks, exactly over where I lay, a-breast of the quarter-deck ladder. One night, the 5th

of April, being terrified in a dream, he awoke in so great a fright that he could not rest in his bed any longer, nor even remain in his cabin; and he went upon deck about four o'clock in the morning extremely agitated. He immediately told those upon the deck of the agonies of his mind, and the dream which occasioned them: in which he said he had seen many things very awful, and had been warned by St. Peter to repent, who told him time was short. This he said had greatly alarmed him, and he was determined to alter his life. People generally mock the fears of others when they are themselves in safety; and some of his shipmates, who heard him, only laughed at him. However, he made a vow that he never would drink strong liquors again; and he immediately got a light, and gave away his sea-store of liquor. After which his agitation still continuing, he began to read the Scriptures, hoping to find some relief; and soon afterwards he laid himself down again on his bed, and endeavoured to compose himself to sleep, but to no purpose; his mind still continuing in a state of agony. By this time it was exactly half after seven in the morning: I was then under the half deck at the great cabin door; and all at once I heard the people in the waist cry out most fearfully— "The Lord have mercy upon us! We are all lost! The Lord have mercy upon us!"—Mr. Mondle, hearing the cries, immediately ran out of his cabin; and we were instantly struck by the Lynne, a forty gun ship, Captain Clark, which nearly ran us down. This ship had just put about, and was by the wind, but had not got full head-way, or we must all have perished: for the wind was brisk. However, before Mr. Mondle had got four steps from his cabin door, she struck our ship, and her cutwater, right in the middle of his bed and cabin, and ran it up to the combings of the quarter-deck-hatchway, and above three feet below water; and in a minute there was not a bit of wood to be seen where Mr. Mondle's cabin stood; and he was so near being killed that some of the splinters tore his face. As Mr. Mondle must inevitably have perished from this accident, had he not been alarmed in the very extraordinary way I have related, I could not help regarding this as an awful interposition of Providence for his preservation.

The two ships for some time swinged alongside of each other; for ours being a fire-ship, our grappling-irons caught the Lynne every way, and the yards and rigging went at an astonishing rate. Our ship was in such a shocking condition that we all thought she would instantly go down, and every one ran for their lives, and got as well as they could on board the Lynne; but our lieutenant being the aggressor, he never quitted the ship. However, on finding she did not sink immediately, the captain came on board again, and encouraged our people to return and try to save her. Many of them came back, but some would not venture. Some of the ships in the fleet, seeing our situation, immediately

sent their boats to our assistance; but it took us the whole day to save the ship with all their help. And by using every possible means, particularly frapping* her together with many hawsers, and putting a great quantity of tallow below water where she was damaged, she was kept together; but had we met with any gale of wind she must have gone to pieces, being in such a crazy condition that we had ships to attend us till we arrived at Belleisle, the place of our destination; and then we had all things taken out of the ship, and she was properly repaired. This escape of Mr. Mondle, which he, as well as myself, always considered as a singular act of Providence, I believe had a great influence on his life and conduct ever afterwards.

Now that I am on this subject, I beg leave to relate another instance or two which strongly raised my belief of the particular interposition of Heaven, and which might not otherwise have found a place here, from their insignificance. I belonged for a few days, in the year 1758, to the Jason, of fifty-four guns, at Plymouth. One night, when I was on board, a woman, with a child at her breast, fell from the upper-deck down into the hold, near the keel. Every one thought that the mother and child must be both dashed to pieces; but, to our great surprise, neither of them was hurt. I myself one day fell headlong from the upper-deck of the Ætna down the after-hold, when the ballast was out; and all who saw me fall called out I was killed; but I received not the least injury. And in the same ship a man fell from the mast-head on the deck without being hurt. In these, and in many more instances, I thought I could very plainly trace the hand of God; without whose permission a sparrow cannot fall. I began to raise my fear from man to Him alone, and to call daily on his holy name, with fear and reverence: and I trust He heard my supplications, and graciously condescended to answer me according to his holy word; and to implant the seeds of piety in me, even one of the meanest of his creatures.

VII.

When we had refitted our ship, and all things were in readiness for attacking the place, the troops were in readiness for attacking the place, the troops on board the transports were ordered to disembark; and my master, as a junior captain, had a share in the command of the landing. This was on the 12th of April. The French were drawn up on the shore,

*Giving a brace or tightening to the tackle, by a complication of ropes.

and had made every disposition to oppose the landing of our men, only a small part of them this day being able to effect it; most of them, after fighting with great bravery, were cut off, and General Crawford, with a number of others, taken prisoners. In this day's engagement we had also our lieutenant killed.

On the 21st of April we renewed our efforts to land the men, all the men of war being stationed along the shore to cover it, and fired at the French batteries and breastworks from early in the morning till about four o'clock in the evening, when our soldiers effected a safe landing. They immediately attacked the French, and, after a sharp encounter, forced them from the batteries. Before the enemy retreated they blew up several of them, lest they should fall into our hands. Our men then proceeded to besiege the citadel, and my master was ordered on shore to superintend the landing of all the materials necessary for carrying on the siege; in this service I mostly attended him. While I was there I visited different parts of the island; and one day, particularly, my curiosity almost cost me my life. I wanted very much to see the mode of charging the mortars and letting off the shells; and for that purpose I went to an English battery, but very few yards from the walls of the citadel. There, indeed, I had an opportunity of completely gratifying myself in seeing the whole operation; but not without running a very great risk, both from the English shells that burst while I was there, and likewise from those of the French. One of the largest of their shells burst within nine or ten yards of me: there was a single rock close by, about the size of a butt; and I got instant shelter under it in time to avoid the fury of the shell. Where it burst the earth was torn in such a manner that two or three butts might easily have gone into the hole it made, and it threw great quantities of stones and dirt to a considerable distance. Three shots were also fired at me and another boy who was along with me; one of them in particular seemed

Wing'd with red lightning and impetuous rage;

for, with a most dreadful sound, it hissed close by me, and struck a rock at a little distance, which it shattered to pieces. When I saw in what perilous circumstances I was, I attempted to return the nearest way I could find and thereby I got between the English and the French centinels. An English sergeant, who commanded the out-posts, seeing me, and surprised how I came there (which was by stealth along the sea-shore), reprimanded me severely for it, and instantly took the centinel off his post into custody, for his negligence in suffering me to pass the lines.

While I was in this situation I observed, at a little distance, a French horse, belonging to some islanders, and I determined to mount him for

the greater expedition in getting off. Accordingly I took some cord, which I had about me, and making a kind of bridle, I put it round the horse's head, and the tame beast very quietly suffered me to tie him thus and mount him. As soon as I was on his back, I began to kick and beat him, and try every means to make him move quickly, but all to very little purpose: I could not drive him out of a slow pace. While I was creeping along, still within reach of the enemy's shot, I met a servant well mounted on an English horse. I immediately stopped; and, crying, told him my case, and begged of him to help me, and this he effectually did; for, having a fine large whip, he began to lash my horse so severely, that he set off full speed with me towards the sea, while I was quite unable to hold or manage him. In this manner I went along till I came to a craggy precipice. I could not stop my horse; and my mind was filled with apprehensions of my deplorable fate should he go down the precipice, which he appeared fully disposed to do: I therefore thought I had better throw myself off him at once, which I did immediately with great dexterity, and fortunately escaped unhurt. As soon as I found myself at liberty I made the best of my way to the ship, determined not to be so fool-hardy in future.

VIII.

We continued to besiege the citadel till June, when it surrendered. During the siege I have counted above sixty shells and carcases in the air at once. When this place was taken I went through the citadel, and into the bomb-proofs under it, cut in the solid rock; and I thought it a surprising place, both for strength and building; notwithstanding, our shots and shells had made amazing devastation, and ruinous heaps all around it.

After the taking of this island, our ships with some others, commanded by Commodore Stanhope, in the Swiftsure, went to Basse-road, where we blocked up a French fleet. Our ships were there from June till February following; and in that time I saw great many scenes of war, and stratagems, on both sides, to destroy each other's fleet. Sometimes we would attack the French with some ships of the line; at other times with boats; and frequently we made prizes. Once or twice the French attacked us, by throwing shells with their bomb-vessels; one day as a French vessel was throwing shells at our ships, she broke from her springs, behind the isle of I de Re: the tide being complicated, she came within a gunshot of the Nassau; but the Nassau could not bring a gun to bear upon her, and thereby the Frenchman got off. We were

twice attacked by their fire-floats, which they chained together, and then let them float down with the tide; but each time we sent boats with grapplings, and towed them safe out of the fleet.

We had different commanders at this place: Commodores Stanhope, Dennis, Lord Howe, &c. From hence, before the Spanish war began, our ship and the Wasp sloop were sent to St. Sebastian, in Spain, by Commodore Stanhope; and Commodore Dennis afterwards sent us as a cartel to Bayonne, in France,* after which† we went, in February 1762, to Belleisle, and there stayed till the summer, when we left it, and returned to Portsmouth.

After our ship was fitted out again for service, in September she went to Guernsey, where I was very glad to see my old hostess, now a widow, and my former little charming companion, her daughter. I spent some time here very happily with them till October, when we had orders to repair to Portsmouth. We parted from each other with a great deal of affection; and I promised to return soon, and see them again; not knowing what all powerful fate had determined for me.

Our ship having arrived at Portsmouth, we went into the harbour and remained there till the end of November, when we heard great talk about a peace; and, to our very great joy, in the beginning of December, we had orders to go up to London with our ship, to be paid off. We received this news with loud huzzas, and every other demonstration of gladness: and nothing but mirth was to be seen through every part of the ship. I too was not without my share of the general joy on this occasion. I thought now of nothing but being freed, and working for myself, and thereby getting money to enable me to get a good education. For I always had a great desire to be able at least to read and write; and while I was on shipboard I had endeavoured to improve myself in both. While in the Ætna, particularly, the captains' clerk taught me to write, and gave me a smattering of arithmetic, as far as the Rule of Three.

There was also one Daniel Queen, about forty years of age, a man

*Among others, whom we brought from Bayonne, were two gentlemen, who had been in the West-Indies, where they sold slaves; and they confessed they had made, at one time, a false bill of sale, and sold two Portuguese white men among a lot of slaves.

†Some people have it, that sometimes shortly before persons die, their ward has been seen:—that is, some spirit exactly in their likeness, though they are themselves at other places at the same time. One day while we were at Bayonne, Mr. Mondle saw one of our men, as he thought, in the gun-room; and, a little after, coming on the quarter-deck, he spoke of the circumstance of this man, to some of the officers. They told him that the man was then out of the ship, in one of the boats with the Lieutenant; but Mr. Mondle would not believe it, and we searched the ship, when we found that the man was actually out of her; and when the boat returned some time afterwards, we found the man had been drowned at the very time Mr. Mondle thought he saw him.

very well educated, who messed with me on board this ship, and he likewise dressed and attended the captain. Fortunately this man soon became very much attached to me, and took great pains to instruct me in many things. He taught me to shave, and dress hair a little, and also to read in the Bible, explaining many passages to me, which I did not comprehend. I was wonderfully surprised to see the laws and rules of my own country written almost exactly here; a circumstance which, I believe, tended to impress our manners and customs more deeply on my memory. I used to tell him of this resemblance; and many a time we have sat up the whole night together at this employment. In short, he was like a father to me; and some used even to call me after his name: they also styled me "the black Christian." Indeed I almost loved him with the affection of a son. Many things I have denied myself, that he might have them; and when I used to play at marbles or any other game, and won a few halfpence, or got some money for shaving any one, I used to buy him a little sugar or tobacco, as far as my stock of money would go. He used to say that he and I never should part, and that when our ship was paid off, as I was as free as himself or any other man on board, he would instruct me in his business, by which I might gain a good livelihood. This gave me new life and spirits; and my heart burned within me, while I thought the time long till I obtained my freedom. For though my master had not promised it to me, yet, besides the assurances I had often received that he had no right to detain me, he always treated me with the greatest kindness, and reposed in me an unbounded confidence. He even paid attention to my morals; and would never suffer me to deceive him, or tell lies, of which he used to tell me the consequences; and that if I did so, God would not love me. So that from all this tenderness I had never once supposed, in all my dreams of freedom, that he would think of detaining me any longer than I wished.

IX.

In pursuance of our orders we sailed from Portsmouth for the Thames, and arrived at Deptford the 10th of December, where we cast anchor just as it was high water. The ship was up about half an hour, when my master ordered the barge to be manned; and, all in an instant, without having before given me the least reason to suspect any thing of the matter, he forced me into the barge, saying, I was going to leave him, but he would take care that I did not. I was so struck with the unexpectedness of this proceeding, that for some time I did not make a

reply; only I made an offer to go for my books and chest of clothes, but he swore I should not move out of his sight; and if I did, he would cut my throat, at the same time taking out his hanger. I began, however, to collect myself; and, plucking up courage, I told him that I was free, and he could not by law serve me so. But this only enraged him the more; and he continued to swear, and said he would soon let me know whether he would or not; and at that instant sprung himself into the barge, from the ship, to the astonishment and sorrow of all on board.

The tide, rather unluckily for me, had just turned downward, so that we quickly fell down the river along with it, till we came among some outwardbound West Indiamen; for he was resolved to put me on board the first vessel he could get to receive me. The boat's crew, who pulled against their will, became quite faint at different times, and would have gone ashore, but he would not let them. Some of them strove then to cheer me, and told me he could not sell me, and that they would stand by me, which revived me a little, and I still entertained hopes; for as they pulled me along he asked some vessels to receive me, and they refused.

But, just as we had got a little below Gravesend, we came alongside of a ship going away the next tide for the West-Indies; her name was the Charming Sally, Captain James Doran. My master went on board and agreed with him for me; and in little time I was sent for into the cabin. When I came there Captain Doran asked me if I knew him: I answered I did not; 'Then,' said he, 'you are now my slave.' I told him my master could not sell me to him nor to any one else. 'Why,' said he, 'did not your master buy you?' I confessed he did. 'But I have served him,' said I, 'many years, and he has taken all my wages and prize-money, for I only got one sixpence during the war. Besides this I have been baptized; and, by the laws of the land, no man has a right to sell me:' And I added, that I had heard a lawyer, and others, at different times tell my master so. They both then said, that those people who told me so, were not my friends: but I replied—it was very extraordinary that the other people did not know the law as well as they. Upon this, Captain Doran said I talked too much English, and if I did not behave myself well and be quiet, he had a method on board to make me. I was too well convinced of his power over me to doubt what he said; and my former sufferings in the slave-ship presenting themselves to my mind, the recollection of them made me shudder. However, before I retired I told them, that as I could not get any right among men here, I hoped I should hereafter in Heaven, and I immediately left the cabin, filled with resentment and sorrow.

The only coat I had with me my master took away with him, and said, 'If your prize-money had been £10,000, I had a right to it all, and would have taken it.' I had about nine guineas, which, during my long sea-faring

life, I had scraped together from trifling perquisites and little ventures; and I hid it that instant, lest my master should take that from me likewise, still hoping that, by some means or other, I should make my escape to the shore. Indeed some of my old shipmates told me not to despair, for they would get me back again; and that, as soon as they could get their pay, they would immediately come to Portsmouth to me, where this ship was going. But, alas! all my hopes were baffled, and the hour of my deliverance was, as yet, far off. My master, having soon concluded his bargain with the captain, came out of the cabin, and he and his people got into the boat and put off. I followed them with aching eyes as long as I could, and when they were out of sight I threw myself on the deck, with a heart ready to burst with sorrow and anguish.

CHAPTER V.

The author's reflections on his situation—Is deceived by a promise of being delivered—His despair at sailing for the West-Indies—Arrives at Montserrat, where he is sold to Mr. King—Various interesting instances of oppression, cruelty, and extortion, which the author saw practised upon the slaves in the West-Indies during his captivity, from the year 1763 to 1766—Address on it to the Planters.

I.

THUS, AT the moment I expected all my toils to end, was I plunged, as I supposed, in a new slavery; in comparison of which all my service hitherto had been perfect freedom; and whose horrors, always present to my mind, now rushed on it with tenfold aggravation. I wept very bitterly for some time; and began to think that I must have done something to displease the Lord, that he thus punished me so severely. This filled me with painful reflections on my past conduct. I recollected that, on the morning of our arrival at Deptford, I had very rashly sworn that as soon as we reached London, I would spend the day in rambling and sport. My conscience smote me for this unguarded expression: I felt that the Lord was able to disappoint me in all things, and immediately considered my present situation as a judgment of Heaven, on account of my presumption in swearing. I therefore, with contrition of heart, acknowledged my transgression to God, and poured out my soul before Him with unfeigned repentance, and with earnest supplications I besought Him not to abandon me in my distress, nor cast me from his mercy for ever. In a little time my grief, spent with its own violence, began to subside; and after the first confusion of my thoughts was over, I reflected with more calmness on my present condition. I considered

that trials and disappointments are sometimes for our good; and I thought God might perhaps have permitted this, in order to teach me wisdom and resignation. For he had hitherto shadowed me with the wings of his mercy and by his invisible, but powerful hand, had brought me the way I knew not. These reflections gave me a little comfort, and I arose at last from the deck with dejection and sorrow in my countenance, yet mixed with some faint hope that the *Lord would appear* for my deliverance.

II.

Soon afterwards, as my new master was going on shore, he called me to him, and told me to behave myself well, and do the business of the ship the same as any of the rest of the boys, and that I should fare the better for it; but I made him no answer. I was then asked if I could swim, and I said, "No." However, I was made to go under the deck, and was carefully watched. The next tide the ship got under way, and soon arrived at the Mother Bank, Portsmouth; where she waited few days for some of the West-India convoy. While here I tried every means I could devise amongst the people of the ship to get me a boat from the shore, as there was none suffered to come alongside of the ship; and their own, whenever it was used, was hoisted in again immediately. A sailor on board took a guinea from me, on pretence of getting me a boat; and promised me, time after time, that it was hourly to come off. When he had the watch upon deck I watched also, and looked long enough, but all in vain; I could never see either the boat or my guinea again. And, what I thought was still the worst of all, the fellow gave information, as I afterwards found, all the while to the mates of my intention to go off if possible; but, rogue-like, he never told them he had got a guinea from me to procure my escape. However, after we had sailed, and his trick was made known to the ship's crew, I had some satisfaction in seeing him detested and despised by them all for his behaviour to me.

I was still in hopes that my old shipmates would not forget their promise to come for me to Portsmouth; and, indeed, at last, but not till the day before we sailed, some of them did come there, and sent me off some oranges, and other tokens of their regard. They also sent me word they would come off to me themselves the next day, or the day after: and a lady also who lived in Gosport, wrote to me that she would come and take me out of the ship at the same time. This lady had been once very intimate with my former master. I used to sell and take care of a great deal of property for her, in different ships; and in return she always

shewed great friendship for me, and used to tell my master she would take me away to live with her. But, unfortunately for me, a disagreement soon afterwards took place between them; and she was succeeded in my master's good graces by another lady, who appeared sole mistress of the Ætna, and mostly lodged on board. I was not so great a favourite with this lady as with the former; she had conceived a pique against me, on some occasion when she was on board, and she did not fail to instigate my master to treat me in the manner he did.*

III.

However, the next morning, the 30th of December, the wind being brisk and easterly, the Æolus frigate, which was to escort the convoy, made a signal for sailing. All the ships then got up their anchors; and before any of my friends had an opportunity to come off to my relief, to my inexpressible anguish, our ship had got under way. What tumultuous emotions agitated my soul when the convoy got under sail, and I a prisoner on board, now without hope! I kept my swimming eyes upon the land in a state of unutterable grief; not knowing what to do, and despairing how to help myself. While my mind was in this situation, the fleet sailed on, and in one day's time I lost sight of the wished-for land. In the first expressions of my grief, I reproached my fate, and wished I had never been born. I was ready to curse the tide that bore us; the gale that wafted my prison, and even the ship that conducted us; and, in the despair of the moment, I called on death to relieve me from the horrors I felt and dreaded, that I might be in that place.

> Where slaves are free, and men oppress no more.
> Fool that I was, inur'd so long to pain,
> To trust to hope, or dream of joy again!
> * * * * * * * * * * *
>
> Now dragg'd once more beyond the western main,
> To groan beneath some dastard planter's chain;
> Where my poor countrymen in bondage wait
> The long enfranchisément of ling'ring fate:

*Thus was I sacrificed to the envy and resentment of this woman, for knowing that the other lady designed to take me into her service; which, had I got once on shore, she would not have been able to prevent. She felt her pride alarmed at the superiority of her rival in being attended by a black servant: it was not less to prevent this, than to be revenged on me, that she caused the captain to treat me thus cruelly.

> Hard ling'ring fate! while, ere the dawn of day,
> Rous'd by the lash they go their cheerless way;
> And as their souls with shame and anguish burn,
> Salute with groans unwelcome morn's return,
> And, chiding ev'ry hour the slow-pac'd sun,
> Pursue their toils till all his race is run.
> No eye to mark their suff'rings with a tear;
> No friend to comfort, and no hope to cheer:
> Then, like the dull unpity'd brutes, repair
> To stalls as wretched, and as coarse a fare;
> Thank heaven one day of mis'ry was o'er,
> Then sink to sleep, and wish to wake no more.*

The turbulence of my emotions, however, naturally gave way to calmer thoughts, and I soon perceived what fate had decreed no mortal on earth could prevent. The convoy sailed on without any accident, with a pleasant gale and smooth sea, for six weeks, till February, when one morning the Æolus ran down a brig, one of the convoy, and she instantly went down and was engulfed in the dark recess of the ocean. The convoy was immediately thrown into great confusion till it was daylight; and the Æolus illuminated with lights to prevent farther mischief. On the 13th of February 1763, from the mast-head, we descried our destined island, Montserrat, and soon after I beheld those

> Regions of sorrow, doleful shades, where peace
> And rest can rarely dwell. Hope never comes
> That comes to all, but torture without end
> Still urges.

At the sight of this land of bondage, a fresh horror ran through all my frame, and chilled me to the heart. My former slavery now rose in dreadful review to my mind, and displayed nothing but misery, stripes, and chains; and in the first paroxysm of my grief, I called upon God's thunder, and his avenging power, to direct the stroke of death to me, rather than permit me to become a slave, and to be sold from lord to lord.

In this state of my mind our ship came to an anchor, and soon after

*"The Dying Negro," a poem originally published in 1773. Perhaps it may not be deemed impertinent here to add, that this elegant and pathetic little poem, was occasioned by the following incident, as appears from the advertisement prefixed to it:—'A black who, a few days before, had run away from his master, and got himself christened, with intent to marry a white woman, his fellow-servant, being taken and sent on board a ship in the Thames, took an opportunity of shooting himself through the head.'

discharged her cargo. I now knew what it was to work hard; I was made to help to unload the ship. And to comfort me in my distress, at that time two of the sailors robbed me of all my money, and ran away from the ship. I had been so long used to an European climate, that at first I felt the scorching West-India sun very painful, while the dashing surf would toss the boat and the people in it, frequently above high-water-mark. Sometimes our limbs were broken with this, or even attended with instant death, and I was day by day mangled and torn.

IV.

About the middle of May, when the ship was got ready to sail for England, I all the time believing that fate's blackest clouds were gathering over my head, and expecting that their bursting would mix me with the dead, Captain Doran sent for me on shore one morning; and I was told by the messenger that my fate was determined. With trembling steps and a fluttering heart I came to the captain, and found with him one Mr. Robert King, a quaker, and the first merchant in the place. The captain then told me my former master had sent me there to be sold; but that he had desired him to get me the best master he could, as he told him I was a very deserving boy, which Captain Doran said he found to be true, and if he were to stay in the West-Indies he would be glad to keep me himself; but he could not venture to take me to London, for he was very sure that when I came there, I would leave him. I at that instant burst out a crying, and begged much of him to take me with him to England, but all to no purpose. He told me he had got me the very best master in the whole island, with whom I should be as happy as if I were in England, and for that reason he chose to let him have me, though he could sell me to his own brother-in-law for a great deal more money than what he got from that gentleman. My new master, Mr. King, then made a reply, and said the reason he had bought me was on account of my good character; and, as he had not the least doubt of my good behaviour, I should be very well off with him. He also told me he did not live in the West-Indies, but at Philadelphia, where he was soon going; and, as I understood something of the rules of arithmetic, when we got there he would put me to school, and fit me for a clerk. This conversation relieved my mind a little, and I left those gentlemen considerably more at ease in myself than when I came to them; and I was very thankful to Captain Doran, and even to my old master, for the character they had given me; a character which I afterwards found of infinite service to me.

I went on board again, and took leave of all my shipmates, and the next day the ship sailed. When she weighed anchor I went to the waterside, and looked at her with a very wishful and aching heart, following her with my eyes until she was totally out of sight. I was so bowed down with grief, that I could not hold up my head for many months; and if my new master had not been kind to me, I believe I should have died under it at last. And indeed I soon found that he fully deserved the good character which Capt. Doran had given me of him; for he possessed a most amiable disposition and temper, and was very charitable and humane. If any of his slaves behaved amiss, he did not beat or use them ill, but parted with them. This made them afraid of disobliging him; and as he treated his slaves better than any other man on the island, so he was better and more faithfully served by them in return. By this kind treatment I did at last endeavour to compose myself; and with fortitude, though moneyless, determined to face whatever fate had decreed for me. Mr. King soon asked me what I could do, and at the same time said he did not mean to treat me as a common slave. I told him I knew something of seamanship, and could shave and dress hair pretty well; I could refine wines, which I had learned on shipboard, where I had often done it; and that I could write, and understood arithmetic tolerably well as far as the Rule of Three. He then asked me if I knew any thing of gauging; and, on my answering that I did not, he said one of his clerks should teach me to gauge.

V.

Mr. King dealt in all manner of merchandize, and kept from one to six clerks. He loaded many vessels in a year; particularly to Philadelphia, where he was born, and was connected with a great mercantile house in that city. He had besides many vessels and doggers, of different sizes, which used to go about the island; and others to collect rum, sugar, and other goods. I understood pulling and managing those boats very well; and this hard work, which was the first that he set me to, in the sugar seasons used to be my constant employment. I have rowed the boat and slaved at the oars, from one hour to sixteen in the twenty-four; during which I had fifteen pence sterling per day to live on, though sometimes only ten pence. However, this was much more than was allowed to other slaves that used to work often with me, and belonged to other gentlemen on the island: these poor souls had never more than nine pence a day, and seldom more than six pence, from their masters or owners, though

they earned them three or four pisterines.* For it is a common practice in the West-Indies for men to purchase slaves, though they have not plantations themselves, in order to let them out to planters and merchants, at so much a piece by the day, and they give what they choose, out of this produce of their daily work; to their slaves for subsistence. This allowance is often very scanty.

My master often gave the owners of these slaves two and a half of these pieces per day, and found the poor fellows in victuals himself, because he thought their owners did not feed them well enough, according to the work they did. The slaves used to like this very well; and, as they knew my master to be a man of feeling, they were always glad to work for him in preference to any other gentleman; some of whom, after they had been paid for their poor people's labours, would not give them their allowance out of it. Many times have I seen these unfortunate wretches beaten for asking for their pay; and often severely flogged by their owners, if they did not bring them their daily or weekly money exactly to the time; though the poor creatures were obliged to wait on the gentlemen they had worked for, sometimes more than half the day before they could get their pay, and this generally on Sundays, when they wanted the time for themselves. In particular, I knew a countryman of mine, who once did not bring the weekly money directly that it was earned; and though he brought it the same day to his master, yet he was staked to the ground for his pretended negligence, and was just going to receive a hundred lashes, but for a gentleman who begged him off fifty.

This poor man was very industrious, and by his frugality had saved so much money, by working on shipboard, that he had got a white man to buy him a boat, unknown to his master. Some time after he had this little estate, the governor wanted a boat to bring his sugar from different parts of the island; and, knowing this to be a negro-man's boat, he seized upon it for himself, and would not pay the owner a farthing. The man on this went to his master, and complained to him of this act of the governor; but the only satisfaction he received was to be damned very heartily by his master, who asked him how dared any of his negroes to have a boat. If the justly-merited ruin of the governor's fortune could be any gratification to the poor man he had thus robbed, he was not without consolation. Extortion and rapine are poor providers; and some time after this, the governor died in the King's Bench, in England, as I was told, in great poverty. The last war favoured this poor negro-man, and he found some means to escape from his christian master: he came to England, where I saw him afterwards several times. Such treatment as this often drives

*These pisterines are of the value of a shilling.

these miserable wretches to despair, and they run away from their masters at the hazard of their lives. Many of them, in this place, unable to get their pay when they have earned it, and fearing to be flogged, as usual, if they return home without it, run away where they can for shelter, and a reward is often offered to bring them in dead or alive. My master used sometimes, in these cases, to agree with their owners, and to settle with them himself; and thereby he saved many of them a flogging.

VI.

Once, for a few days, I was let out to fit a vessel, and I had no victuals allowed me by either party; at last I told my master of this treatment, and he took me away from it. In many of the estates, on the different islands where I used to be sent for rum or sugar, they would not deliver it to me, or to any other negro; he was therefore obliged to send a white man along with me to those places; and then he used to pay him from six to ten pisterines a day. From being thus employed, during the time I served Mr. King, in going about the different estates on the island, I had all the opportunity I could wish for to see the dreadful usage of the poor men—usage that reconciled me to my situation, and made me bless God for the hands into which I had fallen.

I had the good fortune to please my master in every department in which he employed me; and there was scarcely any part of his business, or household affairs, in which I was not occasionally engaged. I often supplied the place of a clerk, in receiving and delivering cargoes to the ships, in tending stores, and delivering goods; and, besides this, I used to shave and dress my master, when convenient, and take care of his horse; and when it was necessary, which was very often, I worked likewise on board of his different vessels. By these means I became very useful to my master, and saved him, as he used to acknowledge, above a hundred pounds a year. Nor did he scruple to say I was of more advantage to him than any of his clerks; tho' their usual wages in the West-Indies are from sixty to a hundred pounds current a year.

I have sometimes heard it asserted that a negro cannot earn his master the first cost; but nothing can be further from the truth. I suppose nine tenths of the mechanics throughout the West-Indies are negro slaves; and I well know the coopers among them earn two dollars a-day; the carpenters the same, and oftentimes more; also the masons, smiths, and fishermen, &c. and I have known many slaves whose masters would not take a thousand pounds current for them. But surely this assertion refutes itself: for, if it be true, why do the planters and merchants pay

such a price for slaves? And, above all, why do those, who make this assertion, exclaim the most loudly against the abolition of the slave trade? So much are men blinded, and to such inconsistent arguments are they driven by mistaken interest! I grant, indeed, that slaves are sometimes, by half-feeding, half-clothing, over-working, and stripes, reduced so low, that they are turned out as unfit for service, and left to perish in the woods, or to expire on a dunghill.

My master was several times offered by different gentlemen one hundred guineas for me; but he always told them he would not sell me, to my great joy: and I used to double my diligence and care for fear of getting into the hands of these men, who did not allow a valuable slave the common support of life. Many of them used to find fault with my master for feeding his slaves so well as he did; although I often went hungry, and an Englishman might think my fare very indifferent: but he used to tell them he always would do it, because the slaves thereby looked better and did more work.

While I was thus employed by my master, I was often a witness to cruelties of every kind, which were exercised on my unhappy fellowslaves. I used frequently to have different cargoes of new negroes in my care for sale; and it was almost a constant practice with our clerks, and other whites, to commit violent depredations on the chastity of the female slaves; and to these atrocities I was, though with reluctance, obliged to submit at all times, being unable to help them. When we have had some of these slaves on board my master's vessels to carry them to other islands, or to America, I have known our mates commit these acts most shamefully, to the disgrace not of christians only, but of men. I have even known them gratify their brutal passion with females not ten years old; and these abominations some of them practised to such a scandalous excess, that one of our captains discharged the mate and others on that account. And yet in Montserrat I have seen a negro-man staked to the ground, and cut most shockingly, and then his ears cut off, bit by bit, because he had been connected with a white woman, who was a common prostitute! As if it were no crime in the whites to rob an innocent African girl of her virtue; but most heinous in a black man only to gratify a passion of nature, where the temptation was offered by one of a different color, though the most abandoned woman of her species.

VII.

One Mr. D——, told me he had sold 41,000 negroes, and he once cut off a negro-man's leg for running away. I asked him if the man had died in the operation, how he, as a christian, could answer, for the horrid

act, before God. And he told me, answering was a thing of another world; what he thought and did were policy. I told him that the christian doctrine taught us "to do unto others as we would that others should do unto us." He then said that his scheme had the desired effect—it cured that man and some others of running away.

Another negro-man was half hanged, and then burnt, for attempting to poison a cruel overseer. Thus, by repeated cruelties, are the wretched first urged to despair, and then murdered, because they still retain so much of human nature about them as to wish to put an end to their misery, and to retaliate on their tyrants! These overseers are, indeed, for the most part, persons of the worst character of any denomination of men in the West-Indies. Unfortunately, many humane gentlemen, by not residing on their estates, are obliged to leave the management of them in the hands of these human butchers, who cut and mangle the slaves in a shocking manner, on the most trivial occasions, and alto-gether treat them, in every respect, like brutes. They pay no regard to the situation of pregnant women, nor the least attention to the lodging of the field negroes. Their huts, which ought to be well covered, and the place dry where they take their short repose, are often open sheds, built in damp places; so that, when the poor creatures return tired from the toils of the field, they contract many disorders, from being exposed to the damp air in this uncomfortable state, while they are heated, and their pores are open.

The neglect certainly conspires with many others to cause a decrease in the births, as well as in the lives of the grown negroes. I can quote many instances of gentlemen who reside on their own estates in the West-Indies, and then the scene is quite changed; the negroes are treated with lenity and proper care, by which their lives are prolonged, and their masters profited. To the honour of humanity, I know several gentlemen who managed their estates in this manner, and found that benevolence was their true interest. And, among many I could mention in Montserrat,* whose slaves looked remarkably well, and never needed any fresh supplies of negroes (and there are many other estates, espe-cially in Barbadoes, which, from such judicious treatment, need no fresh stock of negroes at any time), I have the honour of knowing a most worthy and humane gentleman, who is a native of Barbadoes, and has estates there.† This gentleman has written a treatise on the usage of his own slaves. He allows them two hours for refreshment at mid-day, and many other indulgences and comforts, particularly in their lying; and, besides this, he raises more provisions on his estate than they can destroy;

*Mr. Dubury, and many others, in Montserrat.
†Sir Philip Gibbes, Bart. Barbadoes.

so that by these attentions he saves the lives of his negroes, and keeps them healthy, and as happy as the condition of slavery can admit. I myself, as shall appear in the sequel, managed an estate, where, by such attentions, the negroes were uncommonly cheerful and healthy, and did more work by half than by the common mode of treatment they usually do. For want, therefore, of such care and attention to the poor negroes, and otherwise oppressed as they are, it is no wonder that the decrease should require 20,000 new negroes annually to fill up the vacant places of the dead.

Even in Barbadoes, notwithstanding those humane exceptions which I have mentioned and others with which I am acquainted that justly make it quoted as a place where slaves meet with the best treatment, and need fewest recruits of any in the West-Indies; yet this island requires 1,000 negroes annually to keep up the original stock, which is only 80,000. So that the whole term of a negro's life may be said to be there, but sixteen years!* And yet the climate here is in every respect the same as that from which they are taken, except in being more wholesome. Do the British colonies decrease in this manner? And yet what a prodigious difference is there between an English and West-India climate?

VIII.

While I was in Montserrat I knew a negro-man, one Emanuel Sankey, who endeavoured to escape from his miserable bondage, by concealing himself on board of a London ship. But fate did not favour the poor oppressed man; for, being discovered when the vessel was under sail, he was delivered up again to his master. This christian master immediately pinned the wretch to the ground, at each wrist and ankle, and then took some sticks of sealing wax, lighted them, and dropped it all over his back. There was another master noted for cruelty:—I believe he had not a slave but had been cut, and pieces fairly taken out of the flesh: and after they had been punished thus, he used to make them get into a long wooden box, or case, he had for that purpose, and shut them up during pleasure. It was just about the height and breadth of man; and the poor wretches had no room when in the case to move.

It was very common in several of the islands, particularly in St. Kitt's,

*See Anthony Benezet's "Some Account of Guinea, with an Inquiry into the Slave Trade," p. 16.

for the slaves to be branded with the initial letters of their master's name, and a load of heavy iron hooks hung about their necks. Indeed on the most trivial occasions they were loaded with chains, and often instruments of torture were added. The iron muzzle, thumb-screws, &c. are so well known as not to need a description, and were sometimes applied for the slightest faults. I have seen a negro beaten till some of his bones were broken, for only letting a pot boil over. It is not uncommon, after a flogging, to make slaves go on their knees and thank their owners, and pray, or rather say, "God bless you." I have often asked many of the men slaves (who used to go several miles to their wives, and late in the night, after having been wearied with a hard day's labour) why they went so far for wives, and did not take them of their own master's negro-women, and particularly those who lived together as household slaves. Their answers have ever been—"Because when the master or mistress choose to punish the women, they make the husbands flog their own wives, and that we could not bear to do." Is it surprising such usage should drive the poor creatures to despair, and make them seek a refuge in death, from those evils which render their lives intolerable—while

> With shudd'ring horror pale, and eyes aghast,
> They view their lamentable lot, and find
> No rest?

This they frequently do. A negro-man, on board a vessel of my master's, while I belonged to her, having been put in irons for some trifling misdemeanour, and kept in that state some days, being weary of life, took an opportunity of jumping over-board into the sea; however he was picked up without being drowned. Another, whose life was also a burden to him, resolved to starve himself to death, and refused to eat any victuals: this procured him a severe flogging; and he also on the first occasion that offered, jumped overboard at Charles Town, but was saved.

Nor is there any greater reward shewn to the little property than there is to the persons and lives of the negroes. I have already related an instance or two of particular oppression, out of many which I have witnessed; but the following is frequent in all the islands:—The wretched field-slaves, after toiling all the day for an unfeeling owner, who gives them but little victuals, steal sometimes a few moments from rest or refreshment to gather some small portion of grass, according as their time will admit. This they commonly tie up in a parcel; either a bits worth (sixpence) or half a bit's worth, and bring it to town, or to the market to sell. Nothing is more common than for the white people, on this occasion, to take the grass from them without paying for it; and not only so, but too often also, to my knowledge, our clerks and many others,

at the same time have committed acts of violence on the poor, wretched, and helpless females; whom I have seen for hours stand crying to no purpose, and get no redress or pay of any kind. Is not this one common and crying sin enough to bring down God's judgment on the islands? He tells us the oppressor and the oppressed are both in his hands; and if these are not the poor, the broken-hearted, the blind, the captive, the bruised, of which our Saviour speaks, who are they?

One of these depredators once, in St. Eustatia, came on board of our vessel, and bought some fowls and pigs of me; and a whole day after his departure with the things, he returned and wanted his money back:—I refused to give it; and, he not seeing my captain on board, began the common pranks with me; and swore he would even break open my chest and take my money. I therefore expected, as my captain was absent, that he would be as good as his word: and he was just proceeding to strike me, when fortunately a British seaman on board, whose heart had not been debauched by a West-India climate, interposed and prevented him. But had the cruel man struck me, I certainly should have defended myself, at the hazard of my life. For what is life to a man thus oppressed? He went away, however, swearing; and threatened that whenever he caught me a-shore he would shoot me, and pay for me afterwards.

IX.

The small account, in which the life of a negro is held in the West-Indies, is so universally known, that it might seem impertinent to quote the following extract, if some people had not been hardly enough of late to assert, that negroes are on the same footing in that respect as Europeans. By the 329th Act, page 125, of the Assembly of Barbadoes, it is enacted 'That if any negro, or other slave, under punishment by his master, or his order, for running away, or any other crime or misdemeanour towards his said master, unfortunately shall suffer in life or member, no person whatsoever shall be liable to a fine; but if any man shall out of *wantonness, or only of bloody-mindedness, or cruel intention, wilfully kill a negro, or other slave, of his own, he shall pay into the public treasury £15. sterling.*' And it is the same in most, if not all, of the West-India islands. Is not this one of the many acts of the islands which call loudly for redress? And do not the Assembly, which enacted it, deserve the appellation of savages and brutes rather than of christians and men? It is an act at once unmerciful, unjust, and unwise; which for cruelty would disgrace an assembly of those who are called barbarians; and for its injustice and insanity would shock the morality and common sense of a Samaide or Hottentot.

Shocking as this and many other acts of the bloody West-India code at first view appear, how is the iniquity of it heightened when we consider to whom it may be extended! Mr. James Tobin, a zealous labourer in the vineyard of slavery, gives an account* of a French planter, of his acquaintance, in the island of Martinico, who shewed him many mulattoes working in the fields like beasts of burden; and he told Mr. Tobin these *were all the produce of his own loins!* And I myself have known similar instances. Pray, reader, are these sons and daughters of the French planter less his children by being begotten on black women? And what must be the virtue of those legislators, and the feelings of those fathers, who estimate the lives of their sons, however begotten, at no more than fifteen pounds; though they should be murdered, as the act says, *out of wantonness and bloody-mindedness?* But is not the slave-trade entirely a war with the heart of man? And surely that which is begun by breaking down the barriers of virtue, involves in its continuance destruction to every principle, and buries all sentiments in ruin!

I have often seen slaves, particularly those who were meager, in different islands, put into scales and weighed; and then sold from three-pence to six-pence or nine-pence a pound. My master, however, whose humanity was shocked at this mode, used to sell such by the lump. And at or after a sale, even those negroes born in the islands it is not uncommon to see taken from their wives, wives from their husbands, and children from their parents, and sent off to other islands, and wherever else their merciless lords choose; and, probably, never more, during life, see each other! Oftentimes my heart has bled at these partings; when the friends of the departed have been at the water-side, and, with sighs and tears, have kept their eyes fixed on the vessel till it went out of sight.

A poor Creole negro I know well, who, after having been often thus transported from island to island, at last resided in Montserrat. This man used to tell me many melancholy tales of himself. Generally, after he had done working for his master, he used to employ his few leisure moments to go a fishing. When he had caught any fish, his master would frequently take them from him without paying him; and at other times some other white people would serve him in the same manner. One day he said to me very movingly, 'Sometimes when a white man take away my fish I go to my maser, and he get me my right; and when my maser, by strength, take away my fishes, what me must do? I can't go to any body to be righted; then,' said the poor man, looking up above, 'I must look up to God Mighty in the top for right,' This artless tale moved me much, and I could not help feeling the just cause Moses had in redressing his

*In his "Cursory Remarks."

brother against the Egyptian. I exhorted the man to look up still to the God in the top, since there was no redress below. Though I little thought then that I myself should more than once experience such imposition, and need the same exhortation hereafter, in my own transactions in the islands; and that even this poor man and I should some time after, suffer together in the same manner, as shall be related hereafter.

X.

Nor was such usage as this confined to particular places or individuals; for, in all the different islands in which I have been (and I have visited no less than fifteen) the treatment of the slaves was nearly the same; so nearly, indeed, that the history of an island, or even a plantation, with a few such exceptions as I have mentioned, might serve for a history of the whole. Such a tendency has the slave-trade to debauch men's minds, and harden them to every feeling of humanity! For I will not suppose that the dealers in slaves are born worse than other men. No; it is the fatality of this mistaken avarice, that it corrupts the milk of human kindness and turns it into gall. And, had the pursuits of those men been different, they might have been as generous, as tender-hearted, and just, as they are unfeeling, rapacious and cruel. Surely this traffic cannot be good, which spreads like a pestilence, and taints what it touches! Which violates that first natural right of mankind, equality, and independency; and gives one man a dominion over his fellows which God could never intend! For it raises the owner to a state as far above man as it depresses the slave below it; and, with the presumption of human pride, sets distinction between them, immeasurable in extent, and endless in duration! Yet how mistaken is the avarice even of the planters. Are slaves more useful by being thus humbled to the condition of brutes, than they would be if suffered to enjoy the privileges of men? The freedom which diffuses health and prosperity throughout Britain answers you—"No." When you make men slaves, you deprive them of half their virtue, you set them, in your own conduct, an example of fraud, rapine, and cruelty, and compel them to live with you in a state of war; and yet you complain that they are not honest or faithful! You stupefy them with stripes, and think it necessary to keep them in a state of ignorance; and yet you assert that they are incapable of learning; that their minds are such a barren soil or moor that culture would be lost on them; and that they came from a climate, where nature, though prodigal of her bounties in a degree unknown to yourselves, has left man alone scant and unfinished, and incapable of enjoying the

treasures she has poured out for him!—An assertion at once impious and absurd. Why do you use those instruments of torture? Are they fit to be applied by one rational being to another? And are ye not struck with shame and mortification, to see the partakers of your nature reduced so low? But, above all, are there no dangers attending this mode of treatment? Are you not hourly in dread of an insurrection? Nor would it be surprising: for when

> No peace is given
> To us enslav'd, but custody severe;
> And stripes and arbitrary punishment
> Inflicted—What peace can we return?
> But to our power, hostility and hate,
> Untam'd reluctance, and revenge, tho' slow,
> Yet ever plotting how the conqueror least
> May reap his conquest, and may least rejoice
> In doing what we most in suff'ring feel?
>
> MILTON.

But by changing your conduct, and treating your slaves as men, every cause of fear would be banished. They would be faithful, honest, intelligent and vigorous; and peace, prosperity, and happiness, would attend you.

CHAPTER VI.

*Some account of Brimstone-hill in Montserrat—The author surprised by
two earthquakes—Favourable change in the author's situation—He
commences merchant with three-pence—His various success in dealing
in the different islands, and America, and the impositions he meets
with in his transactions with white people—A curious imposition on
human nature—Danger of the surfs in the West-Indies—Remarkable
instance of kidnapping a free mulatto—The author is nearly murdered
by Dr. Perkins, in Savannah.*

I.

IN THE preceding chapter I have set before the reader a few of those
many instances of oppression, extortion, and cruelty, to which I have
been a witness in the West-Indies; but were I to enumerate them all, the
catalogue would be tedious and disgusting. The punishments of the
slaves on every trifling occasion are so frequent, and so well known,
together with the different instruments with which they are tortured,
that it cannot any longer afford novelty to recite them; and they are too
shocking to yield delight either to the writer or the reader. I shall there-
fore hereafter only mention such as incidentally befel myself in the
course of my adventures.

In the variety of departments in which I was employed by my master,
I had an opportunity of seeing many curious scenes in different islands;
but, above all, I was struck with a celebrated curiosity called Brimstone-
hill, which is a high and steep mountain, some few miles from the town
of Plymouth, in Montserrat. I had often heard of some wonders that
were to be seen on this hill, and I went once with some white and black
people to visit it. When we arrived at the top, I saw under different cliffs
great flakes of brimstone, occasioned by the steams of various little ponds,
which were then boiling naturally in the earth. Some of these ponds
were as white as milk, some quite blue, and many others of different

colours. I had taken some potatoes with me, and I put them into different ponds, and in a few minutes they were well boiled. I tasted some of them, but they were very sulphurous; and the silver shoe-buckles, and all the other things we had among us of that metal, were, in a little time, turned as black as lead.

Whilst I was in the island, one night I felt a strange sensation, on being told that the house where I lived was haunted by spirits! And once, at midnight, as I was sleeping on a large chest, I felt the whole building shake in an uncommon and astonishing manner; so much so, that it shook me off the chest where I then lay. I was exceedingly frightened, and thought it was the visitation of the spirits. It threw me into such a tremor as is not to be described. I instantly covered my head all over as I lay, and did not know what to think or do; and in this consternation, a gentleman, who lay in the next room just by me, came out, and I was glad to hear him, and made a sham cough, and he asked me if I felt the earthquake. I told him I was shaken off the chest where I lay, but did not know what occasioned it; and he told me it was an earthquake, and that it shook him out of his bed. On hearing this I became easy in my mind.

At another time a circumstance of this kind happened, when I was on board of a vessel in Montserrat-Road, at midnight, as we were asleep, and it shook the vessel in the most unaccountable manner imaginable, and to me it seemed as when a vessel or a boat runs on gravel, as near as I can describe it. Many things on board were moved out of their places, but happily no damage was done.

II.

About the end of the year 1763, kind Providence seemed to be rather more favourable to me. One of my master's vessels, a Bermudas sloop, about sixty tons burden, was commanded by one Capt. Thomas Farmer, an Englishman, a very alert and active man, who gained my master a great deal of money, by his good management in carrying passengers from one island to another. But very often his sailors used to get drunk and run away from the vessel, which hindered him in his business very much. This man had taken a liking to me; and many different times begged of my master to let me go a trip with him as a sailor; but he would tell him he could not spare me though the vessel sometimes could not go for want of hands; for sailors were generally very scarce in the island. However, at last, from necessity or force, my master was prevailed on, though very reluctantly, to let me go with this captain; but he gave him great charge to take care that I did not run away, for if I

did he would make him pay for me. This being the case, the captain had for some time a sharp eye upon me whenever the vessel anchored; and as soon as she returned I was sent for on shore again. Thus was I slaving as it were for life, sometimes at one thing, and sometimes at another; so that the captain and I were nearly the most useful men in my master's employment. I also became so useful to the captain on shipboard, that, many times, when he used to ask for me to go with him, though it should be but for twenty-four hours, to some of the islands near us, my master would answer he could not spare me; at which the captain would swear, and would not go the trip, and tell my master that I was better to him on board than any three white men he had. For they used to behave ill in many respects, particularly in get-ting drunk, and then they frequently got the boat stove, so as to hinder the vessel from coming back so soon as she might have done. This my master knew very well; and at last, by the captain's constant entreaties, after I had been several times with him, one day, to my great joy, told me the captain would not let him rest, and asked whether I would go aboard as a sailor, or stay on shore and mind the stores, for he could not bear any longer to be plagued in this manner. I was very happy at this proposal, for I immediately thought I might in time stand a chance, by being on board, to get a little money, or possibly make my escape if I should be used ill. I also expected to get better food, and in a greater abundance; for I had oftentimes felt much hunger, though my master treated his slaves, as I have observed, uncommonly well. I therefore, without hesitation, answered him, that I would go and be a sailor, if he pleased. Accordingly I was ordered on board directly. Nevertheless, between the vessel and the shore, when she was in port, I had little or no rest, as my master always wished to have me along with him. Indeed he was a very pleasant gentleman, and but for my expectations on shipboard, I should not have thought of leaving him. But the captain liked me also very much, and I was entirely his right-hand man. I did all I could to deserve his favour, and in return I received better treatment from him, than I believe, any other, in my situation, ever met with in the West-Indies.

III.

After I had been sailing for some time with this captain, at length I endeavoured to try my luck and commence merchant. I had but a very small capital to begin with; for one single half bit, which is equal to

three-pence in England, made up my whole stock. However I trusted to the Lord to be with me; and at one of our trips to St. Eustatia, a Dutch island, I bought a glass tumbler with my half bit, and when I came to Montserrat I sold it for a bit, or six-pence. Luckily we made several successive trips to St. Eustatia, which was a general mart for the West-Indies, about twenty leagues from Montserrat; and in our next, finding my tumbler so profitable, with this one bit I bought two tumblers more; and when I came back I sold them for two bits, equal to a shilling sterling. When we went again I bought with these two bits four more of these glasses, which I sold for four bits of our return to Montserrat; and in our next voyage to St. Eustatia, I bought two glasses with one bit, and with the other three I bought a jug of Geneva, nearly three pints in measure. When we came to Montserrat, I sold the gin for eight bits, and the tumblers for two, so that my capital now amounted in all to a dollar, well husbanded, and acquired in the space of a month or six weeks, when I blessed the Lord that I was so rich.

As we sailed to different islands, I laid this money out in various things occasionally, and it used to turn to very good account, especially when we went to Guadaloupe, Grenada, and the rest of the French islands. Thus was I going all about the islands upwards of four years, and ever trading as I went, during which I experienced many instances of ill-usage, and have seen many injuries done to other negroes in our dealings with whites. Amidst our recreations, when we have been dancing and merry-making, they without cause, have molested and insulted us. Indeed I was more than once obliged to look up to God on high, as I had advised the poor fisherman some time before.

And I had not been long trading for myself in the manner above related, when I experienced the like trial in company with him as follows: This man being used to the water, was, upon an emergency, put on board of us by his master to work as another hand, on a voyage to Santa Cruz; and at our sailing he had brought his little all for a venture, which consisted of six bits' worth of limes and oranges in a bag; I had also my whole stock, about twelve bits' worth of the same kind of goods, separate in two bags; for we had heard that these fruits sold well in that island. When we came there, in some little convenient time, he and I went on shore with our fruits to sell them; but we had scarcely landed when we were met by two white men, who presently took our three bags from us. We could not at first guess what they meant to do; and for some time we thought they were jesting with us; but they soon let us know otherwise, for they took our ventures immediately to a house hard by, and adjoining the fort, while we followed all the way begging of them to give us our fruits, but in vain. They not only

refused to return them, but they swore at us, and threatened if we did not immediately depart they would flog us well. We told them those three bags were our all, that we brought them with us to sell, and that we came from Montserrat, and shewed them the vessel. But this was rather against us, as they *now saw we were strangers as well as slaves*. They still therefore swore, and desired us to be gone, and even took sticks to beat us; while we, seeing that they meant what they said, went off in the greatest confusion and despair. Thus, in the very minute of gaining more by three times than I ever did by any venture in my life before, was I deprived of every farthing I was worth. An insupportable misfortune! But how to help ourselves we knew not. In our consternation we went to the commanding officer of the fort, and told him how we had been served by some of his people; but we obtained not the least redress. He answered our complaints only by a volley of imprecations against us, and immediately took a horse-whip, in order to chastise us; so that we were obliged to turn out much faster than we came in. I then, in the agony of distress and indignation, wished that the ire of God, in his forked lightning, might transfix these cruel oppressors among the dead. We however returned to the house, and begged and besought them again and again for our fruits, till at last some other people being in the house, asked, if we would be contented if they kept one bag and gave us the other two. We, seeing no remedy whatever, consented to this; and they, observing one bag to have both kinds of fruit in it, which belonged to my companion, kept that; and the other two, being mine, they gave us back. As soon as I got them, I ran as fast as I could, and got the first negro-man I could to help me off. My companion stayed a little longer to plead; he told them that the bag they had was his, and that it was all he was worth in the world. But this was of no avail, and he was obliged to return without it. The poor old man wringing his hands cried bitterly for his loss; and, indeed, he then did look up to God on high, which so moved me with pity for him, that I gave him nearly one third of my fruits. We then proceeded to the markets to sell them; and Providence was more favourable than we could have expected, for we sold our fruits uncommonly well; I got for mine about thirty-seven bits. Such a surprising reverse of fortune, in so short a time, seemed like a dream, and proved no small encouragement for me to trust the Lord in any situation. My captain afterwards frequently used to take my part, and get me my right, when I had been plundered or used ill by these tender christian depredators; among whom I have shuddered to observe the unceasing blasphemous execrations which are wantonly thrown out by persons of all ages and conditions, not only without occasion, but even as if they were indulgences and pleasures.

IV.

At one of our trips to St. Kitt's, I had eleven bits of my own; and my friendly captain lent me five more, with which I bought a Bible. I was very glad to get this book, which I could scarcely meet with any where. I think there were none sold in Montserrat; and, much to my grief, from being forced out of the Ætna, in the manner I have related, my Bible, and the "Guide to the Indians," the two books I loved above all others, were left behind.

While I was in St. Kitt's, a very curious imposition on human nature took place:—A white man wanted to marry, in the church, a free black woman that had land and slaves in Montserrat: but the clergyman told him it was against the law of the place to marry a white and a black in the church. The man then asked to be married on the water, to which the parson consented, and the lovers went in one boat, and the parson and clerk in another, and thus the ceremony was performed. After this the loving pair came on board our vessel, and my captain treated them extremely well, and brought them safe to Montserrat.

The reader cannot but judge of the irksomeness of this situation to a mind like mine, in being daily exposed to new hardships and impositions, after having seen many better days, and been, as it were, in a state of freedom and plenty; added to which, every part of the world in which I had hitherto been, seemed to me a paradise in comparison of the West-Indies. My mind was therefore hourly replete with inventions and thoughts of being freed, and, if possible, by honest and honourable means; for I always remembered the old adage, and I trust that it has ever been my ruling principle, that *Honesty is the best policy*; and like-wise that other golden precept—*To do unto all men as I would they should do unto me*. However, as I was from early years a predestinarian, I thought whatever fate had determined must ever come to pass; and therefore, if ever it were my lot to be freed, nothing could prevent me, although I should at present see no means or hope to obtain my free-dom; on the other hand, if it were my fate not to be freed, I never should be so; and all my endeavours for that purpose would be fruitless. In the midst of these thoughts I therefore looked up with prayers anx-iously to God for my liberty; and at the same time used every honest means, and did all that was possible on my part, to obtain it.

In process of time I became master of a few pounds, and in a fair way of making more, which my friendly captain knew very well: this occasioned him sometimes to take liberties with me; but whenever he treated me waspishly I used plainly to tell him my mind, and that I would die before I would be imposed upon as other negroes were; and that to me life had lost

its relish when liberty was gone. This I said, although I foresaw my then well-being, or future hopes of freedom (humanly speaking) depended on this man. However, as he could not bear the thoughts of my not sailing with him, he always became mild on my threats. I therefore continued with him; and, from my great attention to his orders and his business, I gained him credit, and through his kindness to me I at last procured my liberty.

While I thus went on, filled with the thoughts of freedom, and resisting oppression as well as I was able, my life hung daily in suspense, particularly in the surfs I have formerly mentioned, as I could not swim. These are extremely violent throughout the West-Indies, and I was ever exposed to their howling rage and devouring fury in all the islands. I have seen them strike and toss a boat right up an end, and maim several on board. Once in the Grenada islands, when I and about eight others were pulling a large boat with two puncheons of water in it, a surf struck us, and drove the boat and all in it about half a stone's throw, among some trees, and above the highwater mark. We were obliged to get all the assistance we could, from the nearest estate, to mend the boat, and launch it into the water again. At Montserrat one night, in pressing hard to get off the shore on board, the punt was overset with us four times; the first time I was very near being drowned; however the jacket I had on kept me up above water a little time, while I called on a man near me, who was a good swimmer, and told him I could not swim. He then made haste to me, and, just as I was sinking, he caught hold of me, and brought me to sounding, and then he went and brought the punt also. As soon as we had turned the water out of her, least we should be used ill for being absent, we attempted again three times more, and as often the horrid surfs served us as at first; but at last, the fifth time we attempted, we gained our point, at the imminent hazard of our lives.

One day also, at Old Road, in Montserrat, our captain, and three men besides myself, were going in a large canoe, in quest of rum and sugar, when a single surf tossed the canoe an amazing distance from the water, and some of us near a stone's throw from each other: most of us were very much bruised; so that I and many more often said, and really thought, that there was not such another place under the heavens as this. I longed therefore much to leave it, and daily wished to see my master's promise performed of going to Philadelphia.

V.

While we lay in this place, a very cruel thing happened on board of our sloop, which filled me with horror; though I found afterwards such practices were frequent. There was a very clever and decent free young

mulatto-man who sailed a long time with us: he had a free woman for his wife, by whom he had a child; and she was then living on shore, and all very happy. Our captain and mate, and other people on board, and several elsewhere, even the natives of Bermudas, then with us, all knew this young man from a child that he was always free, and no one had ever claimed him as their property. However, as might too often overcomes right in these parts, it happened that a Bermudas captain, whose vessel lay there for a few days in the road, came on board of us, and seeing the mulatto-man, whose name was Joseph Clipson, he told him he was not free, and that he had orders from his master to bring him to Bermudas. The poor man could not believe the captain to be in earnest; but he was very soon undeceived, his men laying violent hands on him; and although he shewed a certificate of his being born free in St. Kitt's, and most people on board knew that he served his time to boat-building and always passed for a free man, yet he was forcibly taken out of our vessel. He then asked to be carried ashore, before the secretary or magistrates, and these infernal invaders of human rights promised him he should; but, instead of that, they carried him on board of the other vessel; and the next day, without giving the poor man any hearing ashore, or suffering him even to see his wife or child, he was carried away, and probably doomed never more in this world to see them again.

Nor was this the only instance of this kind of barbarity to which I was a witness. I have since often seen in Jamaica and other islands, free men, whom I have known in America, thus villainously trepanned and kept in bondage. I have heard of two similar practices even in Philadelphia: and were it not for the benevolence of the Quakers in that city, many of the sable race, who now breathe the air of liberty, would, I believe, be groaning under some planter's chains. These things opened my mind to a new scene of horror, to which I had been before a stranger. Hitherto I had thought only slavery dreadful; but the state of a free negro appeared to me now equally so at least, and in some respects even worse; for they live in constant alarm for their liberty, which is but nominal; and they are universally insulted and plundered without the possibility of redress; such being the equity of the West-Indian laws, that no free negro's evidence will be admitted in their courts of justice. In this situation is it surprising that slaves, when mildly treated, should prefer even the misery of slavery to such a mockery of freedom? I was now completely disgusted with the West-Indies, and thought I never should be entirely free till I had left them.

> With thoughts like these my anxious boding mind,
> Recall'd those pleasing scenes I left behind;
> Scenes where fair Liberty in bright array

Makes darkness bright, and e'en illumines day;
Where nor complexion, wealth, nor station can
Protect the wretch who makes a slave of man.

I determined to make every exertion to obtain my freedom, and to return to Old England. For this purpose I thought a knowledge of Navigation might be of use to me; for, though I did not intend to run away unless I should be ill used, yet, in such a case, if I understood navigation, I might attempt my escape in our sloop, which was one of the swiftest sailing vessels in the West-Indies, and I could be at no loss for hands to join me. Had I made this attempt, I had intended to go in her to England; but this, as I said, was only to be in the event of my meeting with any ill usage. I therefore employed the mate of our vessel to teach me Navigation, for which I agreed to give him twenty-four dollars, and actually paid him part of the money down; though when the captain, some time after, came to know that the mate was to have such a sum for teaching me, he rebuked him, and said it was a shame for him to take any money from me. However, my progress in this useful art was much retarded by the constancy of our work.

VI.

Had I wished to run away I did not want opportunities, which frequently presented themselves; and particularly at one time, soon after this. When we were at the island of Guadaloupe there was a large fleet of merchantmen bound for Old France; and seamen then being very scarce, they gave from fifteen to twenty pounds a man for the run. Our mate and all the white sailors left our vessel on this account, and went aboard of the French ships. They would have had me also to go with them, for they regarded me, and swore to protect me, if I would go: and, as the fleet was to sail the next day, I really believe I could have got safe to Europe at that time. However, as my master was kind, I would not attempt to leave him; still remembering the old maxim, that *honesty is the best policy*, I suffered them to go without me. Indeed my captain was much afraid of my leaving him and the vessel at that time, as I had so fair an opportunity: but, I thank God, this fidelity of mine turned out much to my advantage hereafter, when I did not in the least think of it; and made me so much in favour with the captain, that he used now and then to teach me some parts of Navigation himself. But some of our passengers, and others, seeing this, found much fault with him for it, saying it was a very dangerous thing to let a negro know Navigation; and thus I was hindered again in my pursuits.

About the latter end of the year 1764, my master bought a larger sloop, called the Prudence, about seventy or eighty tons, of which my captain had the command. I went with him into this vessel, and we took a load of new slaves for Georgia and Charles Town. My master now left me entirely to the captain, though he still wished me to be with him; but I, who always much wished to lose sight of the West-Indies, was not a little rejoiced at the thoughts of seeing any other country. Therefore, relying on the goodness of my captain, I got ready all the little venture I could; and, when the vessel was ready, we sailed to my great joy. When we got to our destined places, Georgia and Charles Town, I expected I should have an opportunity of selling my little property to advantage; but here, particularly in Charles Town, I met with buyers, white men, who imposed on me as in other places. Notwithstanding, I was resolved to have fortitude: thinking no lot or trial too hard when kind Heaven is the rewarder.

We soon got loaded again, and returned to Montserrat; and there, amongst the rest of the islands, I sold my goods well; and in this manner I continued trading during the year 1764; meeting with various scenes of imposition, as usual. After this, my master fitted out his vessel for Philadelphia, in the year 1765; and during the time of loading her, and getting ready for the voyage, I worked with double alacrity, from the hope of getting money enough by these voyages to buy my freedom, in time, if it should please God; and also to see the city of Philadelphia, having heard a great deal about it for some years past; besides which I had always longed to prove my master's promise the first day I came to him. In the midst of these elevated ideas, and while I was about getting my little merchandise in readiness, one Sunday my master sent for me to his house. When I came there I found him and the captain together; and, on my going in, I was struck with astonishment at his telling me, he heard that I meant to run away from him when I got to Philadelphia;—"And therefore," said he, "I must sell you again: you cost me a great deal of money, no less than forty pounds sterling; and it will not do to lose so much. You are a valuable fellow," continued he, "and I can any day get for you one hundred guineas, from many gentlemen in this island." And then he told me of Captain Doran's brother-in-law, a severe master, who ever wanted to buy me to make me his overseer.

My captain also said, he could get much more than a hundred guineas for me in Carolina. This I knew to be a fact; for the gentleman that wanted to buy me, came off several times on board of us, and spoke to me to live with him, and said he would use me well. When I asked to what work he would put me, he said, as I was a sailor, he would make me a captain of one of his rice vessels. But I refused: and fearing at the same time, by a sudden turn I saw in the captain's temper, he might

mean to sell me, I told the gentleman I would not live with him on any condition, and that I certainly would run away with his vessel: but he said, he did not fear that, as he would catch me again: and then he told me how cruelly he would serve me if I should do so. My captain, however, gave him to understand that I knew something of Navigation: so he thought better of it; and, to my great joy, he went away. I now told my master, I did not say I would run away in Philadelphia, neither did I mean it, as he did not use me ill, nor yet the captain; for if they did, I certainly would have made some attempts before now; but as I thought that if it were God's will I ever should be freed it would be so, and, on the contrary, if it was not his will it would not happen; so I hoped if ever I were freed, whilst I was used well, it should be by honest means; but as I could not help myself, he must do as he pleased; I could only hope and trust in the God of Heaven; and at that instant my mind was big with inventions, and full of schemes to escape.

I then appealed to the captain whether he ever saw any sign of my making the least attempt to run away; and asked him if I did not always come on board according to the time for which he gave me liberty; and more particularly, when all our men left us at Guadaloupe, and went on board the French fleet, and advised me to go with them, whether I might not, and that he could not have got me again. To my no small surprise, and very great joy, the captain confirmed every syllable I said, and even more; for he said he had tried different times to see if I would make any attempt of this kind, both at St. Eustatia and in America, and he never found that I made the smallest; but, on the contrary, I always came on board according to his orders;—and he did really believe, if ever I meant to run away, that, as I could never have had a better opportunity, I would have done it the night the mate and all the people left our vessel at Guadaloupe. The captain then informed my master, who had been thus imposed on by our mate (though I did not know who was my enemy), the reason the mate had for imposing this lie upon him; which was, because I had acquainted the captain with the provisions the mate had given away or taken out of the vessel.

This speech of the captain was like life to the dead to me, and instantly my soul glorified God: and still more so on hearing my master immediately say that I was a sensible fellow, and he never did intend to use me as a common slave; and that, but for the entreaties of the captain, and his character of me, he would not have let me go from the stores about as I had done: that also, in so doing, he thought by carrying one little thing or other to different places to sell I might make money: that he intended to encourage me in this, by crediting me with half a puncheon of rum and half a hogshead of sugar at a time: so that, from being careful, I might have money enough, in some time, to purchase my freedom:

and, when that was the case, I might depend upon it he would let me
have it for forty pounds sterling money, which was only the same price
he gave for me. This soon gladdened my poor heart beyond measure;
though indeed it was no more than the idea I had formed in my mind
of my master long before, and I immediately made him this reply: 'Sir,
I always had that very thought of you; indeed I had; and that made me
so diligent in serving you.' He then gave me a large piece of silver coin,
such as I had never seen or had before, and told me to get ready for the
voyage, and he would credit me with a tierce of sugar and another of rum;
he also said that he had two amiable sisters in Philadelphia, from whom
I might get some necessary things. Upon this my noble captain desired
me to go a board: and, knowing the African Metal, he charged me not
to say any thing of this matter to any body; and he promised that the
lying mate should not go with him any more.

VII.

This was a change indeed; in the same hour to feel the most exquis-
ite pain, and, in the turn of a moment, the fullest joy. It caused in me
such sensations as I was only able to express in my looks; my heart was
so overpowered with gratitude that I could have kissed both of their feet.
When I left the room I immediately went, or rather flew, to the vessel,
which being loaded, my master, as good as his word, trusted me with a
tierce of rum and another of sugar, when we sailed, and arrived safe at
the elegant town of Philadelphia. I soon sold my goods here pretty well;
and in this charming town I found every thing plentiful and cheap.

While I was in this place a very extraordinary occurrence befel me. I
had been told one evening of a WISE WOMAN, a Mrs. Davis, who
revealed secrets, foretold events, &c. I put little faith in this story at first,
as I could not conceive that any mortal could foresee the future disposals
of Providence, nor did I believe in any other revelation than that of the
Holy Scriptures. However, I was greatly astonished at seeing this
woman in a dream that night, though a person I never before beheld in
my life. This made such an impression on me, that I could not get the
idea next day out of my mind, and I then became as anxious to see her
as I was before indifferent. Accordingly in the evening, after we left off
working, I inquired where she lived, and being directed to her, to my
inexpressible surprise, beheld the very woman in the very same dress
she appeared to me to wear in the vision. She immediately told me I
had dreamed of her the preceding night; related to me many things that
had happened with a correctness that astonished me; and finally told

me I should not be long a slave. This was the more agreeable news, as I believed it the more readily than her having so faithfully related the past incidents of my life. She said I should be twice in very great danger of my life within eighteen months, which if I escaped, I should afterwards go on well; so, giving me her blessing, we parted. After staying here some time till our vessel was loaded and I had bought in my little traffic, we sailed from this agreeable spot for Montserrat, once more to encounter the raging surfs.

We arrived safe at Montserrat, where we discharged our cargo, and soon after that we took slaves on board for St. Eustatia, and from thence to Georgia. I had always exerted myself, and did double work, in order to make our voyages as short as possible; and from thus over-working myself while we were at Georgia I caught a fever and ague. I was very ill for eleven days, and near dying; eternity was now exceedingly impressed on my mind, and I feared very much that awful event. I prayed the Lord therefore to spare me; and I made a promise in my mind to God, that I would be good if ever I should recover. At length, from having an eminent doctor to attend me, I was restored again to health; soon after we got the vessel loaded, and set off for Montserrat. During the passage, as I was perfectly restored, and had much business of the vessel to mind, all my endeavours to keep up my integrity, and perform my promise to God, began to fail; and, in spite of all I could do, as we drew nearer and nearer to the islands, my resolutions more and more declined, as if the very air of that country or climate seemed fatal to piety. When we were safe arrived at Montserrat, and I had got ashore, I forgot my former resolutions. Alas! how prone is the heart to leave that God it wishes to love! And how strongly do the things of this world strike the senses and captivate the soul!

After our vessel was discharged, we soon got her ready, and took in, as usual, some of the poor oppressed natives of Africa, and other negroes; we then set off again for Georgia and Charlestown. We arrived at Georgia, and having landed part of our cargo, proceeded to Charlestown with the remainder. While we were there I saw the town illuminated; the guns were fired, and bonfires and other demonstrations of joy shewn, on account of the repeal of the stamp-act. Here I disposed of some goods on my own account; the white men buying them with smooth promises and fair words, giving me, however, but very indifferent payment.

There was one gentleman particularly who bought a puncheon of rum of me, and gave me a great deal of trouble. Although I used the interest of my friendly captain, I could obtain nothing for it, and could not oblige him to pay me. This vexed me much, not knowing how to act. I lost some time in seeking after this Christian; and though, when

the Sabbath came, which the negroes usually make their holiday, I was inclined to go to public worship yet I was obliged to hire some black men to help to pull a boat across the water to go in quest of this gentleman. When I found him, after much entreaty both from myself and my worthy captain, he at last paid me in dollars, some of them, however, were copper, and of consequence of no value. But he took advantage of my being a negroman, and obliged me to put up with those or none, although I objected to them. Immediately after, as I was trying to pass them in the market amongst other white men, I was abused for offering to pass bad coin, and though I shewed them the man I had got them from, I was within one minute of being tied up and flogged without either judge or jury. However, by the help of a good pair of heels, I ran off and so escaped the bastinadoes I should have received. I got on board as fast as I could, but still continued in fear of them until we sailed, which, I thank God, we did, not long after; and I have never been amongst them since.

VIII.

We soon came to Georgia, where we were to complete our lading; and here worse fate than ever attended me: for one Sunday night, as I was with some negroes, in their master's yard, in the town of Savannah, it happened that their master, one Doctor Perkins, who was a very severe and cruel man, came in, drunk; and not liking to see any strange negroes in his yard, he and a ruffian of a white man he had in his service, beset me in an instant, and both of them struck me with the first weapons they could get hold of. I cried out as long as I could for help and mercy; but though I gave a good account of myself, and he knew my captain, who lodged hard by him, it was to no purpose. They beat and mangled me in a shameful manner, leaving me nearly dead. I lost so much blood from the wounds I received that I lay quite motionless, and was so benumbed that I could not feel any thing for many hours. Early in the morning they took me away to the jail.

As I did not return to the ship all night, my captain not knowing where I was, and being uneasy that I did not then make my appearance, made inquiry after me; and having found where I was, he immediately came to me. As soon as the good man saw me so cut and mangled, he could not forbear weeping. He soon got me out of jail to his lodgings, and immediately sent for the best doctors in the place, who at first declared it as their opinion that I could not recover. My captain on this went to all the lawyers in the town for their advice, but they told him

they could do nothing for me as I was a negro. He then went to Doctor Perkins, the hero who had vanquished me, and menaced him, swearing he would be revenged of him, and challenged him to fight. But cowardice is ever the companion of cruelty—and the doctor refused.

However by the skilfulness of one Dr. Brady of that place, I began at last to amend. But although I was so sore and bad, with the wounds I had all over me, that I could not rest in any posture; yet I was in more pain on account of the captain's uneasiness about me than I otherwise should have been. The worthy man nursed and watched me all the hours of the night; and I was, through his attention and that of the doctor, able to get out of bed in about sixteen or eighteen days. All this time I was very much wanted on board, as I used frequently to go up and down the river for rafts, and other parts of our cargo, and stow them, when the mate was sick or absent. In about four weeks I was able to go on duty; and in a fortnight after, having got in all our lading, our vessel set sail for Montserrat, and in less than three weeks we arrived there safe, towards the end of the year. This ended my adventures in 1765; for I did not leave Montserrat again till the beginning of the following year.

CHAPTER VII.

The author's disgust at the West-Indies—Forms schemes to obtain his freedom—Ludicrous disappointment he and his captain meet with in Georgia—At last, by several successful voyages he acquires a sum of money sufficient to purchase it—Applies to his master, who accepts it, and grants his manumission, to his great joy—He afterwards enters as a freeman on board one of Mr. King's ships, and sails for Georgia—Impositions on free negroes as usual—His venture of turkies—Sails for Montserrat, and on his passage, his friend, the Captain, falls ill and dies.

I.

EVERY DAY now brought me nearer my freedom, and I was impatient till we proceeded again to sea, that I might have an opportunity of getting a sum large enough to purchase it. I was not long ungratified; for in the beginning of the year 1766, my master bought another sloop, named the Nancy, the largest I had ever seen. She was partly laden, and was to proceed to Philadelphia. Our captain had his choice of three, and I was well pleased he chose this, which was the largest; for, from his having a large vessel, I had more room, and could carry a larger quantity of goods with me. Accordingly, when we had delivered our old vessel, the Prudence, and completed the lading of the Nancy, having made near three hundred per cent. by four barrels of pork I brought from Charlestown, I laid in as large a cargo as I could, trusting to God's Providence to prosper my undertaking. With these views I sailed for Philadelphia. On our passage, when we drew near the land, I was for the first time surprised at the sight of some whales, having never seen any such large sea-monsters before; and, as we sailed by the land, one

morning I saw a puppy whale close by the vessel; it was about the length of a wherry-boat, and it followed us all the day until we got within the Capes. We arrived safe and in good time at Philadelphia, and I sold my goods there chiefly to the Quakers. They always appeared to be a very honest and discreet sort of people, and never attempted to impose on me; I therefore liked them, and ever after chose to deal with them in preference to any others.

One Sunday morning while I was here, as I was going to church, I chanced to pass a meeting-house. The doors being open, and the house full of people, it excited my curiosity to go in. When I entered the house, to my great surprise, I saw a very tall woman standing in the midst of them, speaking in an audible voice something which I could not understand. Having never seen any thing of this kind before, I stood and stared about me for some time, wondering at this odd scene. As soon as it was over, I took an opportunity to make enquiry about the place and people, when I was informed they were called Quakers. I particularly asked what that woman I saw in the midst of them had said, but none of them were pleased to satisfy me; so I quitted them, and soon after, as I was returning, I came to a church crowded with people; the church-yard was full likewise, and a number of people were even mounted on ladders, looking in at the windows. I thought this a strange sight, as I had never seen churches, either in England or the West-Indies, crowded in this manner before. I therefore made bold to ask some people the meaning of all this, and they told me the Rev. George Whitfield was preaching. I had often heard of this gentleman, and had wished to see and hear him; but I had never before had an opportunity. I now therefore resolved to gratify myself with the sight, and pressed in amidst the multitude. When I got into the church I saw this pious man exhorting the people with the greatest fervour and earnestness, and sweating as much as ever I did while in slavery on Montserrat-beach. I was very much struck and impressed with this; I thought it strange I had never seen divines exert themselves in this manner before; and was no longer at a loss to account for the thin congregations they preached to.

II.

When we had discharged our cargo here, and were loaded again, we left this fruitful land once more, and set sail for Montserrat. My traffic had hitherto succeeded so well with me, that I thought, by selling my goods when we arrived at Montserrat, I should have enough to purchase my freedom. But as soon as our vessel arrived there, my master

came on board, and gave orders for us to go to St. Eustatia, and discharge our cargo there, and from thence to proceed for Georgia. I was much disappointed at this; but thinking, as usual, it was of no use to murmur at the decrees of fate, I submitted without repining, and we went to St. Eustatia.

After we had discharged our cargo there, we took in a live cargo, as we call a cargo of slaves. Here I sold my goods tolerably well; but not being able to lay out all my money in this small island to as much advantage as in many other places, I laid out only part, and the remainder I brought away with me neat. We sailed from hence for Georgia, and I was glad when we got there, though I had not much reason to like the place from my last adventure in Savannah; but I longed to get back to Montserrat and procure my freedom, which I expected to be able to purchase when I returned. As soon as we had arrived here I waited on my careful doctor, Mr. Brady, to whom I made the most grateful acknowledgments in my power, for his former kindness and attention during my illness.

While we remained here, an odd circumstance happened to the Captain and me, which disappointed us both a great deal. A silversmith, whom we had brought to this place some voyages before, agreed with the Captain to return to the West-Indies, and promised at the same time to give the Captain a great deal of money, having pretended to take a liking to him, and being, as we thought, very rich. But while we stayed to load our vessel this man was taken ill, in a house where he worked, and in a week's time became very bad. The worse he grew the more he used to speak of giving the Captain what he had promised him, so that he expected something considerable from the death of this man, who had no wife or child, and he attended him day and night.

I used also to go with the Captain, at his own desire, to attend him; especially when we saw there was no appearance of his recovery: and in order to recompence me for my trouble, the Captain promised me ten pounds, when he should get the man's property. I thought this would be of great service to me, although I had nearly money enough to purchase my freedom, if I should get safe this voyage to Montserrat. In this expectation I laid out above eight pounds of my money for a suit of superfine clothes to dance in at my freedom, which I hoped was then at hand. We still continued to attend this man, and were with him even on the last day he lived, till very late at night when we went on board. After we were got to bed, about one or two o'clock in the morning, the Captain was sent for, and was informed the man was dead. On this he came to my bed, and, waking me, informed me of it, and desired me to get up, procure a light, and to go immediately with him. I told him I was very sleepy, and wished he would take somebody else with him; or

else, as the man was dead, and could want no further attendance, to let all things remain as they were till the next morning. 'No, no,' said he, 'we will have the money to-night. I cannot wait till to-morrow; so let us go.' Accordingly I got up and struck a light, and away we both went, and saw the man as dead as we could wish. The Captain said he would give him a grand burial, in gratitude for the promised treasure; and desired that all the things belonging to the deceased might be brought forth. Amongst others there was a nest of trunks, of which he had kept the keys whilst the man was ill; and when they were produced, we opened them with no small eagerness and expectation;—as there were a great number within one another, with much impatience we took them out of each other. At last, when we came to the smallest, and had opened it, we saw it was full of papers, which we supposed to be notes; at the sight of which our hearts leapt for joy; and that instant the Captain, clapping his hands, cried out—'Thank God! here it is!'

But when we began to examine the supposed treasure and long-looked-for bounty, alas! alas! how uncertain and deceitful are all human affairs! what had we found? While we thought we were embracing a substance, we grasped an empty nothing. The whole amount in the nest of trunks was only a dollar and a half; and all that the man possessed would not pay for his coffin! Our sudden and exquisite joy was now succeeded by as sudden and exquisite pain; and my captain and I exhibited, for some time, most ridiculous figures—pictures of chagrin and disappointment! We went away greatly mortified, and left the deceased to do as well as he could for himself, as we had taken so good care of him when alive for nothing.

III.

We set sail once more for Montserrat, and arrived there safe; but much out of humour with our friend, the silversmith. When we had unladen the vessel, and I had sold my venture, finding myself master of about forty-seven pounds, I consulted my true friend, the Captain, how I should proceed in offering my master the money for my freedom. He told me to come on a certain morning, when he and my master would be at breakfast together. Accordingly, on that morning I went, and met the Captain there, as he had appointed. When I went in I made my obeisance to my master, and with my money in my hand, and many fears in my heart, I prayed him to be as good as his offer to me, when he was pleased to promise me my freedom as soon as I could purchase it. This speech seemed to confound him; he began to recoil; and my

heart that instant sunk within me. 'What,' said he, 'give you your freedom? Why, where did you get the money? Have you got forty pounds sterling?' 'Yes, sir,' I answered. 'How did you get it?' replied he. I told him, 'very honestly.' The Captain then said he knew I got the money very honestly and with much industry, and that I was particularly careful. On which my master replied, I got money much faster than he did; and said he would not have made me the promise which he did, had he thought I should have got the money so soon. 'Come, come,' said my worthy Captain, clapping my master on the back, 'Come Robert (which was his name), I think you must let him have his freedom. You have laid your money out very well; you have received good interest for it all this time, and here is now the principal at last. I know GUSTAVUS has earned you more than a hundred a year, and he will still save you money, as he will not leave you. Come, Robert, take the money.' My master then said, he would not be worse than his promise; and, taking the money, told me to go to the Secretary at the Register Office, and get my manumission drawn up.

These words of my master were like a voice from heaven to me: in an instant all my trepidation was turned into unutterable bliss, and I most reverently bowed myself with gratitude, unable to express my feelings, but by the overflowing of my eyes, and a heart replete with thanks to God; while my true and worthy friend, the Captain, congratulated us both with a peculiar degree of heartfelt pleasure. As soon as the first transports of my joy were over, and that I had expressed my thanks to these my worthy friends in the best manner I was able, I rose with a heart full of affection and reverence, and left the room, in order to obey my master's joyful mandate of going to the Register Office. As I was leaving the house I called to mind the words of the Psalmist, in the 126th Psalm, and like him, 'I glorified God in my heart, in whom I trusted.' These words had been impressed on my mind from the very day I was forced from Deptford to the present hour, and I now saw them, as I thought, fulfilled and verified.

My imagination was all rapture as I flew to the Register Office; and in this respect, like the apostle Peter* (whose deliverance from prison was so sudden and extraordinary, that he thought he was in a vision) I could scarcely believe I was awake. Heavens! who could do justice to my feelings at this moment? Not conquering heroes themselves, in the midst of a triumph—Not the tender mother who has just regained her long-lost infant, and presses it to her heart—Not the weary, hungry mariner, at the sight of the desired friendly port—Not the lover, when

*Acts xii. 9.

he once more embraces his beloved mistress, after she has been ravished from his arms!—All within my breast was tumult, wildness, and delirium! My feet scarcely touched the ground; for they were winged with joy, and, like Elijah, as he rose to Heaven, they 'were with lightning sped as I went on.' Every one I met I told of my happiness, and blazed about the virtue of my amiable master and Captain.

When I got to the office and acquainted the Register with my errand, he congratulated me on the occasion, and told me he would draw up my manumission for half-price, which was a guinea. I thanked him for his kindness; and, having received it and paid him, I hastened to my master to get him to sign it, that I might be fully released. Accordingly he signed the manumission that day; so that, before night, I, who had been a slave in the morning, trembling at the will of another, was become my own master, and completely free. I thought this was the happiest day I had ever experienced; and my joy was still heightened by the blessings and prayers of many of the sable race, particularly the aged, to whom my heart had ever been attached with reverence.

As the form of my manumission has something peculiar in it, and expresses the absolute power and dominion one man claims over his fellow, I shall beg leave to present it before my readers at full length.*

IV.

In short, the fair as well as black people immediately styled me by a new appellation,—to me the most desirable in the world,—which was "Freeman," and, at the dances I gave, my Georgia superfine blue clothes made no indifferent appearance, as I thought. Some of the sable females, who formerly stood aloof, now began to relax and appear less coy; but my heart was still fixed on London, where I hoped to be ere long. So that my worthy Captain, and his owner, my late master, finding that the bent of my mind was towards London, said to me, 'We hope you won't leave us, but that you will still be with the vessels.' Here gratitude bowed me down; and none but the generous mind can judge of my feelings, struggling between inclination and duty. However, notwithstanding my wish to be in London, I obediently answered my benefactors that I would go in the vessel, and not leave them; and from that day I was entered on board as an able-bodied seaman, at thirty-six shillings per month, besides what perquisites I could make. My intention

*See Appendix A.

was to make a voyage or two, entirely to please these my honoured patrons; but I determined that the year following, if it pleased God, I would see Old England once more, and surprise my old master, Captain Pascal, who was hourly in my mind; for I still loved him, notwithstanding his usage to me, and I pleased myself with thinking of what he would say when he saw what the Lord had done for me in so short a time, instead of being, as he might perhaps suppose, under the cruel yoke of some planter.

With such reveries I used often to entertain myself, and shorten the time till my return; and now, being as in my original free African style, I embarked on board the Nancy, after having got all things ready for our voyage. In this state of serenity we sailed for St. Eustatia; and having smooth seas and calm weather, we soon arrived there; after taking our cargo on board, we proceeded to Savannah in Georgia, in August, 1766. While we were there, as usual, I used to go for the cargo up the rivers in boats; and, when on this business, I have been frequently beset by Alligators, which were very numerous on that coast and river. I have shot many of them when they have been near getting into our boats; which we have with great difficulty sometimes prevented, and have been very much frightened at them. I have seen a young one sold in Georgia alive for sixpence.

During our stay at this place, one evening a slave belonging to Mr. Read, a merchant of Savannah, came near our vessel, and began to use me very ill. I entreated him, with all the patience of which I was master, to desist, as I knew there was little or no law for a free negro here. But the fellow, instead of taking my advice, persevered in his insults, and even struck me. At this I lost all temper, and fell on him, and beat him soundly. The next morning his master came to our vessel, as we lay alongside the wharf, and desired me to come ashore that he might have me flogged all round the town, for beating his negro slave! I told him he had insulted me, and had given the provocation by first striking me. I had also told my Captain the whole affair that morning, and desired him to go along with me to Mr. Read, to prevent bad consequences; but he said that it did not signify, and if Mr. Read said any thing he would make matters up, and desired me to go to work, which I accordingly did.

The Captain being on board when Mr. Read came and applied to him to deliver me up, he said he knew nothing of the matter, I was a free man. I was astonished and frightened at this, and thought I had better keep where I was, than go ashore and be flogged round the town, without judge or jury. I therefore refused to stir; and Mr. Read went away, swearing he would bring all the constables in the town, for he would have me out of the vessel. When he was gone, I thought his

threat might prove too true to my sorrow; and I was confirmed in this belief, as well by the many instances I had seen of the treatment of free negroes, as from a fact that had happened within my own knowledge here a short time before.

There was a free black man, a carpenter, that I knew, who for asking a gentleman that he had worked for, for the money he had earned, was put into gaol; and afterwards this oppressed man was sent from Georgia, with false accusations, of an intention to set the gentleman's house on fire, and run away with his slaves. I was therefore much embarrassed, and very apprehensive of a flogging at least. I dreaded, of all things, the thoughts of being stripped, as I never in my life had the marks of any violence of that kind. At that instant a rage seized my soul, and for a little I determined to resist the first man that should attempt to lay violent hands on me, or basely use me without a trial; for I would sooner die like a free man, than suffer myself to be scourged, by the hands of ruffians, and my blood drawn like a slave.

The Captain and others, more cautious, advised me to make haste and conceal myself; for they said Mr. Read was a very spiteful man, and he would soon come on board with constables and take me. At first I refused this counsel, being determined to stand my ground; but at length, by the prevailing entreaties of the Captain and Mr. Dixon, with whom we lodged, I went to Mr. Dixon's house, which was a little out of the town, at a place called Yeama-chra. I was but just gone when Mr. Read, and the constables, came for me, and searched the vessel; but, not finding me there, he swore he would have me dead or alive. I was secreted about five days; however the good character which my Captain always gave me, as well as some other gentlemen, who also knew me, procured me some friends. At last some of them told my Captain that he did not use me well, in suffering me thus to be imposed upon, and said they would see me redressed, and get me on board some other vessel. My Captain, on this, immediately went to Mr. Read, and told him, that ever since I eloped from the vessel his work had been neglected, and he could not go on with her loading, himself and mate not being well; and as I had managed things on board for them, my absence must have retarded his voyage, and consequently hurt the owner. He therefore begged of him to forgive me, as he said he never heard any complaint of me before, during the several years I had been with him. After repeated entreaties, Mr. Read said I might go to hell; and that he would not meddle with me; on which my Captain came immediately to me at his lodging, and telling me how pleasantly matters had gone on, desired me to go on board.

Some of my other friends then asked him if he had got the constable's warrant from them; the Captain said, "No." On this I was desired

by them to stay in the house; and they said they would get me on board of some other vessel before the evening. When the Captain heard this he became almost distracted. He went immediately for the warrant, and, after using every exertion in his power, he at last got it from my hunters; but I had all the expenses to pay.

V.

After I had thanked all my friends for their kindness, I went on board again to my work, of which I had always plenty. We were in haste to complete our lading, and were to carry twenty head of cattle with us to the West-Indies, where they are a very profitable article. In order to encourage me in working, and to make up for the time I had lost, my Captain promised me the privilege of carrying two bullocks of my own with me; this made me work with redoubled ardour. As soon as I had got the vessel loaded, in doing which I was obliged to perform the duty of the mate as well as my own work, and when the bullocks were near coming on board, I asked the Captain leave to bring my two, according to his promise; but, to my great surprise, he told me there was no room for them. I then asked him to permit me to take one; but he said he could not. I was a good deal mortified at this usage, and told him I had no notion that he intended thus to impose on me; nor could I think well of any man that was so much worse than his word. On this we had some disagreement, and I gave him to understand that I intended to leave the vessel. At this he appeared to be very much dejected; and our mate, who had been very sickly, and whose duty had long devolved upon me, advised him to persuade me to stay. In consequence of which he spoke very kindly to me, making many fair promises, telling me that, as the mate was so sickly, he could not do without me; and that, as the safety of the vessel and cargo depended greatly upon me, he therefore hoped that I would not be offended at what had passed between us, and swore he would make up all matters when we arrived in the West-Indies; so I consented to slave on as before.

Soon after this, as the bullocks were coming on board, one of them ran at the Captain, and butted him so furiously in the breast, that he never recovered of the blow. In order to make me some amends for his treatment about the bullocks, the Captain now pressed me very much to take some turkeys, and other fowls, with me, and gave me liberty to take as many as I could find room for; but I told him he knew very well I had never carried any turkeys before, as I always thought they were such tender birds as were not fit to cross the seas. However, he continued

to press me to buy them for once; and, what seemed very surprising to me, the more I was against it, the more he urged my taking them, insomuch that he insured me from all losses that might happen by them, and I was prevailed on to take them. But I thought this very strange, as he had never acted so with me before. This, and not being able to dispose of my paper-money in any other way, induced me at length to take four dozen. The turkeys, however, I was so dissatisfied about that I determined to make no more voyages to this quarter, nor with this Captain; and was very apprehensive that my free voyage would be the worst I had ever made.

We set sail for Montserrat. The Captain and mate had been both complaining of sickness when we sailed, and as we proceeded on our voyage they grew worse. This was about November, and we had not been long at sea before we began to meet with strong northerly gales and rough seas; and in about seven or eight days all the bullocks were near being drowned, and four or five of them died. Our vessel, which had not been tight at first, was much less so now: and, though we were but nine in the whole, including five sailors and myself, yet we were obliged to attend to the pumps, every half or three quarters of an hour. The Captain and mate came on deck as often as they were able, which was now but seldom; for they declined so fast, that they were not well enough to make observations above four or five times the whole passage. The whole care of the vessel rested therefore upon me, and I was obliged to direct her by mere dint of reason, not being able to work a traverse.

The Captain was now very sorry he had not taught me navigation, and protested, if ever he should get well again, he would not fail to do so. But in about seventeen days his illness increased so much, that he was obliged to keep his bed, continuing sensible, however, until the last, constantly having the owner's interest at heart; for this just and benevolent man ever appeared much concerned about the welfare of what he was intrusted with. When this dear friend found the symptoms of death approaching, he called me by my name; and, when I came to him, he asked (with almost his last breath) if he had ever done me any harm. 'God forbid I should think so!' I replied, 'I should then be the most ungrateful of wretches to the best of benefactors.' While I was thus expressing my affection and sorrow by his bedside, he expired without saying another word, and the day following we committed his body to the deep. Every man on board loved him, and regretted his death; but I was exceedingly affected at it, and found that I did not know, till he was gone, the strength of my regard for him. Indeed I had every reason in the world to be attached to him; for, besides that he was in general mild, affable, generous, faithful, benevolent, and just, he was to me a friend and father; and had it pleased

Providence that he had died but five months before, I verily believe I should not have obtained my freedom when I did; and it is not improbable that I might not have been able to get it at any rate afterwards.

VI.

The Captain being dead, the mate came on the deck, and made such observations as he was able, but to no purpose. In the course of a few days more, the few bullocks that remained were found dead; but the turkeys I had, though on the deck, and exposed to so much wet and bad weather, did well, and I afterwards gained near three hundred per cent. on the sale of them. So that in the event it proved a happy circumstance for me that I had not bought the bullocks I intended, for they must have perished with the rest. I could not help looking upon this, otherwise trifling, circumstance, as a particular providence of God; and was accordingly thankful. The care of the vessel took up all my time, and engaged my attention entirely. As we were now out of the variable winds, I thought I should not be much puzzled to hit the islands. I was persuaded I steered right for Antigua, which I wished to reach, as the nearest to us; and in the course of nine or ten days we made that island to our great joy, and the day after we came safe to Montserrat.

Many were surprised when they heard of my conducting the sloop into the port; and I now obtained a new appellation, and was called "Captain." This elated me not a little, and it was quite flattering to my vanity to be thus styled by as high a title as any sable freeman in this place possessed. When the death of the Captain became known, he was much regretted by all who knew him; for he was a man universally respected. At the same time the sable Captain lost no fame; for the success I had met with increased the affection of my friends in no small measure; and I was offered, by a gentleman of the place, the command of his sloop, to go amongst the islands, but I refused.

CHAPTER VIII.

The author, to oblige Mr. King, once more embarks for Georgia, in the Nancy—A new Captain is appointed—They sail, and steer a new course—Three remarkable dreams—The vessel is wrecked on Bahama Banks; but the crew are preserved, principally by means of the author—He sets out from an island with the Captain, in a small boat, in quest of a ship—Their distress—Meet with a wrecker—Sail for Providence—Are overtaken again by a terrible storm, and are all near perishing—Arrive at New Providence—The author, after some time, sails from thence to Georgia—Meets with another storm, and is obliged to put back and refit—Arrives at Georgia—Meets new impositions— Two white men attempt to kidnap him—Officiates as a parson at a funeral ceremony—Bids adieu to Georgia, and sails for Martinico.

I.

As I had now, by the death of my Captain, lost my great benefactor and friend, I had little inducement to remain longer in the West-Indies, except my gratitude to Mr. King, which I thought I had pretty well discharged in bringing back his vessel safe, and delivering his cargo to his satisfaction. I began to think of leaving this part of the world, of which I had been long tired, and of returning to England, where my heart had always been; but Mr. King still pressed me very much to stay with his vessel: and he had done so much for me, that I found myself unable to refuse his requests, and consented to go another voyage to Georgia, as the mate, from his ill state of health, was quite useless in the vessel. Accordingly a new Captain was appointed, whose name was William Phillips, an old acquaintance of mine; and, having refitted our vessel, and taken several slaves on board, we set sail for St. Eustatia, where we

stayed but a few days: and on the 30th of January, 1767, we steered for Georgia. Our new Captain boasted strangely of his skill in navigating and conducting a vessel; and in consequence of this he steered a new course, several points more to the westward than we ever did before;— this appeared to me very extraordinary.

On the 4th of February, which was soon after we had got into our new course, I dreamed the ship was wrecked amidst the surfs and rocks, and that I was the means of saving every one on board; and on the night following I dreamed the very same dream. These dreams, however, made no impression on my mind; and the next evening, it being my watch below, I was pumping the vessel a little after eight o'clock, just before I went off the deck, as is the custom; and being weary with the duty of the day, and tired at the pump (for we made a good deal of water), I began to express my impatience, and uttered with an oath, 'Damn the vessel's bottom out!' But my conscience instantly smote me for the expression. When I left the deck I went to bed, and had scarcely fallen asleep when I dreamed the same dream again about the ship as I had dreamed the two preceding nights.

At twelve o'clock the watch was changed; and, as I had always the charge of the captain's watch, I then went upon deck. At half after one in the morning, the man at the helm saw something under the lee-beam that the sea washed against, and he immediately called to me that there was a grampus, and desired me to look at it. Accordingly I stood up, and observed it for some time; but, when I saw the sea wash against it again and again, I said it was not a fish but a rock. Being soon certain of this, I went down to the Captain, and with some confusion told him the danger we were in, and desired him to come upon deck immediately. He said *it was very well*, and I went up again. As soon as I was upon deck, the wind, which had been pretty high, having abated a little, the vessel began to be carried sideways towards the rock, by means of the current. Still the Captain did not appear. I therefore went to him again, and told him the vessel was then near a large rock, and desired he would come up with all speed. He said he would, and I returned on the deck. When I was upon the deck again, I saw we were not above a pistol-shot from the rock, and I heard the noise of the breakers all around us. I was exceedingly alarmed at this; and the Captain having not yet come on the deck, I lost all patience; and, growing quite enraged, I ran down to him again, and asked him why he did not come up, and what he could mean by all this? 'The breakers,' said I, 'are around us, and the vessel is almost on the rock.' With that he came on the deck with me, and tried to put the vessel about, and get her out of the current; but all to no purpose, the wind being very small. We then called all hands up immediately; and after a little we got up one end of

a cable, and fastened it to the anchor. By this time the surf was foaming round us, and made a dreadful noise on the breakers, and the very moment we let the anchor go, the vessel struck against the rocks.

II.

One swell now succeeded another, as if it were one wave calling on its fellow. The roaring of the billows increased, and, with one single heave of the swells, the sloop was pierced and transfixed among the rocks!* In a moment a scene of horror presented itself to my mind, such as I never had conceived or experienced before. All my sins stared me in the face; and especially I thought that God had hurled his direful vengeance on my guilty head, for cursing the vessel on which my life depended. My spirits at this forsook me, and I expected every moment to go to the bottom; I determined, if I should still be saved, that I would never swear again. And in the midst of my distress, while the dreadful surfs were dashing with unremitting fury among the rocks, I remembered the Lord, though fearful that I was undeserving of forgiveness, and I thought that as he had often delivered, he might yet deliver; and, calling to mind the many mercies he had shewn me in times past, they gave me some small hope that he might still help me. I then began to think how we might be saved; and, I believe no mind was ever like mine, so replete with inventions and confused with schemes; though how to escape death I knew not.

The captain immediately ordered the hatches to be nailed down on the slaves in the hold, where above twenty of them were, all of whom must unavoidably have perished if he had been obeyed. When he desired

*In his Edition of 1792, the author had inserted, in addition to the plate of *The Nancy foundering on the Bahamas Banks*, 1767, the following quotations from Scripture, which are very applicable to his prophetic dream and his subsequent shipwreck:

Now a thing was secretly brought to me, and mine ear received a little thereof. — In *thoughts from the visions of the night, when deep sleep falleth on men.* JOB iv. 12, 13.

For God speaketh once, yea, twice, yet man perceiveth it not. In a dream, in a vision of the night, when deep sleep falleth upon men, in slumberings upon the bed; then He openeth the ears of men and sealeth their instruction. — Lo, *all these things worketh God oftentimes with man, to bring back his soul from the pit, to be enlightened with the light of the living.* JOB xxxiii. 14–16. 29, 30. *They ran the ship aground; and the fore part struck fast and remained unmovable, but the hinder part was broken by the violence of the waves.* — *Howbeit we must be cast upon a certain island; wherefore, sirs, be of good cheer; for I believe God, that it shall be even as it was told me.* — *And so it came to pass that they escaped all safe to land.* ACTS xxvii. 41, 26, 25, 44.

the men to nail down the hatches, I thought that my sin was the cause of this, and that God would charge me with these people's blood. This thought rushed upon my mind that instant with such violence, that it quite overpowered me, and I fainted. I recovered just as the people were about to nail down the hatches; perceiving which, I desired them to stop. The Captain then said, "it must be done;" I asked him "why?" He said that every one would endeavour to get into the boat, which was but small, and thereby we should be drowned; for it would not have carried above ten at the most. I could no longer restrain my emotion, and I told him he deserved drowning for not knowing how to navigate the vessel; and I believe the people would have tossed him overboard if I had given them the least hint of it. However the hatches were not nailed down; and, as none of us could leave the vessel then, on account of the darkness, and as we knew not where to go, and were convinced besides that the boat could not survive the surfs, we all said we would remain on the dry part of the vessel, and trust to God till day-light appeared, when we should know better what to do.

I then advised to get the boat prepared against morning, and some of us began to set about it; but others abandoned all care of the ship and themselves, and fell to drinking. Our boat had a piece out of her bottom near two feet long, and we had no materials to mend her; however, necessity being the mother of invention, I took some pump leather and nailed it to the broken part, and plastered it over with tallow-grease. And, thus prepared, with the utmost anxiety of mind we watched for day-light, and thought every minute an hour till it appeared. At last it saluted our longing eyes, and kind Providence accompanied its approach with what was no small comfort to us—for the dreadful swells began to subside; and the next thing that we discovered to raise our dropping spirits, was a small key or desolate island, about five or six miles off; but a barrier soon presented itself; for there was not water enough for our boat to go over the reefs, and this threw us again into a sad consternation. But there was no alternative, we were therefore obliged to put but few things in the boat at once; and, what was still worse, all of us were frequently under the necessity of getting out to drag and lift it over the reefs. This cost us much labour and fatigue; and what was yet more distressing, we could not avoid having our legs cut and torn very much with the rocks.

There were only four people that would work with me at the oars; and they consisted of three black men, and a Dutch Creole sailor; and though we went with the boat fives times that day, we had no others to assist us. But had we not worked in this manner, I really believe the people could not have been saved; for not one of the white men did any thing to preserve their lives. Indeed they soon got so drunk that they

were not able; but lay about the deck like swine, so that we were at last obliged to lift them into the boat and carry them on shore by force. This want of assistance made our labour intolerably severe; insomuch that, by going on shore so often that day, the skin was partly stripped off my hands. We continued, however, all the day to toil and strain our exertions, till we had brought all on board safe to the shore; so that out of thirty-two people we lost not one.

III.

My dream now returned upon my mind with all its force; it was fulfilled in every part; for our danger was the same I had dreamed of; and I could not help looking on myself as the principal instrument in effecting our deliverance. For, owing to some of our people getting drunk, the rest of us were obliged to double our exertions; and it was fortunate we did, for in a very little time longer the patch of leather on the boat would have been worn out, and she would have been no longer fit for service. Situated as we were, who could think that men should be so careless of the danger they were in? For, if the wind had but raised the swell, as it was when the vessel struck, we must have bid a final farewell to all hopes of deliverance; and though I warned the people who were drinking, and entreated them to embrace the moment of deliverance, nevertheless they persisted, as if not possessed of the least spark of reason. I could not help thinking, that, if any of these people had been lost, God would charge me with their lives; which, perhaps, was one cause of my labouring so hard for their preservation; and indeed every one of them afterwards seemed so sensible of the service I had rendered them, that while we were on the key I was a kind of chieftain amongst them.

I brought some limes, oranges, and lemons on shore; and finding it to be a good soil where we were, I planted several of them as a token to any one that might be cast away hereafter. This key, as we afterwards found, was one of the Bahama islands, which consist of a cluster of large islands, with smaller ones, or keys, as they are called, interspersed among them. It was about a mile in circumference, with a white sandy beach running in a regular order along it. On that part of it where we first attempted to land, there stood some very large birds, called flamingoes: these, from the reflection of the sun, appeared to us at a little distance as large as men; and when they walked backwards and forwards, we could not conceive what they were: our Captain swore they were cannibals. This created a great panic among us; and we held a consultation how to act. The Captain wanted to go to a key that was

within sight, but a great way off; but I was against it, as in so doing we should not be able to save all the people. 'And therefore,' said I, 'let us go on shore here, and perhaps these cannibals may take to the water.' Accordingly we steered towards them, and when we approached them, to our very great joy and no less wonder, they walked off, one after the other, very deliberately; and at last they took to flight, and relieved us entirely from our fears. About the key there were turtles, and several sorts of fish, in such abundance that we caught them without bait, which was a great relief to us after the salt provisions on board. There was also a large rock on the beach about ten feet high, which was in the form of a punch-bowl at the top: this we could not help thinking Providence had ordained to supply us with rain-water; and it was something singular that, if we did not take it when it rained, in some little time after it would turn as salt as sea-water.

IV.

Our first care, after refreshment, was to make ourselves tents to lodge in, which we did as well as we could with some sails we had brought from the ship. We then began to think how we might get from this uninhabited place; and we determined to repair our boat, which was very much shattered, and to put to sea in quest of a ship, or some inhabited island. It took us up eleven days before we could get the boat ready for sea, in the manner we wanted it, with a sail and other necessaries. Having got all things prepared, the Captain wanted me to stay on shore, while he went to sea in quest of a vessel to take all the people off the key. But this I refused; and the Captain, and myself, with five more, set off in the boat towards New Providence. We had no more than two musketload of gunpowder with us, if any thing should happen; and our stock of provisions consisted of three gallons of rum, four of water, some salt beef, some biscuit; and in this manner we proceeded to sea.

On the second day of our voyage, we came to an island called Abbico, the largest of the Bahama islands. We were much in want of water; for by this time our water was expended, and we were exceedingly fatigued; in pulling two days in the heat of the sun; and it being late in the evening, we hauled the boat ashore to try for water, and to remain during the night: when we came ashore we searched for water, but could find none. When it was dark, we made a fire around us for fear of the wild beasts, as the place was an entire thick wood, and we took it by turns to watch. In this situation we found very little rest, and waited with impatience for the morning. As soon as the light appeared,

we set off again with our boat, in hopes of finding assistance during the day. We were now much dejected and weakened by pulling the boat; for our sail was of no use, and we were almost famished for want of fresh water to drink. We had nothing left to eat but salt beef, and that we could not use without water.

In this situation we toiled all day in sight of the island, which was very long; in the evening, seeing no relief, we made shore again, and fastened our boat. We then went to look for fresh water, being quite faint for the want of it; and we dug and searched about for some all the remainder of the evening, but could not find one drop; so that our dejection at this period became excessive, and our terror so great, that we expected nothing but death to deliver us. We could not touch our beef, which was salt as brine, without fresh water; and we were in the greatest terror from the apprehension of wild beasts. When unwelcome night came, we acted as on the night before; and the next morning we set off again from the island in hopes of seeing some vessel. In this manner we toiled, as well as we were able, till four o'clock, during which we passed several keys, but could not meet with a ship; and, still famishing with thirst, went ashore on one of those keys again, in hopes of finding some water. Here we found some leaves with a few drops of water on them, which we lapped with much eagerness; we then dug in several places, but without success.

As we were digging holes in search of water, there came forth some very thick and black stuff; but none of us could touch it, except the poor Dutch creole, who drank about a quart of it as eagerly as if it had been wine. We tried to catch fish, but could not; and we now began to repine at our fate, and abandon ourselves to despair; when, in the midst of our murmuring, the captain all at once cried out, 'A sail! a sail! a sail!' This gladdening sound was like a reprieve to a convict, and we all instantly turned to look at it;—but in a little time some of us began to be afraid it was not a sail. However at a venture we embarked, and steered after it; and, in half an hour, to our unspeakable joy, we plainly saw that it was a vessel. At this our drooping spirits revived, and we made towards her with all the speed imaginable. When we came near to her we found she was a little sloop, about the size of a Gravesend hoy, and quite full of people;—a circumstance of which we could not make out the meaning. Our Captain, who was a Welchman, swore that they were pirates, and would kill us. I said "be that as it might, we must board her, if we were to die by it; and, if they should not receive us kindly, we must oppose them, as well as we could; for there was no alternative between their perishing and ours." This counsel was immediately taken; and I really believe that the Captain, myself, and the Dutchman would then

have faced twenty men. We had two cutlasses and a musket, that I brought in the boat, and in this situation we rowed alongside and immediately boarded her. I believe there were about forty hands on board; but how great our surprise, as soon we got on board, to find that the major part of them were in the same predicament as ourselves!

They belonged to a whaling schooner, that was wrecked, two days before us, about nine miles to the north of our vessel. When she was wrecked, some of them had taken to their boats, and had left some of their people and property on a key as we had done, and were going, like us, to New Providence in quest of a ship, when they met with this little sloop, called a wrecker; whose employment in those seas is to look after wrecks. They were then going to take the remainder of the people belonging to the schooner; for which the wrecker was to have all things belonging to the vessel, and likewise their people's help to get all they could out of her, and were then to carry the crew to New Providence.

V.

We told the people of the wrecker the condition of our vessel; and we made the same agreement with them as the schooner's people had done; and, on their complying, we begged of them to go to our key directly, because our people were in want of water. They agreed, therefore, to go along with us first; and in two days we arrived at the key, to the inexpressible joy of the people that we had left behind, as they had been reduced to great extremities for want of water in our absence. Luckily for us, the wrecker had now more people on board than she could carry or victual for any moderate length of time; they therefore hired the schooner's people to work on the wreck, and we left them our boat, and embarked for New Providence.

Nothing could have been more fortunate than our meeting with this wrecker; for New Providence was at such a distance, we never could have reached it in our boat. The island of Abbico was much longer than we expected; and it was not till after sailing for three or four days, that we got safe to the farther end of it, towards New Providence. When arrived there we watered, and got a good many lobsters and other shell-fish; which proved a great relief to us, as our provisions and water were almost exhausted. We then proceeded on our voyage; but the day after we left the island, and late in the evening, while we were yet amongst the Bahama keys, we were overtaken by a violent gale of wind which obliged us to cut away the mast. The vessel was very near

foundering; for she parted from her anchors and struck several times on the shoals. We here expected her every minute to go to pieces, and each moment to be our last: so much so, that my old captain, and sickly useless mate, and several others, fainted; and death stared us in the face on every side.

All the swearers on board now began to call on the God of Heaven to assist them: and, sure enough, beyond our comprehension, He did assist us, and in a miraculous manner delivered us! In the very height of our extremity the wind lulled for a few minutes; and although the swell was high, beyond expression, two men, who were expert swimmers, attempted to go to the buoy of the anchor, which we still saw in the water at some distance, in a little punt that belonged to the wrecker, which was not large enough to carry more than two. She filled at different times in their endeavours to get into her, alongside of our vessel; and nothing but death appeared before them and us; but, however, they said they might as well die that way as any other. A coil of very small rope, with a little buoy, was put in along with them; and, at last, they got the punt clear from the vessel, and these two intrepid water heroes paddled away for life towards the buoy of the anchor.

Our eyes were fixed on them all the time, expecting every minute to be their last: and the prayers of all those that remained in their senses, were offered up to God, on their behalf, for a speedy deliverance, and for our own, which depended on them; and He heard and answered us! These two men at last reached the buoy; and, having fastened the punt to it, they tied one end of their rope to the small buoy that they had in the punt, and sent it adrift towards the vessel. We on board, observing this, threw out boat-hooks and leads fastened to lines, in order to catch the buoy: at last we caught it, and fastened a hawser to the end of the small rope. We then gave them a sign to pull, and they pulled the hawser to them and fastened it to the buoy; which being done, we hauled for our lives; and, through the mercy of God, we got again from the shoals into deep water, and the punt got safe to the vessel.

It is impossible for any to conceive our heart-felt joy, at this second deliverance from ruin, but those who have suffered the same hardships. Those whose strength and senses were gone, came to themselves, and were now as elated as they were before depressed. Two days after this the wind ceased, and the water became smooth. The punt then went on shore, and we cut down some trees; and having found our mast and mended it, we brought it on board, and fixed it up. As soon as we had done this we got up the anchor, and away we went once more for New Providence, which in three days more we reached safe, after having been above three weeks in a situation from which we did not expect to escape with life.

VI.

The inhabitants here were very kind to us; and having learned our situation, they shewed us a great deal of hospitality and friendship. Soon after this, every one of my old fellow-sufferers, that were free, parted from us, and shaped their course as inclination led them. One merchant, who had a large sloop, seeing our condition, and knowing we wanted to go to Georgia, told four of us that his vessel was going there; and offered us our passage free, on condition of our helping to load and work the vessel. As we could not get any wages, and found it very hard to get off the place, we consented to his proposal; and went on board and helped to load the sloop, though we had only our victuals allowed us. When entirely loaded, he told us she was going to Jamaica first, where we must go if we went in her. This, however, I refused; but my fellow-sufferers, not having any money to help themselves with, were obliged by necessity to accept of the offer, and to steer the course, though they did not like it.

We stayed in New Providence about seventeen or eighteen days; during which time I met with many friends, who gave me encouragement to stay there with them, but I declined it; though, had not my heart been fixed on England, I should have stayed, as I liked the place extremely, and there were some free black people here who were very happy, and we passed our time pleasantly together, with the melodious sound of the catguts, under the lime and lemon trees. At length Captain Phillips hired a sloop to carry him and some of the slaves, that he could not sell here, to Georgia; and I agreed to go with him in the vessel, meaning now to take my farewell of that place. When the vessel was ready, we all embarked; and I took my leave of New Providence, not without regret.

We sailed about four o'clock in the morning, with a fair wind, for Georgia; and, about eleven o'clock the same morning, a sudden and short gale sprung up and blew away most of our sails; and, as we were still among the keys, in a very few minutes it dashed the sloop against the rocks. Luckily for us the water was deep; and the sea was not so angry, but that, after having for sometime laboured hard, and being many in number, we were saved through God's mercy: and, by using our greatest exertions, we got the vessel off. The next day we returned to Providence, where we soon got her again refitted. Some of the people swore that we had spells set upon us, by somebody in Montserrat; and others said that we had witches and wizards amongst the poor helpless slaves; and that we never should arrive safe at Georgia. But these things did not deter me; I said, 'Let us again face the winds and seas, and swear not, but trust

to God, and he will deliver us.' We therefore once more set sail: and with hard labour, in seven days' time, arrived safe at Georgia.

After our arrival we went up to the town of Savannah; and the same evening I went to a friend's house to lodge, whose name was Mosa, a black man. We were very happy at meeting each other; and, after supper, we had a light, until between nine and ten o'clock at night. About that time the watch or patrol came by, and, discerning a light in the house, they knocked at the door; we opened it, and they came in and sat down, and drank some punch with us; they also begged some limes of me, as they understood I had some, which I readily gave them. A little after this, they told me I must go to the watch-house with them; this surprised me a good deal after our kindness to them, and I asked them, 'Why so?' They said, that all negroes, who had a light in their houses after nine o'clock were to be taken into custody, and either pay some dollars or be flogged. Some of these people knew that I was a free man; but, as the man of the house was not free, and had his master to protect him, they did not take the same liberty with him they did with me. I told them that I was a free man, and just arrived from Providence; that we were not making any noise, and that I was not a stranger in that place, but was very well known there; 'Besides,' said I, 'what will you do with me?' — 'That you shall see,' replied they; 'but you must go to the watch-house with us.'

Now, whether they meant to get money from me or not, I was at a loss to know; but I thought immediately of the oranges and limes at Santa Cruz; and seeing that nothing would pacify them, I went with them to the watch-house, where I remained during the night. Early the next morning these imposing ruffians flogged a negro-man and woman that they had in the watch-house, and then they told me that I must be flogged too. I asked why; and if there was no law for free men; and told them if there was, I would have it put in force against them. But this only exasperated them the more, and they instantly swore they would serve me as Dr. Perkins had done; and were going to lay violent hands on me; when one of them, more humane than the rest, said, that as I was a free man they could not justify stripping me by law. I then immediately sent for Dr. Brady, who was known to be a honest and worthy man; and, on his coming to my assistance, they let me go.

VII.

This was not the only disagreeable incident I met with while I was in this place; for, one day, being a little way out of the town of Savannah, I was beset by two white men, who meant to play their usual tricks with

me in the way of kidnapping. As soon as these men accosted me, one of them said to the other, 'This is the very fellow we are looking for, that you lost:' and the other swore immediately that I was the identical person. On this they made up to me, and were about to handle me, but I told them to be still and keep off, for I had seen those tricks played upon other free blacks, and they must not think to serve me so. At this they paused a little, and one said to the other, "It will not do;" and the other answered that I talked too good English. I replied I believed I did; and I had also with me a revengeful stick equal to the occasion; and my mind was likewise good. Happily, however it was not used: and, after we had talked together a little in this manner, the rogues left me.

I stayed in Savannah some time, anxiously trying to get to Montserrat, once more to see Mr. King, my old master; and then to take a final farewell of the American quarter of the globe. At last I met with a sloop called the Speedwell, Captain John Bunton, which belonged to Grenada, and was bound to Martinico, a French island, with a cargo of rice, and I shipped myself on board of her.

Before I left Georgia, a black woman, who had a child lying dead, being very tenacious of the church burial-service, and not able to get any white person to perform it, applied to me for that purpose. I told her I was no parson; and besides, that the service over the dead did not affect the soul. This however did not satisfy her; she still urged me very hard. I therefore complied with her entreaties, and at last consented to act the parson for the first time in my life. As she was much respected, there was a great company both of white and black people at the grave. I then, accordingly, assumed my new vocation, and performed the funeral ceremony to the satisfaction of all present; after which I bade adieu to Georgia, and sailed for Martinico.

CHAPTER IX.

The author arrives at Martinico—Meets with new difficulties—Gets to Montserrat, where he takes leave of his old master, and sails for England—Meets Capt. Pascal—Learns the French horn—Hires himself with Dr. Irving, where he learns to freshen sea water—Leaves the Dr. and goes a voyage to Turkey and Portugal: and afterwards goes a voyage to Grenada, and another to Jamaica—Returns to the Dr. and they embark together on a voyage to the North Pole, with the Hon. Captain Phipps—Some account of that voyage, and the dangers the author was in—He returns to England.

I.

I THUS took a final leave of Georgia; for the treatment I had received in it disgusted me very much against the place; and when I left it and sailed for Martinico, I determined never more to revisit it. My new Captain conducted his vessel safer than my former one; and after an agreeable voyage, we got safe to our intended port. While I was on this island I went about a good deal, and found it very pleasant; in particular, I admired the town of St. Pierre, which is the principal one in the island, and built more like an European town than any I had seen in the West-Indies. In general also, slaves were better treated, had more holidays, and looked better than those in the English islands. After we had done our business here, I wanted my discharge, which was necessary; for it was then the month of May, and I wished much to be at Montserrat to bid farewell to Mr. King, and all my other friends there, in time to sail for old England in the July fleet. But, alas! I had put a

great stumbling block in my own way, by which I was near losing my passage that season to England. I had lent my Captain some money, which I now wanted, to enable me to prosecute my intentions. This I told him; but when I applied for it, though I urged the necessity of my occasion I met with so much shuffling from him, that I began at last to be afraid of losing my money, as I could not recover it by law. For I have already mentioned, that throughout the West Indies no black man's testimony is admitted, on any occasion, against any white person whatever, and therefore my own oath would have been of no use. I was obliged, therefore, to remain with him till he might be disposed to return it to me.

Thus we sailed from Martinico for the Grenades. I frequently pressed the Captain for my money, to no purpose; and, to render my condition worse, when we got there, the Captain and his owners quarrelled. So that my situation became daily more irksome; for besides that we on board had little or no victuals allowed us, and I could not get my money nor wages, I could then have gotten my passage free to Montserrat had I been able to accept it. The worst of all was, that it was growing late in July, and the ships in the islands must sail by the 26th of that month. At last, however, with a great many entreaties, I got my money from the Captain, and took the first vessel I could meet with for St. Eustatia. From thence I went in another to Basseterre in St. Kitt's where I arrived on the 19th of July.

On the 22d, having met with a vessel bound to Montserrat, I wanted to go in her; but the Captain and others would not take me on board until I should advertise myself, and give notice of my going off the island. I told them of my haste to be in Montserrat; and that the time then would not admit of advertising, it being late in the evening, and the vessel about to sail; but he insisted it was necessary, and otherwise he said he would not take me. This reduced me to great perplexity; for if I should be compelled to submit to this degrading necessity, which every black freeman is under, of advertising himself like a slave, when he leaves an island, and which I thought a gross imposition upon any freeman, I feared I should miss that opportunity of going to Montserrat, and then I could not get to England that year. The vessel was just going off, and no time could be lost; I immediately therefore set about it, with a heavy heart, to try whom I could get to befriend me in complying with the demands of the Captain. Luckily I found, in a few minutes, some gentlemen of Montserrat whom I knew; and having told them my situation, I requested their friendly assistance in helping me off the island. Some of them, on this, went with me to the Captain, and satisfied him of my freedom; and, to my very great joy, he desired me to go on board.

II.

We then set sail, and the next day, the 23d, I arrived at the wished-for place, after an absence of six months, in which I had more than once experienced the delivering hand of Providence, when all human means of escaping destruction seemed hopeless. I saw my friends with a gladness of heart which was increased by my absence and the dangers I had escaped; and I was received with great friendship by them all, but particularly by Mr. King, to whom I related the fate of his sloop, the Nancy, and the causes of her being wrecked. I now learned with extreme sorrow, that his house was washed away during my absence, by the bursting of a pond at the top of a mountain that was opposite the town of Plymouth. It swept great part of the town away, and Mr. King lost a great deal of property from the inundation, and nearly his life. When I told him I intended to go to London that season, and that I had come to visit him before my departure, the good man expressed a great deal of affection for me and sorrow that I should leave him, and warmly advised me to stay there; insisting, as I was much respected by all the gentlemen in the place, that I might do very well, and in a short time have land and slaves of my own. I thanked him for this instance of his friendship; but, as I wished very much to be in London, I declined remaining any longer there, and begged he would excuse me. I then requested he would be kind enough to give me a certificate of my behaviour while in his service, with which he very readily complied, and gave me the following:

Montserrat, 26th of the Seventh Month, 1767.
 The bearer hereof, GUSTAVUS VASSA, was my slave for upwards of three years, during which he has always behaved himself well, and discharged his duty with honesty and assiduity.
ROBERT KING.

 To all whom this may concern.

Having obtained this, I parted from my kind master, after many sincere professions of gratitude and regard, and prepared for my departure for London. I immediately agreed to go with one Capt. John Hamer, for seven guineas (the passage to London), on board a ship called the Andromache; and on the 24th and 25th, I had free dances, as they are called, with some of my friends and countrymen, previous to my setting off; after which I took leave of all my friends, and on the 26th I embarked for London, exceedingly glad to see myself once more on board of a ship; and still more so, in steering the course I had long wished for. With a light heart I bade Montserrat farewell, and never had

had better try it.' I told him then that I would try it, which enraged him very much; however, out of regard to the ladies, I remained still, and never made any farther demand of my right.

Some time afterwards, these friendly ladies asked me what I meant to do with myself, and how they could assist me. I thanked them, and said, if they pleased, I would be their servant; but if not, I had thirty-seven guineas, which would support me for some time, and I would be much obliged to them to recommend me to some person who would teach me a trade whereby I might earn my living. They answered me very politely, that they were sorry it did not suit them to take me as their servant, and asked me what business I should like to learn. I said "hair dressing." They then promised to assist me in this; and soon after they recommended me to a gentleman, whom I had known before, one Captain O'Hara, who treated me with much kindness, and procured me a master, a hair dresser, in Coventry Court, Haymarket, with whom he placed me.

I was with this man from September till the February following. In that time we had a neighbour in the same Court, who taught the French-horn. He used to blow it so well that I was charmed with it, and agreed with him to teach me to blow it. Accordingly he took me in hand, and began to instruct me, and I soon learned all the three parts. I took great delight in blowing on this instrument, the evenings being long; and, besides that I was fond of it, I did not like to be idle, and it filled up my vacant hours innocently. At this time also I agreed with the Rev. Mr. Gregory, who lived in the same court, where he kept an academy and an evening school, to improve me in Arithmetic. This he did as far as Barter and Alligation; so that all the time I was here I was entirely employed.

In February 1768, I hired myself to Dr. Charles Irving, in Pall-mall, so celebrated for his successful experiments in making sea water fresh; and here I had plenty of hair-dressing to improve my hand. This gentleman was an excellent master; he was exceedingly kind and good-tempered; and allowed me in the evenings to attend my schools, which I esteemed a great blessing; therefore I thanked God and him for it, and used all diligence to improve the opportunity. This diligence and attention recommended me to the notice and care of my three preceptors, who, on their parts, bestowed a great deal of pains in my instruction, and besides were all very kind to me. My wages, however, which were by two thirds less than ever I had in my life (for I had only £12 per annum), I soon found would not be sufficient to defray this extraordinary expence of masters and my own necessary expences. My old thirty-seven guineas had by this time worn all away to one. I thought it best therefore to try the sea again in quest of more money, as I had been bred to it, and had hitherto found the profession of it successful. I had also, a very great desire to see Turkey, and I now determined to gratify it.

my feet on it since: and with it I bade adieu to the sound of the cruel whip, and all other dreadful instruments of torture; adieu to the offensive sight of the violated chastity of the sable females, which has too often accosted my eyes; adieu to oppressions; (although to me less severe than most of my countrymen) and adieu to the angry, howling, dashing surfs. I wished for a grateful and thankful heart to praise the Lord God on high for all his mercies! In this ecstacy I steered the ship all night.

III.

We had a most prosperous voyage, and, at the end of seven weeks, arrived at Cherry Garden stairs. Thus were my longing eyes once more gratified with a sight of London, after having been absent from it above four years. I immediately received my wages, and I never had earned seven guineas so quickly in my life before; I had thirty-seven guineas in all, when I got cleared of the ship. I now entered upon a scene quite new to me, but full of hope. In this situation my first thoughts were to look out for some of my former friends, and amongst the first of those were the Miss Guerins. As soon as I had regaled myself I went in quest of those kind ladies, whom I was very impatient to see, and, with some difficulty and perseverance, I found them at May's-hill, Greenwich. They were most agreeably surprised to see me, and I quite overjoyed at meeting with them. I told them my history, at which they expressed great wonder, and freely acknowledged it did their cousin, Captain Pascal, no honour. He then visited there frequently; and I met him, four or five days after, in Greenwich park. When he saw me, he appeared a good deal surprised, and asked me how I came back. I answered, "In a ship." To which he replied dryly, 'I suppose you did not walk back to London on the water.' As I saw, by his manner, that he did not seem to be sorry for his behaviour to me, and that I had not much reason to expect any favour from him, I told him that he had used me very ill, after I had been such a faithful servant to him for so many years; on which, without saying any more, he turned about and went away. A few days after this I met Captain Pascal at Miss Guerin's house, and asked him for my prize-money. He said there was none due to me; for, if my prize-money had been £10,000, he had a right to it all. I told him I was informed otherwise: on which he bade me defiance; and, in a bantering tone, desired me to commence a law-suit against him for it; 'There are lawyers enough,' said he, 'that will take the cause in hand, and you

Accordingly, in the month of May, 1768, I told the doctor of my wish to go to sea again, to which he made no opposition; and we parted on friendly terms. The same day I went into the city in quest of a master. I was extremely fortunate in my enquiry; for I soon heard of a gentleman who had a ship going to Italy and Turkey, and he wanted a man who could dress hair well. I was overjoyed at this, and went immediately on board of his ship, as I had been directed, which I found to be fitted up with great taste, and I already foreboded no small pleasure in sailing in her. Not finding the gentleman on board, I was directed to his lodgings, where I met with him the next day, and gave him a specimen of my dressing. He liked it so well that he hired me immediately, so that I was perfectly happy; for the ship, master, and voyage, were entirely to my mind.

IV.

The ship was called the Delaware, and my master's name was John Jolly, a neat, smart, good-humoured man, just such a one as I wished to serve. We sailed from England in July following, and our voyage was extremely pleasant. We went to Villa Franca, Nice, and Leghorn; and in all these places I was charmed with the richness and beauty of the countries, and struck with the elegant buildings with which they abound. We had always in them plenty of extraordinary good wines and rich fruits, of which I was very fond; and I had frequent occasions of gratifying both my taste and curiosity; for my Captain always lodged on shore in those places, which afforded me opportunities to see the country around. I also learned navigation of the mate, of which I was very fond.

When we left Italy we had delightful sailing among the Archipelago islands, and from thence to Smyrna in Turkey. This is a very ancient city, the houses are built of stone, and most of them have graves adjoining to them, so that they sometimes present the appearance of church-yards. Provisions are very plentiful in this city, and good wine less than a penny a pint. The grapes, pomegranates, and many other fruits, were also the richest and largest I ever saw or tasted. The natives are good-looking and strong made, and always treated me with great civility. In general, I believe, they are fond of black people; and several of them gave me pressing invitations to stay amongst them, although they keep the Franks, or Christians, separate, and do not suffer them to dwell immediately amongst them. I was astonished at not seeing women in any of their shops, and very rarely any in the streets; and whenever I did, they were covered with a veil from head to foot, so that I could not see

their faces, except when any of them, out of curiosity, uncovered them to look at me, which they sometimes did. I was surprised to see how the Greeks are, in some measure, kept under by the Turks, as the negroes are in the West Indies by the white people. The less refined Greeks, as I have already hinted, dance here in the same manner as we do in our nation.

On the whole, during our stay here, which was about five months, I liked the place and the Turks extremely well. I could not help observing one remarkable circumstance there: — the tails of the sheep are flat, and so very large, that I have known the tail even of a lamb to weigh from eleven to thirteen pounds. The fat of them is very white and rich, and is excellent in puddings, for which it is much used. Our ship being at length richly loaded with silk and other articles, we sailed for England.

In May 1769, soon after our return from Turkey, our ship made a delightful voyage to Oporto in Portugal, where we arrived at the time of the carnival. On our arrival, there were sent on board of us thirty-six articles to be observed, with very heavy penalties if we should break any of them: and none of us even dared to go on board any other vessel or on shore, till the Inquisition had sent on board and searched for every thing illegal, especially Bibles. All we had were produced, and certain other things were sent on shore till the ships were going away: and any person, in whose custody a Bible was found concealed, was to be imprisoned and flogged, and sent into slavery for ten years.

I saw here many magnificent sights, particularly the garden of Eden, where many of the clergy and laity went in procession in their several orders with the host, and sung Te Deum. I had a great curiosity to go into some of their churches, but could not gain admittance without using the necessary sprinkling of holy water at my entrance. From curiosity, and a wish to be holy, I therefore complied with this ceremony; but its virtues were lost upon me, for I found myself nothing the better for it. This place abounds with plenty of all kinds of provisions. The town is well built and pretty, and commands a fine prospect. Our ship having taken in a load of wine and other commodities, we sailed for London, and arrived there in July following.

V.

Our next voyage was to the Mediterranean. The ship was again got ready, and we sailed in September for Genoa. This is one of the finest cities I ever saw; some of the edifices were of beautiful marble, and made a most notable appearance; and many had very curious fountains before them. The churches were rich and magnificent, and curiously

adorned both in the inside and out. But all this grandeur was, in my eyes, disgraced by the galley-slaves, whose condition, both there and in other parts of Italy, is truly piteous and wretched. After we had staid there some weeks, during which we bought many different things we wanted, and got them very cheap, we sailed to Naples, a charming city and remarkably clean. The bay is the most beautiful I ever saw; the moles for shipping are excellent. I thought it extraordinary to see grand operas acted here on Sunday nights, and even attended by their Majesties. I too, like these great ones, went to those sights, and vainly served God in the day while I thus served mammon effectually at night.

While we remained here, there happened an eruption of Mount Vesuvius, of which I had a perfect view. It was extremely awful; and we were so near that the ashes from it used to be thick on our deck. After we had transacted our business at Naples, we sailed with a fair wind once more for Smyrna, and arrived there in December. A seraskier, or officer, took a liking to me here, and wanted me to stay, offering me two wives. But I refused the temptation, thinking one was as much as some could manage, and more than others would venture on. The merchants here travel in caravans or large companies. I have seen many caravans from India, with some hundreds of camels, laden with different goods. The people of these caravans are quite brown. Among other articles, they brought with them a great quantity of locusts, which are a kind of pulse, sweet and pleasant to the palate, and in shape resembling French beans, but longer. Each kind of goods is sold in a street by itself, and I always found the Turks very honest in their dealings. They let no Christians into their mosques, or churches; for which I was very sorry, being always fond of going to see the different modes of worship of the people wherever I went.

The plague broke out while we were in Smyrna; and we stopped taking goods into the ship till it was over. She was then richly laden, and we sailed, in March 1770, for England. One day, on our passage, we met with an accident, which was near burning the ship: A black cook, in melting some fat, overset the pan into the fire under the deck, which immediately began to blaze, and the flame went up very high under the fore-top. With the fright the poor cook became almost white, and altogether speechless. Happily, however, we got the fire out without doing much mischief. After various delays in this passage, we arrived in Sandgate creek in July; and, at the latter end of the year, some new event occurred, so that my noble Captain, the ship, and I, all separated.

In April 1771, I shipped myself as a steward with Captain William Robertson, of the ship Grenada Planter, once more to try my fortune in the West Indies; and we sailed from London for Madeira, Barbadoes, and the Grenades. When we were at this last place, having some goods

to sell, I met once more with my former kind of West-India customers. A white man, an islander, bought some goods of me to the amount of some pounds, and made me many fair promises, as usual, but without any intention of paying me. He had likewise bought goods from some more of our people, whom he intended to serve in the same manner; but still he amused us with promises. However, when our ship was loaded and near sailing, this honest buyer discovered no intention or sign of paying for any thing he had bought of us; but, on the contrary, when I asked him for my money, he threatened me and another black man he had bought goods of, so that we found we were like to get more blows than payment. On this we went to complain to one Mr. Mac Intosh, a justice of the peace; we told his worship of the man's villainous tricks, and begged that he would be kind enough to see us redressed. But being negroes, although free, we could not get any remedy; and our ship being then just upon the point of sailing, we knew not how to help ourselves, though we thought it hard to lose our property in this manner. Luckily for us, however, this man was also indebted to three white sailors, who could not get a farthing from him; they therefore readily joined us, and we all went together in search of him. When we found where he was, I took him out of a house and threatened him with vengeance; on which, finding he was likely to be handled roughly, the rogue offered each of us some small allowance, but nothing near our demands. This exasperated us much more; and some were for cutting his ears off; but he begged hard for mercy, which was at last granted him, after we had entirely stripped him. We then let him go, for which he thanked us, glad to get off so easily, and ran into the bushes, after having wished us a good voyage. We then repaired on board, and shortly after set sail for England.

VI.

I cannot help remarking here a very narrow escape we had from being blown up, owing to a piece of negligence of mine. Just as our ship was under sail, I went down under the cabin, to do some business, and had a lighted candle in my hand, which, in my hurry, without thinking, I held in a barrel of gunpowder. It remained in the powder, until it was near catching fire, when, fortunately, I observed it, and snatched it out in time, and providentially no harm happened; but I was so overcome with terror, that I immediately fainted at this deliverance.

In twenty-eight days' time we arrived in England, and I got clear of the ship. But being still of a roving disposition, and desirous of seeing as

many different parts of the world as I could, I shipped myself soon after, in the same year, as steward, on board of a fine large ship, called the Jamaica, Captain David Watt, and we sailed from England in December 1771, for Nevis and Jamaica. I found Jamaica to be a very fine large island, well-peopled, and the most considerable of the West-India islands. There was a vast number of negroes here, whom I found, as usual, exceedingly imposed upon by the white people, and the slaves punished as in the other islands. There are negroes whose business it is to flog slaves; they go about to different people for employment, and the usual pay is from one to four bits. I saw many cruel punishments inflicted on the slaves in the short time I stayed here. In particular I was present when a poor fellow was tied up, and kept hanging by the wrists at some distance from the ground, and then some half-hundred weights were fixed to his ancles, in which posture he was flogged most unmercifully. — There were also, as I heard, two different masters noted for cruelty on the island, who had staked up two negroes naked, and in two hours the vermin stung them to death. I heard gentleman, whom I knew, tell my Captain, that he passed sentence on a negroe man to be burnt alive for attempting to poison an overseer.

I pass over numerous instances, in order to relieve the reader by a milder scene of roguery. Before I had been long on the island, one Mr. Smith, at Port Morant, bought goods of me to the amount of £25 sterling: but when I demanded payment from him, he was each time going to beat me, and threatened to put me in gaol. One time he would say I was going to set his house on fire; at another he would swear I was going to run away with his slaves. I was astonished at this usage from a person who was in the situation of a gentleman; but I had no alternative, and was therefore obliged to submit. When I came to Kingston, I was surprised to see the number of Africans who were assembled together on Sundays; particularly at a large commodious place, called Spring Bath. Here each different nation of Africa meets and dances after the manner of their own country. They still retain most of their native customs: they bury their dead, and put victuals, pipes, and tobacco, and other things in the grave with the corpse, in the same manner as in Africa.

Our ship having got her loading, we sailed for London, where we arrived in the August following. On my return to London, I waited on my old and good master, Dr. Irving, who made me an offer of his service again. Being now tired of the sea, I gladly accepted it. I was very happy in living with this gentleman once more; during which time we were daily employed in reducing old Neptune's dominions, by purifying the briny element, and making it fresh. Thus I went on till May 1773, when I was roused by the sound of fame to seek new adventures, and find, towards the North Pole, what our Creator never intended we should, a

passage to India. An expedition was fitting out to explore a north-east passage, conducted by the Hon. Constantine John Phipps, since Lord Mulgrave, in his Majesty's sloop of war the Race Horse.

VII.

My master being anxious for the reputation of this adventure, we therefore prepared every thing for our voyage, and I attended him on board the Race Horse, the 24th day of May, 1773. We proceeded to Sheerness, where we were joined by his Majesty's sloop the Carcass, commanded by Captain Lutwidge. On the 4th of June we sailed towards our destined place, the Pole; and on the 15th of the same month we were off Shetland. On this day I had a great and unexpected deliverance from an accident which was near blowing up the ship, and destroying the crew, which made me ever after, during the voyage, uncommonly cautious. The ship was so filled that there was very little room for any one on board; which placed me in a very awkward situation. I had resolved to keep a journal of this singular and interesting voyage; and I had no other place for this purpose but a little cabin, or the doctor's store-room, where I slept. This little place was stuffed with all manner of combustibles, particularly with tow and aquafortis, and many other dangerous things. Unfortunately it happened in the evening, as I was writing my journal, that I had occasion to take the candle out of the lanthorn, and a spark having touched a single thread of the tow, all the rest caught the flame, and immediately the whole was in a blaze. I beheld nothing but present death before me, and expected to be the first to perish in the flames. In a moment the alarm was spread, and many people who were near, ran to assist in putting out the fire.

All this time I was in the very midst of the flames; my shirt, and the handkerchief on my neck, were burnt, and I was almost smothered with the smoke. But through God's mercy, as I was nearly giving up all hopes, some people brought blankets and mattresses and threw them on the flames: by which means, in a short time, the fire was put out. I was severely reprimanded and menaced by such of the officers as knew it; and strictly charged never more to go there with a light; and, indeed, my fears made me give heed to this command for a little time; but at last, not being able to write my journal in any other part of the ship, I was tempted again to venture, by stealth, with a light in the same cabin, though not without considerable fear and dread on my mind.

On the 20th of June we began to use Dr. Irving's apparatus for making salt water fresh. I used to attend the distillery; I frequently purified from twenty-six to forty gallons a day. The water thus distilled was perfectly

pure, well tasted, and free from salt; and was used on various occasions on board the ship. On the 28th of June, being in lat. 78° we made Greenland, where I was surprised to see the sun did not set. The weather now became extremely cold; and as we sailed between north and east, which was our course, we saw many very high and curious mountains of ice; and also a great number of very large whales, which used to come close to our ship, and blow the water up to a very great height in the air. One morning we had vast quantities of sea-horses about the ship, which neighed exactly like any other horses. We fired some harpoon guns amongst them in order to take some, but we could not get any.

On the 30th, the Captain of a Greenland ship came on board, and told us of three ships that were lost in the ice; however, we still held on our course till July the 11th, when we were stopped by one compact impenetrable body of ice. We ran along it from east to west above ten degrees; and on the 27th we got as far north as 80°, 37'; and in 19 or 20 degrees east longitude from London. On the 29th and 30th of July, we saw one continued plain of smooth unbroken ice bounded only by the horizon, and we fastened to a piece of ice that was eight yards eleven inches thick. We had generally sunshine, and constant day-light; which gave cheerfulness and novelty to the whole of this striking, grand, and uncommon scene; and, to heighten it still more, the reflection of the sun from the ice gave the clouds a most beautiful appearance.

We killed many different animals at this time, and, among the rest, nine bears. Though they had nothing in their paunches but water, yet they were all very fat. We used to decoy them to the ship sometimes by burning feathers or skins. I thought them coarse eating, but some of the ship's company relished them very much. Some of our people once, in a boat, fired at and wounded a sea-horse, which dived immediately; and in a little time after brought up with it a number of others. They all joined in an attack upon the boat, and were with difficulty prevented from staving or oversetting her; but a boat from the Carcass having come to assist ours, and joined it, they dispersed after having wrested an oar from one of the men. One of the ship's boats had before been attacked in the same manner, but happily no harm was done. Though we wounded several of these animals we got but one.

VIII.

We remained hereabouts until the 1st of August, when the two ships got completely fastened in the ice occasioned by the loose ice that set in from the sea. This made our situation very dreadful and alarming; so that on the 7th day we were in very great apprehension of having the

ship squeezed to pieces. The officers held a council to know what was best to do in order to save our lives, and it was determined that we should endeavour to escape by dragging our boats along the ice towards the sea; which, however, was farther off than any of us thought. This determination filled us with extreme dejection, and confounded us with despair; for we had very little prospect of escaping with life. However, we sawed some of the ice about the ships, to keep it from hurting them, and thus kept them in a kind of pond. We then began to drag the boats, as well as we could, towards the sea; but, after two or three days' labour we made very little progress; so that some of our hearts totally failed us, and I really began to give up myself for lost, when I saw our surrounding calamities.

While we were at this hard labour, I once fell into a pond we had made amongst some loose ice, and was very near being drowned; but providentially some people were near who gave me immediate assistance, and thereby I escaped drowning. Our deplorable condition, which kept up the constant apprehension of our perishing in the ice, brought me gradually to think of eternity in such a manner as I had never done before. I had the fears of death hourly upon me, and shuddered at the thoughts of meeting the grim king of terrors in the natural state I then was in, and was exceedingly doubtful of a happy eternity, if I should die in it. I had no hopes of my life being prolonged for any time; for we saw that our existence could not be long on the ice after leaving the ships, which were now out of sight, and some miles from the boats. Our appearance now became truly lamentable; pale dejection seized every countenance; many, who had been before blasphemers, in this our distress began to call on the good God of heaven for his help; and, in the time of our utter need He heard us, and, against hope or human probability, He delivered us!

It was the eleventh day of the ships being thus fastened, and the fourth of our drawing the boats in this manner, that the wind changed to the E. N. E. The weather immediately became mild and the ice broke towards the sea, which was to the S. W. of us. Many of us, on this, got on board again, and with all our might we hove the ships into every open water we could find and made all the sail on them in our power; and now, having a prospect of success, we made signals for the boats and the remainder of the people. This seemed to us like a reprieve from death; and happy was the man who could first get on board of any ship, or the first boat he could meet. We proceeded in this manner till we got into open water again, which we accomplished in about thirty hours, to our infinite joy and gladness of heart. As soon as we were out of danger, we came to anchor and refitted; and on the 19th of August we sailed from this uninhabited extremity of the world, where the inhospitable

climate affords neither food nor shelter, and not a tree or shrub of any kind grows amongst its barren rocks; but where all is one desolate and expanded waste of ice, which even the constant beams of the sun, for six months in the year, cannot penetrate or dissolve. The sun now being on the decline, the days shortened as we sailed to the southward: and, on the 28th, in lat. 73°, it was dark by ten o'clock at night. September the 10th, in latitude 58°, 59', we met a very severe gale of wind and high seas, and shipped a great deal of water in the space of ten hours. This made us labour exceedingly hard at all our pumps a whole day, and one sea, which struck the ship with more force than any thing I ever met with of the kind before, laid her under water for some time, so that we thought she would have gone down. Two boats were washed from the booms, and the long boat from the chucks: all other movable things on the decks were also washed away; among which were many curious things of different kinds which we had brought from Greenland; and in order to lighten the ship we were obliged to toss some of our guns overboard. We saw a ship, at the same time, in very great distress, and her masts gone; but we were unable to assist her. We now lost sight of the Carcass till the 26th, when we saw land about Orfordness, off which place she joined us. From thence we sailed for London, and on the 30th came up to Deptford. And thus ended our Arctic voyage, to the no small joy of all on board, after having been absent four months, in which time, at the imminent hazard of our lives, we explored nearly as far towards the Pole as 81 degrees north, and 20 degrees east longitude; being much farther, by all accounts, than any navigator had ever ventured before; in which we fully proved the impracticability of finding a passage that way to India.

CHAPTER X.

The author leaves Dr. Irving, and engages on board a Turkey ship—
Account of a black man's being kidnapped on board, and sent to the
West-Indies, and the author's fruitless endeavours to procure his
freedom—Some account of the manner of the author's conversion to
the faith of Jesus Christ.

I.

OUR VOYAGE to the North Pole being ended, I returned to London with
Dr. Irving; with whom I continued for some time, during which I began
seriously to reflect on the dangers I had escaped, particularly those of
my last voyage, which made a lasting impression on my mind, and, by
the grace of God, proved afterwards a mercy to me; it caused me to
reflect deeply on my eternal state, and to seek the Lord with full pur-
pose of heart ere it was too late. I rejoiced greatly; and heartily thanked
the Lord for directing me to London, where I was determined to work
out my own salvation, and, in so doing, procure a title to heaven; this
being the result of a mind blinded by ignorance and sin.

In process of time I left my master, Dr. Irving, the purifier of waters.
I lodged in Coventry Court, Haymarket, where I was continually
oppressed and much concerned about the salvation of my soul, and was
determined in my own strength to be a first-rate Christian. I used every
means for this purpose; and not being able to find any person amongst
those with whom I was then acquainted, that acquiesced with me in
point of religion, or, in scripture language, that *would shew me any good*,
I was much dejected, and knew not where to seek relief; however, I first
frequented the neighbouring churches, St. James's and others, two or
three times a day for many weeks. Still I came away dissatisfied; something

was wanting that I could not obtain, and I really found more heart-felt relief in reading my Bible at home than in attending the church; and, being resolved to be saved, I pursued other methods. First I went among the people called Quakers, whose meeting at times was held in silence, and I remained as much in the dark as ever. I then searched into the Roman Catholic principles; but was not in the least edified. I at length had recourse to the Jews, which availed me nothing, as the fear of eternity daily harassed my mind, and I knew not where to seek shelter from the wrath to come.

II.

However, this was my conclusion, at all events, to read the Four Evangelists, and whatever sect or party I found adhering thereto, such I would join. Thus I went on heavily without any guide to direct me the way that leadeth to eternal life. I asked different people questions about the manner of going to heaven, and was told different ways. Here I was much staggered, and could not find any at that time more righteous than myself, or indeed so much inclined to devotion. I thought we should not all be saved (this is agreeable to the scriptures), nor would all be damned. I found none among the circle of my acquaintance that kept wholly the Ten Commandments. So righteous was I in my own eyes, that I was convinced I excelled many of them in that point, by keeping eight out of ten; and finding those, who in general termed themselves Christians, not so honest nor so good in their morals as the Turks, I really thought the Turks were in a safer way of salvation than my neighbours; so that between hopes and fears I went on, and the chief comforts I enjoyed were in the musical French-horn, which I then practised, and also dressing of hair. Such was my situation some months, experiencing the dishonesty of many people here. I determined at last to set out for Turkey, and there to end my days.

It was now early in the spring 1774. I sought for a master, and found a captain John Hughes, commander of a ship called the Anglicania, fitting out in the river Thames, and bound to Smyrna in Turkey. I shipped myself with him as steward; at the same time I recommended to him a very clever black man, John Annis, as a cook. This man was on board the ship near two months doing his duty: he had formerly lived many years with Mr. William Kirkpatrick, a gentleman of the island of St. Kitt's, from whom he parted by consent, though he afterwards tried many schemes to inveigle the poor man. He had applied to many Captains, who traded to St. Kitt's, to trepan him; and when all their

attempts and schemes of kidnapping proved abortive, Mr. Kirkpatrick came to our ship at Union Stairs, on Easter Monday, April the 4th, with two wherry-boats and six men, having learned that the man was on board; and tied, and forcibly took him away from the ship, in the presence of the crew and the chief mate, who had detained him after he had information to come away. I believe this was a combined piece of business: but be that as it may, it certainly reflected great disgrace on the mate and Captain also; who, although they had desired the oppressed man to stay on board, yet notwithstanding this vile act on the man who had served him, he did not in the least assist to recover him, or pay me a farthing of his wages, which was about Five Pounds. I proved the only friend he had who attempted to regain him his liberty, if possible, having known the want of liberty myself. I sent, as soon as I could, to Gravesend, and got knowledge of the ship in which he was; but, unluckily, she had sailed the first tide after he was put on board. My intention was then immediately to apprehend Mr. Kirkpatrick, who was about setting off for Scotland; and having obtained a *habeas corpus* for him, and got a tipstaff to go with me to St. Paul's church-yard, where he lived, he, suspecting something of this kind, set a watch to look out. My being known to them obliged me to use the following deception: I whitened my face, that they might not know me; and this had the desired effect. He did not go out of his house that night, and next morning I contrived a well plotted stratagem, notwithstanding he had a gentleman in his house to personate him. My direction to the tipstaff had the desired effect; he got admittance into the house, and conducted him to a judge, according to the writ. When he came there, his plea was, that he had not the body in custody, on which he was admitted to bail. I proceeded immediately to that well-known philanthropist, Granville Sharp, Esq. who received me with the utmost kindness, and gave me every instruction that was needful on the occasion. I left him in full hope that I should gain the unhappy man his liberty, with the warmest sense of gratitude towards Mr. Sharp for his kindness. But, alas! my attorney proved unfaithful: he took my money, lost me many months' employ, and did not the least good in the cause. When the poor man arrived at St. Kitt's, he was, according to custom, staked to the ground with four pins through a cord, two on his wrists, and two on his ancles; was cut and flogged most unmercifully, and afterwards loaded cruelly with irons about his neck. I had two very moving letters from him, while he was in this situation; and I made attempts to go after him at a great hazard, but was sadly disappointed: I also was told of it by some very respectable families, now in London, who saw him in St. Kitt's, in the same state, in which he remained till kind death released him out of the hands of his tyrants.

III.

During this disagreeable business I was under strong convictions of sin, and thought that my state was worse than any man's; my mind was unaccountably disturbed; I often wished for death, though at the same time convinced that I was altogether unprepared for that awful summons. Suffering much by villains in the late cause, and being much concerned about the state of my soul, these things (but particularly the latter) brought me very low; so that I became a burden to myself, and viewed all things around me as emptiness and vanity, which could give no satisfaction to a troubled conscience. I was again determined to go to Turkey, and resolved, at that time, never more to return to England. I engaged as steward on board a Turkeyman, the Wester Hall, Captain Lina; but was prevented by means of my late Captain, Mr. Hughes, and others. All this appeared to be against me, and the only comfort I then experienced was in reading the holy scriptures, where I saw that 'there is no new thing under the sun.' (Eccles. i. 9.) And what was appointed for me I must submit to. Thus I continued to travel in much heaviness, and frequently murmured against the Almighty, particularly in his providential dealings; and, awful to think! I began to blaspheme, and wished often to be any thing but a human being.

In these severe conflicts the Lord answered me by awful 'visions of the night, when deep sleep falleth upon men, in slumbering upon the bed.' (Job xxxiii. 15.) He was pleased, in much mercy, to give me to see, and in some measure understand, the great and awful scene of the judgment-day that 'no unclean person, no unholy thing, can enter into the kingdom of God.' (Eph. v. 5.) I would then, if it had been possible, have changed my nature with the meanest worm on the earth; and was ready to say to the mountains and rocks, 'fall on me.' (Rev. vi. 16.) But all in vain! I then in the greatest agony requested the Divine Creator, that he would grant me a small space of time to repent of my follies and vile iniquities, which I felt to be grievous. The Lord, in his manifold mercies, was pleased to grant my request; and being yet in a state of time, the sense of God's mercies was so great on my mind when I awoke, that my strength entirely failed me for many minutes, and I was exceedingly weak. This was the first spiritual mercy I ever was sensible of; and being on praying ground, as soon as I recovered a little strength, and got out of bed and dressed myself, I invoked Heaven from my inmost soul, and fervently begged that God would never again permit me to blaspheme his most holy name. The Lord, who is long-suffering, and full of compassion to such poor rebels as we are, condescended to hear and answer. I felt that I was altogether unholy, and saw clearly

what a bad use I had made of the faculties I was endowed with; they were given me to glorify God with; I thought, therefore, I had better want them here, and enter into life eternal, than abuse them and be cast into hell-fire.

I prayed to be directed, if there were any holier persons than those with whom I was acquainted, that the Lord would point them out to me. I appealed to the Searcher of hearts, whether I did not wish to love him more, and serve him better. Notwithstanding all this, the reader may easily discern, if a believer, that I was still in nature's darkness. At length I hated the house in which I lodged, because God's most holy name was blasphemed in it; then I saw the word of God verified, viz. 'Before they call, I will answer; and while they are yet speaking, I will hear.'

I had a great desire to read the Bible the whole day at home; but not having a convenient place for retirement, I left the house in the day, rather than stay amongst the wicked ones; and that day, as I was walking, it pleased God to direct me to a house where there was an old sea-faring man, who experienced much of the love of God shed abroad in his heart. He began to discourse with me, and, as I desired to love the Lord, his conversation rejoiced me greatly; and indeed I had never heard before the love of Christ to believers set forth in such a manner, and in so clear a point of view. Here I had more questions to put to the man, than his time would permit him to answer; and in that memorable hour there came in a dissenting minister; he joined our discourse, and asked me some few questions; among others, *where I heard the gospel preached.* I knew not what he meant by "hearing the gospel;" I told him I had read the gospel; and he asked me, *where I went to church, or whether I went at all or not.* To which I replied 'I attend St. James's, St. Martin's, and St. Ann's Soho.' — 'So,' said he, 'you are a churchman?' I answered, I was. He then invited me to a love-feast at his chapel that evening. I accepted the offer, and thanked him; and soon after he went away, I had some further discourse with the old Christian, added to some profitable reading, which made me exceedingly happy. When I left him he reminded me of coming to the feast; I assured him I would be there. Thus we parted, and I weighed over the heavenly conversation that had passed between these two men, which cheered my then heavy and drooping spirit more than any thing I had met with for many months.

However, I thought the time long in going to my supposed banquet. I also wished much for the company of these friendly men; their company pleased me much: and I thought the gentleman very kind in asking me, a stranger, to a feast; but how singular did it appear to me, to have it in a chapel! When the wished-for hour came I went, and happily the old man was there, who kindly seated me, as he belonged to the place. I was much astonished to see the place filled with people, and no signs of eating and

drinking. There were many ministers in the company. At last they began by giving out hymns, and, between the singing, the ministers engaged in prayer: in short, I knew not what to make of this sight, having never seen any thing of the kind in my life before now. Some of the guests began to speak their experience, agreeably to what I read in the Scriptures: much was said by every speaker of the providence of God, and his unspeakable mercies to each of them. This I knew in a great measure, and could most heartily join them. But when they spoke of a future state, they seemed to be altogether certain of their calling and election of God; and that no one could ever separate them from the love of Christ, or pluck them out of his hands. This filled me with utter consternation, intermingled with admiration. I was so amazed as not to know what to think of the company; my heart was attracted, and my affections were enlarged; I wished to be as happy as they, and was persuaded in my mind that they were different from the world, that lieth in wickedness. (I John v. 19.) Their language and singing, &c. did well harmonize; I was entirely overcome, and wished to live and die thus. Lastly, some persons produced some neat baskets full of buns, which they distributed about; and each person communicated with his neighbour, and sipped water out of different mugs, which they handed about to all who were present.

This kind of Christian fellowship I had never seen, nor ever thought of seeing on earth. It fully reminded me of what I had read in the holy Scriptures, of the primitive Christians, who loved each other and broke bread, in partaking of it, even from house to house. This entertainment (which lasted about four hours) ended in singing and prayer. It was the first soul-feast I ever was present at. These last twenty-four hours produced me things spiritual and temporal, sleeping and waking, judgment and mercy, that I could not but admire the goodness of God, in directing the blind, blasphemous sinner in the path that he knew not of, even among the just; and instead of judgment he hath shewed mercy, and will hear and answer the prayers and supplications of every returning prodigal.

O! to grace how great a debtor
Daily I'm constrain'd to be!

IV.

After this I was resolved to win heaven, if possible; and if I perished I thought it should be at the feet of Jesus, in praying to him for salvation. After having been an eye-witness to some of the happiness which attended

those who feared God, I knew not how, with any propriety, to return to my lodgings, where the name of God was continually profaned, at which I felt the greatest horror; I paused in my mind for some time, not knowing what to do; whether to hire a bed elsewhere, or go home again. At last, fearing an evil report might arise, I went home, with a farewell to card-playing and vain jesting, &c. I saw that time was very short, eternity long, and very near; and I viewed those persons alone blessed, who were found ready at midnight call, or when the judge of all, both quick and dead, cometh.

The next day I took courage, and went to Holborn, to see my new and worthy acquaintance, the old man, Mr. C——. He and his wife, a gracious woman, were at work in silk-weaving; they seemed mutually happy, and both quite glad to see me, and I more to see them. I sat down and we conversed much about soul matters, &c. Their discourse was amazingly delightful, edifying, and pleasant. I knew not at last how to leave this agreeable pair, till time summoned me away. As I was departing, they lent me a little book, entitled "The Conversion of an Indian." It was in questions and answers. The poor man came over the sea to London, to enquire after the Christian's God whom, through rich mercy, he found, and had not his journey in vain. The above book was of great use to me, and at that time was a means of strengthening my faith; in parting, they both invited me to call on them when I pleased. This delighted me, and I took care to make all the improvement from it I could; and so far I thanked God for such company and desires. I prayed that the many evils I felt within might be done away, and that I might be weaned from my former carnal acquaintances. This was quickly heard and answered, and I was soon connected with those who the scripture calls "the excellent of the earth." I heard the gospel preached, and the thoughts of my heart and actions were laid open by the preachers, and the way of salvation by Christ alone was evidently set forth.

Thus I went on happily for near two months: and I once heard, during this period, a reverend gentleman, Mr. G——, speak of a man who had departed this life in full assurance of his going to glory. I was much astonished at the assertion; and did very deliberately inquire how he could get at this knowledge. I was answered fully, agreeably to what I read in the oracles of truth: and was told also, that if I did not experience the new birth, and the pardon of my sins, through the blood of Christ, before I died, I could not enter the kingdom of heaven.

I knew not what to think of this report, as I thought I kept eight commandments out of ten: then my worthy interpreter told me I did not do it, nor could I; and he added, that no man ever did or could keep the commandments, without offending in one point. I thought this sounded very strangely; it puzzled me much for many weeks; for I

thought it a hard saying. I then asked my friend Mr. L——d, who was clerk in a chapel, *why the commandments of God were given, if we could not be saved by them.* To which he replied, 'The law is a school-master to bring us to Christ,' who alone could, and did keep the commandments, and fulfilled all their requirements for his elect people, even those to whom he had given a living faith, and the sins of those chosen vessels *were already* atoned for, and forgiven them whilst living; and if I did not experience the same before my exit, the Lord would say at that great day to me, "Go, ye cursed," &c. &c. for God would appear faithful in his judgments to the wicked, as he would be faithful in shewing mercy to those who were ordained to it before the world was; therefore Christ Jesus seemed to be all in all to that man's soul.

V.

I was much wounded at this discourse, and brought into such a dilemma as I never expected. I asked him, if *he* was to die that moment, whether he was sure to enter the kingdom of God: and added, 'Do you *know* that your sins are forgiven you?' He answered in the affirmative. Then confusion, anger, and discontent seized me, and I staggered much at this sort of doctrine: it brought me to a stand, not knowing what to believe, whether salvation by works, or by faith only in Christ. I requested him to tell me how I might know when my sins were forgiven me. He assured me he could not, and that none but God alone could do this. I told him it was very mysterious; but he said it was really matter of fact, and quoted many portions of a scripture immediately to the point, to which I could make no reply. He then desired me to pray to God to shew me these things. I answered I prayed to God every day. He said, 'I perceive you are a church-man.' I answered I was. He then entreated me to beg of God *to shew me what I was, and the true state of my soul.* I thought the prayer very short and odd; so we parted for that time.

I weighed all these things over, and could not help thinking how it was possible for a man to know his sins were forgiven him in this life. I wished that God would reveal this self-same thing to me. In a short time after this, I went to Westminster chapel: The Rev. Mr. P—— preached from Lam. iii 39. It was a wonderful sermon; he clearly shewed that a living man had no cause to complain for the punishments of his sins; he evidently justified the Lord in all his dealings with the sons of men; he also shewed the justice of God in the eternal punishment of the wicked and impenitent. The discourse seemed to me like a two-edged

sword cutting all ways. It afforded me much joy, intermingled with many fears about my soul; and when it was ended he gave it out that he intended, the ensuing week, to examine all those who meant to attend the Lord's table. Now I thought much of my good works, and at the same time was doubtful of my being a proper object to receive the sacrament; I was full of meditation till the day of examining.

However I went to the chapel; and, though much distressed, I addressed the reverend gentleman, thinking if I was not right, he would endeavour to convince me of it. When I conversed with him, the first thing he asked me was, *What I knew of Christ*. I told him I believed in him, and had been baptized in his name. 'Then,' said he, 'when were you brought to the knowledge of God? and how were you convinced of sin?' I knew not what he meant by these questions. I told him I kept eight commandments out of ten; but that I sometimes swore on board of ship, and sometimes when on shore, and broke the sabbath. He then asked me if I could read. I answered 'Yes.' 'Then,' said he, 'do you read in the Bible, *He that offends in one point is guilty of all?*' I said, 'Yes.' Then he assured me, that one sin, unatoned for, was as sufficient to damn a soul, as one leak was to sink a ship. Here I was struck with awe; for the minister exhorted me much, and reminded me of the shortness of time, and the length of eternity; and that no unregenerate soul, or any thing unclean, could enter the kingdom of Heaven.

He did not admit me as a communicant; but recommended me to read the scriptures, and hear the word preached; not to neglect fervent prayer to God, who has promised to hear the supplications of those who seek him in godly sincerity; so I took my leave of him with many thanks, and resolved to follow his advice, so far as the Lord would condescend to enable me.

VI.

During this time I was out of employ; nor was likely to get a situation suitable for me: which obliged me to go once more to sea. I engaged as steward of a ship called the Hope, Captain Richard Strange, bound from London to Cadiz in Spain. In a short time after I was on board I heard the name of God much blasphemed, and I feared greatly least I should catch the horrible infection. I thought if I sinned again, after having life and death set evidently before me, I should certainly go to hell. My mind was uncommonly chagrined, and I murmured much at God's providential dealings with me, and was discontented with the commandments, that I could not be saved by what I had done. I hated

all things, and wished I had never been born: confusion seized me, and I wished to be annihilated.

One day I was standing on the very edge of the stern of the ship, thinking to drown myself, but this scripture was instantaneously impressed on my mind— 'That no murderer hath eternal life abiding in him.' (1 John iii. 15.) Then I paused, and thought myself the unhappiest man living. Again I was convinced that the Lord was better to me than I deserved, and I was better off in the world than many. After this I began to fear death; I fretted, mourned, and prayed, till I became a burthen to others but more so to myself. At length I concluded to beg my bread on shore, rather than go again to sea amongst a people who feared not God, and I entreated the Captain three different times to discharge me; he would not, but each time gave me greater and greater encouragement to continue with him, and all on board shewed me very great civility: notwithstanding all this, I was unwilling to embark again. At last some of my religious friends advised me, by saying it was my lawful calling, consequently it was my duty to obey, and that God was not confined to place, &c. &c. particularly Mr. G. the governor of Tothillfields, Bridewell, who pitied my case, and read the eleventh chapter of the Hebrews to me, with exhortations. He prayed for me, and I believe that he prevailed on my behalf, as my burden was then greatly removed, and I found a heart-felt resignation to the will of God.

The good man gave me a pocket Bible, and Alleine's "Alarm to the unconverted." We parted, and the next day I went on board again. We sailed for Spain, and I found favour with the Captain. It was the fourth of September when we sailed from London, and we had a delightful voyage to Cadiz, where we arrived the twenty-third of the same month. The place is strong, commands a fine prospect, and is very rich. The Spanish galleons frequent that port, and some arrived whilst we were there. I had many opportunities of reading the scriptures. I wrestled hard with God in fervent prayers, who had declared in his word that he would hear the groanings and deep sighs of the poor in spirit. This I found verified, to my utter astonishment and comfort, in the following manner:—On the morning of the sixth of October (I pray you to attend), all that day, I thought I should see or hear something supernatural. I had a secret impulse on my mind of something that was to take place, which drove me, for all that time, to a throne of grace. It pleased God to enable me to wrestle with him as Jacob did: I prayed that if sudden death were to happen, and I perished, it might be at Christ's feet.

In the evening of the same day, as I was reading and meditating on the fourth chapter of the Acts, twelfth verse, under the solemn apprehensions of eternity, and reflecting on my past actions, I began to think I had lived a moral life, and that I had a proper ground to believe I had

an interest in the divine favour; but still meditating on the subject, not knowing whether salvation was to be had partly for our own good deeds, or solely as the sovereign gift of God. In this deep consternation the Lord was pleased to break in upon my soul with his bright beams of heavenly light; and in an instant, as it were, removing the veil, and letting light into a dark place. (Isa. xxv. 7.) I saw clearly, with the eye of faith, the crucified Saviour bleeding on the cross on Mount Calvary: the Scriptures became an unsealed book; I saw myself a condemned criminal under the law, which came with its full force to my conscience, and when 'the commandment came, sin revived, and I died.' I saw the Lord Jesus Christ in his humiliation, loaded, and bearing my reproach, sin, and shame.

I then clearly perceived, that *by the deeds of the law no flesh living could be justified.* I was then convinced, that by the first Adam sin came, and by the second Adam, the Lord Jesus Christ, all that are saved must be made alive. It was given me at that time to know what it was to be born again. (John iii. 5.) I saw the eighth chapter to the Romans, and the doctrines of God's decrees verified, agreeably to his eternal, everlasting, and unchangeable purposes. The word of God was sweet to my taste, yea, sweeter than honey and the honey-comb. Christ was revealed to my soul as the chiefest among ten thousand. — These heavenly moments were really as life to the dead, and what John calls an earnest of the Spirit. (John xvi. 13, 14, &c.) This was indeed unspeakable, and I firmly believe, undeniable to many.

VII.

Now every leading providential circumstance that happened to me, from the day I was taken from my parents to that hour, was then, in my view, as if it had but just then occurred. I was sensible of the invisible hand of God, which guided and protected me, when in truth I knew it not: still the Lord pursued me, although I slighted and disregarded it; this mercy melted me down. When I considered my poor wretched state, I wept, seeing what a great debtor I was to sovereign free grace. Now the Ethiopian was willing to be saved by Jesus Christ, the sinner's only surety, and also to rely on none other person or thing for salvation. Self was obnoxious, and good works I had none; for it is God that worketh in us both to will and to do. Oh! the amazing things of that hour can never be told! It was joy in the Holy Ghost! I felt an astonishing change; the burden of sin, the gaping jaws of hell, and the fears of death, that weighed me down before, now lost their horror; indeed I thought death

would now be the best earthly friend I ever had. Such were my grief and joy as I believe are seldom experienced. I was bathed in tears, and said, "What am I, that God should thus look on me, the vilest of sinners?" I felt a deep concern for my mother and friends, which occasioned me to pray with fresh ardour; and in the abyss of thought, I viewed the unconverted people of the world in a very awful state, being without God and without hope.

It pleased God to pour out on me the spirit of prayer and the grace of supplication, so that in loud acclamations I was enabled to praise and glorify his most holy name. When I got out of the cabin, and told some of the people what the Lord had done for me, alas! who could understand me or believe my report!—None but to whom the arm of the Lord was revealed. I became a barbarian to them in talking of the love of Christ: his name was to me as ointment poured forth; indeed it was sweet to my soul, but to them a rock of offence. I thought my case singular, and every hour a day until I came to London; for I much longed to be with some to whom I could tell of the wonders of God's love towards me, and join in prayer to him whom my soul loved and thirsted after. I had uncommon commotions within, such as few can tell aught about. Now the Bible was my only companion and comfort; I prized it much, with many thanks to God that I could read it for myself, and was not left to be tossed about or led by man's devices and notions. The worth of a soul cannot be told.—May the Lord give the reader an understanding in this!

Whenever I looked in the Bible I saw things new, and many texts were immediately applied to me with great comfort, for I knew that to me was the word of salvation sent. Sure I was, that the Spirit, which indited the word, opened my heart to receive the truth of it as it is in Jesus, that the same Spirit enabled me to act with faith upon the promises which were precious to me, and enable me to believe, to the salvation of my soul. By free grace I was persuaded that I had a part in the first resurrection, and was enlightened with the "light of the living." (Job xxxiii. 30.) I wished for a man of God, with whom I might converse: my soul was like the chariots of Aminadab. (Canticles vi. 12.) These, among others, were the precious promises that were so powerfully applied to me: "All things whatsoever ye shall ask in prayer, believing, ye shall receive." (Matt. xxi. 22.) "Peace I leave with you, my peace I give unto you." (John xiv. 27.) I saw the blessed Redeemer to be the fountain of life, and the well of salvation. I experienced him to be all in all. He had brought me by a way that I knew not, and he had made crooked paths straight. Then in his name I set up my Ebenezer, saying, "Hitherto He hath helped me:" and could say to the sinners about me, "Behold what a Saviour I have!" Thus I was, by the teaching of that

all-glorious Deity, the great One in Three and Three in One, confirmed in the truths of the Bible, those oracles of everlasting truth, on which every soul living must stand or fall eternally, agreeably to Acts iv. 12: "Neither is there salvation in any other: for there is none other name under heaven given among men whereby we must be saved, but only Jesus Christ." May God give the reader a right understanding in these facts! "To him that believeth all things are possible, but to them that are unbelieving nothing is pure." (Titus i. 15.)

During this period we remained at Cadiz until our ship got laden. We sailed about the fourth of November; and, having a good passage, we arrived in London the month following, to my comfort, with heartfelt gratitude to God for his rich and unspeakable mercies.

VIII.

On my return I had but one text which puzzled me, or that the devil endeavoured, to buffet me with, viz. Rom. xi. 6. and, as I had heard of the Rev. Mr. Romaine, and his great knowledge in the scriptures, I wished much to hear him preach. One day I went to Blackfriars church, and, to my great satisfaction and surprise, he preached from that very text. He very clearly shewed the difference between human works and free election, which is according to God's sovereign will and pleasure. These glad tidings set me entirely at liberty, and I went out of the church rejoicing, seeing my spots were those of God's children. I went to Westminster chapel, and saw some of my old friends, who were glad when they perceived the wonderful change that the Lord had wrought in me, particularly Mr. G. Smith, my worthy acquaintance, who was a man of a choice spirit, and had great zeal for the Lord's service. I enjoyed his correspondence till he died in the year 1784. I was again examined in that same chapel, and was received into church-fellowship amongst them; I rejoiced in spirit, making melody in my heart to the God of all my mercies. Now my whole wish was to be dissolved, and to be with Christ. But, alas! I must wait my appointed time.

MISCELLANEOUS VERSES;
OR,
REFLECTIONS ON THE STATE OF MY MIND.

During my first Convictions of the Necessity of believing the Truth, and of experiencing the inestimable Benefits of Christianity.

WELL may I say my life has been
One scene of sorrow and of pain;
From early days I griefs have known,
And as I grew my griefs have grown.

Dangers were always in my path,
And fear of wrath and sometimes death;
While pale dejection in me reign'd,
I often wept, by grief constrain'd.

When taken from my native land,
By an unjust and cruel band,
How did uncommon dread prevail!
My sighs no more I could conceal.

To ease my mind I often strove,
And tried my trouble to remove;
I sung and utter'd sighs between,
Assay'd to stifle guilt with sin.

But O! not all that I could do
Would stop the current of my woe,
Conviction still my vileness shew'd;
How great my guilt; how lost to good!

'Prevented, that I could not die,
Nor could to one sure refuge fly,
An orphan state I had to mourn,
Forsook by all, and left forlorn.'

Those who beheld my downcast mien,
Could never guess by woes unseen;
They by appearance could not know
The troubles that I waded through.

Lust, anger, blasphemy, and pride,
With legions of such ills beside,
Troubled my thoughts, while doubts and fears
Clouded and darken'd most my years.

'Sighs now no more would be confin'd;
They breath'd the trouble of my mind;'
I wish'd for death, but check'd the word,
And often pray'd unto the Lord.

Unhappy, more than some on earth,
I thought the place that gave me birth;
Strange thoughts oppress'd, while I replied,
"Why not in Ethiopia died?

And why thus spar'd, when nigh to hell?"
God only knew—I could not tell!
'A tott'ring fence, a bowing wall,
I thought myself e'er since the fall.'

Oft times I mus'd, and nigh despair,
While birds melodious fill'd the air.
'Thrice happy songsters, ever free!'
How blest were they compar'd to me!

Thus all things added to my pain,
While grief compell'd me to complain;
When sable clouds began to rise,
My mind grew darker than the skies.

The English nation call'd to leave,
How did my breast with sorrow heave!
I long'd for rest—cried "Help me, Lord!
Some mitigation, Lord, afford!"

Yet on, dejected, still I went,
Heart-throbbing woes within me pent;
Nor land, nor sea, could comfort give,
Nor aught my anxious mind relieve.

Weary with troubles, yet unknown
To all but God and self alone,
Numerous months for peace I strove,
Numerous foes I had to prove.

Inur'd to dangers, grief, and woes,
Train'd up 'midst perils, death, and foes,
I said, "Must it thus ever be?
No quiet is permitted me."

Hard hap, and more than heavy lot!
I pray'd to God, "Forget me not:
What thou ordain'st help me to bear;
But, O! deliver from despair!"

Strivings and wrestling seem'd in vain;
Nothing I did could ease my pain;
Then gave I up my work and will,
Confess'd and own'd my doom was hell!

Like some poor pris'ner at the bar,
Conscious of guilt, of sin, and fear,
Arraign'd and self-condemn'd I stood,
'Lost in the world and in my blood!'

Yet here, 'midst blackest clouds confin'd,
A beam from Christ, the day-star, shin'd;
"Surely, thought I, if Jesus please,
He can at once sign my release."

I, ign'rant of his righteousness,
Set up my labours in its place;
'Forgot for why his blood was shed,
And pray'd and fasted in his stead.'

He died for sinners—I am one;
Might not his blood for me atone?
Though I am nothing else but sin,
Yet surely he can make me clean!

Thus light came in, and I believ'd;
Myself forgot, and help receiv'd!
My Saviour then, I know, I found,
For, eas'd from guilt, no more I groan'd.

O, happy hour, in which I ceas'd
To mourn, for then I found a rest!
My soul and Christ were now as one:
Thy light, O Jesus, in me shone.

Bless'd be thy name; for now I know
I and my works can nothing do;
"The Lord alone can ransom man—
For this the spotless Lamb was slain."

When sacrifices, works, and pray'r,
Prov'd vain, and ineffectual were,
"Lo then I come!" the Saviour cried,
And, bleeding, bow'd his head and died.

He died for all who ever saw
No help in them, nor by the law;
I this have seen and gladly own
"Salvation is by Christ alone!"*

*Acts iv. 12.

The author embarks on board a ship bound to Cadiz. Is near being shipwrecked—Goes to Malaga—Remarkably fine Cathedral there—The author disputes with a Popish priest—Picks up eleven miserable men at sea in returning to England—Engages again with Dr. Irving to accompany him to Jamaica and the Musquito shore—Meets with an Indian Prince on board—The author attempts to instruct him in the truths of the Gospel—Frustrated by the bad example of some in the ship—They arrive on the Musquito shore with some slaves they purchased at Jamaica, and begin to cultivate a Plantation—Some account of the manners and customs of the Musquito Indians—Successful device of the author's to quell a riot among them—Curious entertainment given by them to Dr. Irving and the author, who leaves the shore and goes for Jamaica—Is barbarously treated by a man with whom he engaged for his passage—Escapes, and goes to the Musquito Admiral, who treats him kindly—He gets another vessel, and goes on board—Instances of bad treatment—Meets Dr. Irving—Gets to Jamaica—Is cheated by his Captain—Leaves the Doctor, and sails for England.

I.

WHEN OUR ship was got ready for sea again, I was intreated by the Captain to go in her once more; but, as I felt myself as happy as I could wish to be in this life, I for some time refused; however, the advice of my friends at last prevailed; and, in full resignation to the will of God, I again embarked for Cadiz in March 1775. We had a very good passage, without any material accident, until we arrived off the Bay of Cadiz; when one Sunday, just as we were going into the harbour, the

ship struck against a rock, and knocked off a garboard plank, which is the next to the keel. In an instant all hands were in the greatest confusion, and began with loud cries to call on God to have mercy on them. Although I could not swim, and saw no way of escaping death, I felt no dread in my then situation, having no desire to live. I even rejoiced in spirit, thinking this death would be sudden glory. But the fulness of time was not yet come. The people near to me were very much astonished in seeing me thus calm and resigned; but I told them of the peace of God, which, through sovereign grace I enjoyed, and these words were that instant in my mind:

> Christ is my pilot wise, my compass is his word;
> My soul each storm defies, while I have such a Lord.
> I trust his faithfulness and power,
> To save me in the trying hour.
>
> Though rocks and quicksands deep thro' all my passage lie,
> Yet Christ shall safely keep and guide me with his eye.
> How can I sink with such a prop,
> That bears the world and all things up.

At this time there were many large Spanish flukers, or passage-vessels, full of people crossing the channel; a number of them, seeing our condition, came along-side of us. As many hands, as could be employed, began to work; some at our three pumps, and the rest unloading the ship as fast as possible. There being only a single rock called the Porpus on which we struck, we soon got off it, and providentially it was then high water; we therefore run the ship ashore at the nearest place to keep her from sinking. After many tides, with a great deal of care and industry, we got her repaired again. When we had dispatched our business at Cadiz, we went to Gibraltar, and from thence to Malaga, a very pleasant and rich city, where there is one of the finest cathedrals I had ever seen. It had been above fifty years in building, as I had heard, though it was not then quite finished; great part of the inside, however, was completed and highly decorated with the richest marble columns, and many superb paintings; it was lighted occasionally by an amazing number of wax tapers of different sizes, some of which were as thick as a man's thigh; these, however, were only used on some of their grand festivals.

I was very much shocked at the custom of bullbaiting, and other diversions which prevailed here on Sunday evenings, to the great scandal of Christianity and morals. I used to express my abhorrence of it to a priest whom I met with. I had frequent contests about religion with

the reverend father, in which he took great pains to make a proselyte of me to his church; and I no less to convert him to mine. On these occasions I used to produce my Bible, and shew him in what points his church erred. He then said he had been in England, and that every person there read the Bible, which was very wrong; but I answered him, that Christ desired us to search the Scriptures. In his zeal for my conversion, he solicited me to go to one of the universities in Spain, and declared that I should have my education free; and told me, if I got myself made a priest, I might in time become even Pope; and that Pope Benedict was a black man. As I was ever desirous of learning, I paused some time upon this temptation, and thought by being crafty, I might catch some with guile; but I began to think it would only be hypocrisy in me to embrace his offer, as I could not in conscience conform to the opinions of his church. I was therefore enabled to regard the word of God, which says, 'Come out from amongst them;' and I refused Father Vincent's offer. So we parted without conviction on either side.

II.

Having taken at this place some fine wines, fruits, and money, we proceeded to Cadiz, where we took about two tons more of money, &c. and then sailed for England in the month of June. When we were about the north latitude 42°, we had contrary winds for several days, and the ship did not make in that time above six or seven miles straight course. This made the Captain exceedingly fretful and peevish: and I was very sorry to hear God's most holy name often blasphemed by him. One day, as he was in that impious mood, a young gentleman on board, who was a passenger, reproached him, and said *he acted wrong; for we ought to be thankful to God for all things, as we were not in want of any thing on board; and though the wind was contrary for us, yet it was fair for some others, who, perhaps, stood in more need of it than we.* I immediately seconded this young gentleman with some boldness, and said we had not the least cause to murmur, for that the Lord was better to us than we deserved, and that he had done all things well.

I expected that the Captain would be very angry with me for speaking, but he replied not a word. However before that time on the following day, being the 21st. of June, much to our great joy and astonishment, we saw the providential hand of our benign Creator, whose ways with his blind creatures are past finding out. The preceding night I dreamed that I saw a boat immediately off the starboard main shrouds; and exactly

at half-past one o'clock, the following day, at noon while I was below, just as we had dined in the cabin, the man at the helm cried out, "A boat!" which brought my dream that instant into my mind. I was the first man that jumped on the deck; and looking from the shrouds onward, according to my dream, I descried a little boat at some distance: but as the waves were high, it was as much as we could do sometimes to discern her. We however stopped the ship's way, and the boat, which was extremely small, came alongside with eleven miserable men, whom we took on board immediately. To all human appearance, these people must have perished in the course of an hour or less; the boat being small, it barely contained them. When we took them up they were half drowned, and had no victuals, compass, water, or any other necessary; and had only one bit of an oar to steer with, and that right before the wind, so that they were obliged to trust entirely to the mercy of the waves. As soon as we got them all on board, they bowed themselves on their knees, and with hands and voices lifted up to Heaven, thanked God for their deliverance; and I trust that my prayers were not wanting amongst them at the same time. This mercy of the Lord quite melted me, and I recollected his words, which I saw thus verified, in the 107th Psalm: — "O give thanks unto the Lord, for he is good, for his mercy endureth for ever.— Hungry and thirsty, their souls fainted in them. They cried unto the Lord in their trouble, and he delivered them out of their distresses. And he led them forth by the right way, that they might go to a city of habitation. O that men would praise the Lord for his goodness, and for his wonderful works to the children of men. For he satisfieth the longing soul, and filleth the hungry soul with goodness.

"Such as sit in darkness and in the shadow of death: then they cried unto the Lord in their trouble, and he saved them out of their distresses. They that go down to the sea in ships; that do business in great waters; these see the works of the Lord, and his wonders in the deep.— Whoso is wise and will observe these things, even they shall understand the loving-kindness of the Lord."

The poor distressed Captain said, "The Lord is good; for seeing that I am not fit to die, he therefore gave me a space of time to repent." I was very glad to hear this expression, and took an opportunity, when convenient, of talking to him on the providence of God. They told us they were Portuguese, and were in a brig loaded with corn, which shifted that morning at five o'clock, owing to which the vessel sunk that instant with two of the crew; and how these eleven got into the boat, which was lashed to the deck, not one of them could tell. We provided them with every necessary, and brought them all safe to London; and I hope the Lord gave them repentance unto eternal life.

III.

I was happy once more amongst my friends and brethren, till November, when my old friend, the celebrated Dr. Irving, bought a remarkably fine sloop, about 150 tons. He had a mind for a new adventure in cultivating a plantation at Jamaica and the Musquito Shore; he asked me to go with him, and said that he would trust me with his estate in preference to any one. By the advice, therefore, of my friends, I accepted of the offer, knowing that the harvest was fully ripe in those parts, and I hoped to be an instrument under God, of bringing some poor sinner to my well-beloved master, Jesus Christ. Before I embarked, I found with the Dr. four Musquito Indians, who were chiefs in their own country, and were brought here by some English traders for some selfish ends. One of them was the Musquito king's son, a youth of about eighteen years of age; and whilst he was here he was baptized by the name of George. They were going back at the government's expence, after having been in England about a year, during which they learned to speak pretty good English. When I came to talk to them, about eight days before we sailed, I was very much mortified in finding that they had not frequented any churches since they were there to be baptized, nor was any attention paid to their morals. I was very sorry for this mock christianity, and had just an opportunity to take some of them once to church before we sailed.

We embarked in the month of November 1775, on board of the sloop, the Morning Star, Captain David Miller, and sailed for Jamaica. In our passage I took all the pains that I could to instruct the Indian prince in the doctrines of Christianity, of which he was entirely ignorant; and, to my great joy, he was quite attentive, and received with gladness the truths that the Lord enabled me to set forth to him. I taught him, in the compass of eleven days, all the letters; and he could put even two or three of them together, and spell them. I had Fox's Martyrology with cuts, and he used to be very fond of looking into it, and would ask many questions about the Papal cruelties he saw depicted there, which I explained to him. I made such progress with this youth, especially in religion, that when I used to go to bed at different hours of the night, if he was in his bed he would get up on purpose to go to prayer with me, without any other clothes than his shirt; and before he would eat any of his meals amongst the gentlemen in the cabin, he would first come to me to pray, as he called it. I was well pleased at this, and took great delight in him, and used much supplication to God for his conversion. I was in full hope of seeing daily every appearance of that change which I could wish; not knowing the devices of Satan, who had many of his emissaries to sow his tares as fast as I sowed the good seed, and pull down as fast as I built up.

Thus we went on nearly four-fifths of our passage, when Satan at last got the upper hand. Some of his messengers, seeing this poor heathen much advanced in piety, began to ask him _whether I had converted him to Christianity_; laughed and made their jest at him, for which I rebuked them as much as I could. But this treatment caused the prince to halt between two opinions. Some of the true sons of Belial, who did not believe that there was any hereafter, told him never to fear the devil, for there was none existing; and if ever he came to the prince, they desired he might be sent to them. Thus they teazed the poor innocent youth, so that he would not learn his book any more! He would not drink nor carouse with these ungodly actors, nor would he be with me even at prayers. This grieved me very much. I endeavoured to persuade him as well as I could, but he would not come; and entreated him very much to tell me his reasons for acting thus. At last he asked me,—"How comes it that all the white men on board, who can read and write, observe the sun and know all things, yet swear, lie, and get drunk, only excepting yourself?" I answered him, _the reason was that they did not fear God; and that if any one of them died so, they could not go to, or be happy with, God._ He replied _that if a certain person went to hell, he would go to hell too._ I was sorry to hear this; and as he sometimes had the toothache, and also some other persons in the ship at the same time, I asked him, _if their tooth-ache made his easy._ He said, "No." Then I told him if he and these people went to hell together, their pains would not make his any lighter. This had great weight with him; it depressed his spirits much; and he became ever after, during the passage, fond of being alone.

IV.

When we came into the latitude of Martinico and near making the land, one morning we had a brisk gale of wind, and, carrying too much sail, the main mast went over the side. Many people were then all about the deck, and the yards, masts, and rigging, came tumbling all about us, yet there was not one of us in the least hurt; although some were within a hair's breadth of being killed: and particularly, I saw two men, who, by the providential hand of God, were most miraculously preserved from being smashed to pieces. On the 5th of January we made Antigua and Montserrat, and ran along the rest of the islands; and on the 14th we arrived at Jamaica. One Sunday, while we were there, I took the Musquito Prince George to church where he saw the sacrament administered. When we came out we saw all kinds of people, almost

from the church door for the space of half a mile down to the water-side, buying and selling all kinds of commodities: and these acts afforded me greater matter of exhortation to this youth who was much astonished.

Our vessel being ready to sail for the Musquito shore, I went with the Doctor on board a Guineaman, to purchase some slaves to carry with us, and cultivate a plantation; and I chose them all of my own country-men, some of whom came from Lybia. On the 12th of February we sailed from Jamaica, and on the 18th arrived at the Musquito shore, at a place called Dupeupy. All our Indian guests now, after I had admon-ished them, and a few cases of liquor given them by the Doctor, took an affectionate leave of us, and went ashore, where they were met by the Musquito king, and we never saw one of them afterwards. We then sailed to the southward of the shore, to a place called Cape Gracias a Dios, where there was a large lagoon or lake, which received the empty-ing of two or three very fine large rivers, and abounded much in fish and land tortoise. Some of the native Indians came on board of us here; we used them well and told them that we were come to dwell amongst them, at which they seemed pleased. So the Doctor and I, with some others, went with them ashore; and they took us to different places to view the land, in order to choose a place to make a plantation of.

We fixed on a spot near a river's bank, in a rich soil; and having got our necessaries out of the sloop, we began to clear away the woods, and to plant different kinds of vegetables which had a quick growth. While we were employed in this manner, our vessel went northward to Black River to trade. While she was there, a Spanish guarda costa met with and took her. — This proved very hurtful, and a great embarrassment to us. However we went on with the culture of the land. We used to make fires every night all around us, to keep off wild beasts, which, as soon as it was dark, set up a most hideous roaring. Our habitation being far up in the woods, we frequently saw different kinds of animals; but none of them ever hurt us, except poisonous snakes, the bite of which the Doctor used to cure by giving to the patient, as soon as possible, about half a tumbler of strong rum, with a good deal of Cayenne pepper in it. In this manner he cured two natives and one of his own slaves.

V.

The Indians were exceedingly fond of the Doctor, and they had good reason for it; for I believe they never had such an useful man amongst them. They came from all quarters to our dwelling; and some Woolwow, or flat-headed Indians, who lived fifty or sixty miles above our river and

this side of the South Sea, brought us a good deal of silver in exchange for our goods. The principal articles we could get from our neighbouring Indians were turtle oil, and shells, a little silk-grass, and some provisions; but they would not work at any thing for us, except fishing; and a few times they assisted to cut down some trees, in order to build houses, which they did exactly like the Africans, by the joint labour of men, women, and children.

I do not recollect any of them to have had more than two wives. These always accompanied their husbands when they came to our dwelling, and then they generally carried whatever was brought to us, and always squatted down behind their husbands. Whenever we gave them any thing to eat, the men and their wives ate separate. I never saw the least sign of incontinence among them. The women are ornamented with beads, and fond of painting themselves; the men also paint, even to excess, both their faces and shirts: their favourite colour is red. The women generally cultivate the ground, and the men are all fishermen and canoe makers. Upon the whole, I never met any nation that were so simple in their manners as these people, or had so little ornament in their houses. Neither had they, as I ever could learn, one word expressive of an oath. The worst word I ever heard amongst them, when they were quarrelling, was one, that they had got from the English, which was "you rascal." I never saw any mode of worship among them; but in this they were not worse than their European brethren or neighbours; for I am sorry to say that there was not one white person in our dwelling, nor any where else, that I saw in different places I was at on the shore, that was better or more pious than those unenlightened Indians; but they either worked or slept in Sundays: and, to my sorrow, working was too much Sunday's employment with ourselves; so much so, that, in some length of time, we really did not know one day from another. This mode of living laid the foundation of my decamping at last. The natives are well made and warlike; and they particularly boast of having never been conquered by the Spaniards. They are great drinkers of strong liquors, when they can get them. We used to distil rum from pineapples, which were plentiful here; and then we could not get them away from our place. Yet they seemed to be singular, in point of honesty, above any other nation I was ever amongst. The country being hot, we lived under an open shed, where we had all kinds of goods, without a door or lock to any one article; yet we slept in safety, and never lost any thing, or were disturbed. This surprised us a good deal; and the Doctor, myself, and others, used to say if we were to lie in that manner in Europe we should have our throats cut the first night.

The Indian Governor goes once in a certain time all about the

province or district, and has a number of men with him as attendants and assistants. He settles all the differences among the people, like the judge here, and is treated with very great respect. He took care to give us timely notice before he came to our habitation, by sending his stick as a token, for rum, sugar, and gunpowder, which we did not refuse sending; and at the same time we made the utmost preparations to receive his honour and his train.

When he came, with his tribe and all our neighbouring chieftains, we expected to find him a grave reverend judge, solid, and sagacious; but instead of that, before he and his gang came in sight, we heard them very clamorous; and they even had plundered some of our good neighbouring Indians, having intoxicated themselves with our liquor. When they arrived, we did not know what to make of our new guests, and would gladly have dispensed with the honour of their company. However, having no alternative, we feasted them plentifully all the day till the evening; when the Governor, getting quite drunk, grew very unruly, and struck one of our most friendly chiefs, who was our nearest neighbour, and also took his gold-laced hat from him. At this a great commotion took place; and the Doctor interfered to make peace, as we could all understand one another, but to no purpose; and at last they became so outrageous, that the Doctor, fearing he might get into trouble, left the house and made the best of his way to the nearest wood, leaving me to do as well as I could among them.

I was so enraged with the governor, that I could have wished to have seen him tied fast to a tree, and flogged for his behaviour, but I had not people enough to cope with his party. I therefore thought of a stratagem to appease the riot. Recollecting a passage I had read in the life of Columbus, when he was among the Indians in Mexico, or Peru, where, on some occasion, he frightened them, by telling them of certain events in the heavens, I had recourse to the same expedient, and it succeeded beyond my most sanguine expectations. When I had formed my determination, I went in the midst of them, and taking hold of the governor, I pointed up to the heavens. I menaced him and the rest: I told them God lived there, and that he was angry with them, and they must not quarrel so; that they were all brothers, and if they did not leave off and go away quietly, I would take the book (pointing to the Bible), read, and tell God to make them dead. This operated on them like magic. The clamour immediately ceased, and I gave them some rum and a few other things; after which they went away peaceably; and the governor afterwards gave our neighbour, who was called Captain Plasmyah, his hat again. When the Doctor returned, he was exceedingly glad at my success in thus getting rid of our troublesome guest.

VI.

The Musquito people within our vicinity, out of respect to the Doctor, myself, and his people, made entertainments of the grand kind, called in their tongue "tourrie" or "dryckbot." The English of this expression is, "a feast of drinking about," of which it seems a corruption of language. The drink consisted of pine-apples roasted, and casades chewed or beaten in mortars; which, after lying some time, ferments, and becomes so strong as to intoxicate when drank in any quantity. We had timely notice given to us of the entertainment. A white family within five miles of us, told us how the drink was made; I and two others went before the time to the village where the mirth was appointed to be held, and there we saw the whole art of making the drink, and also the kind of animals that were to be eaten there. I cannot say the sight of either the drink or the meat was enticing to me. They had some thousands of pine-apples roasting, which they squeezed, dirt and all, into a canoe they had there for the purpose. The casade-drink, was in beef barrels and other vessels, and looked exactly like hogwash. Men, women, and children were thus employed in roasting the pine-apples and squeezing them with their hands. For food they had many land torpins or tortoises, some dried turtle, and three large alligators alive, and tied fast to the trees. I asked the people *what they were going to do with these alligators*; and I was told *they were to be eaten*. I was much surprised at this, and went home not a little disgusted at the preparations.

When the day of the feast was come, we took some rum with us, and went to the appointed place, where we found a great assemblage of those people, who received us very kindly. The mirth had begun before we came: and they were dancing with music: and the musical instruments were nearly the same as those of any other sable people, but, as I thought, much less melodious than those of any other nation I ever knew. They had many curious gestures in dancing, and a variety of motions and postures of their bodies, which to me were in no wise attracting. The males danced by themselves, and the females also by themselves, as with us. The Doctor shewed his people the example by immediately joining the women's party, though not by their choice. On perceiving the women disgusted, he joined the males.

At night there were great illuminations, by setting fire to many pine-trees, while the dryckbot went round merrily, by calabashes or gourds; but the liquor might more justly be called eating than drinking. One Owden, the oldest father in the vicinity, was dressed in a strange and terrifying form. Around his body were skins adorned with different kinds of feathers, and he had on his head a very large and high headpiece in

the form of a Grenadier's cap, with prickles like a porcupine: and he made a certain noise which resembled the cry of an alligator. Our people skipped amongst them out of complaisance, though some could not drink of their tourrie; but our rum met with customers enough, and was soon gone. The alligators were killed, and some of them roasted. Their manner of roasting is by digging a hole in the earth, and filling it with wood, which they burn to coal, and then they lay sticks across, on which they lay the meat. I had a raw piece of the alligator in my hand: it was very rich: I thought it looked like fresh salmon and it had a most fragrant smell, but I could not eat any of it. This merry-making at last ended without the least discord in any person in the company, although it was made up of different nations and complexions.

VII.

The rainy season came on here about the latter end of May, and continued till August very heavily; so that the rivers overflowed, and our provisions, then in the ground, were washed away. — I thought this was, in some measure, a judgment upon us for working on Sundays, and it hurt my mind very much. I often wished to leave this place and sail for Europe; for our mode of procedure and living, in this heathenish form, was very irksome to me. The word of God saith "What does it avail a man if he gain the whole world, and lose his own soul?" This was much and heavily impressed on my mind; and though I did not know how to speak to the Doctor for my discharge, it was disagreeable for me to stay any longer. But about the middle of June, I took courage enough to ask him for it. He was very unwilling at first to grant me my request; but I gave him so many reasons for it, that at last he consented to my going, and gave me the following certificate of my good behaviour:

The bearer, GUSTAVUS VASSA, has served me several years with strict honesty, sobriety, and fidelity. I can therefore, with justice recommend him for these qualifications, and indeed in every respect I consider him as an excellent servant. I do hereby certify that he always behaved well, and that he is perfectly trust-worthy.

CHARLES IRVING.

Musquito Shore, June 15, 1776.

Though I was much attached to the Doctor, I was happy when he consented. I got every thing ready for my departure, and hired some Indians, with a large canoe, to carry me off. All my poor countrymen, the slaves,

when they heard of my leaving them, were very sorry, as I had always treated them with care and affection, and did every thing I could to comfort the poor creatures, and render their condition easy. Having taken leave of my old friends and companions, on the 18th of June, accompanied by the Doctor, I left that spot of the world, and went southward above 20 miles along the river. There I found a sloop, the Captain of which told me he was going to Jamaica. Having agreed for my passage with him and one of the owners, who was also on board, named Hughes, the Doctor and I parted, not without shedding tears on both sides.

The vessel then sailed along the river till night, when she stopped in a lagoon within the same river. During the night a schooner belonging to the same owners came in, and as she was in want of hands, Hughes, the owner of the sloop, asked me to go in the schooner as a sailor, and said he would give me wages. I thanked him; but I said I wanted to go to Jamaica. He then immediately changed his tone, and swore and abused me very much, and asked how I came to be freed. I told him, and said that I came into that vicinity with Dr. Irving whom he had seen that day. This account was of no use; he still swore exceedingly at me, and cursed the master for a fool that sold me my freedom, and the Doctor for another in letting me go from him. Then he desired me to go in the schooner, or else I should not go out of the sloop as a free man. I said this was very hard, and begged to be put on shore again; but he swore that I should not. I said that I had been twice amongst the Turks, yet had never seen any such usage with them, and much less could I have expected any thing of this kind among the Christians. This incensed him exceedingly; and with a volley of oaths and imprecations, he replied, "Christians! damn you, you are one of St. Paul's men; but, by G——d, except you have St. Paul's or St. Peter's faith, and *walk upon the water to the shore*, you shall not go out of the vessel;" which I now learnt was going amongst the Spaniards towards Carthagena, where he swore he would sell me. I simply asked him *what right he had to sell me?* but, without another word, he made some of his people tie ropes round each of my ancles, and also to each wrist, and another rope round my body, and hoisted me up, without letting my feet touch or rest upon any thing.

Thus I hung, without any crime committed, and without judge or jury, merely because I was a freeman, and could not, by the law, get any redress from a white person in those parts of the world. I was in great pain from my situation, and cried and begged very hard for some mercy, but all in vain. My tyrant, in a rage, brought a musket out of the cabin, and loaded it before me and the crew, and swore that he would shoot me if I cried any more. I had now no alternative; I therefore remained silent, seeing not one white man on board who said a word in my behalf. I hung in that manner from between ten and eleven o'clock

at night till about one in the morning: when, finding my cruel abuser fast asleep, I begged some of his slaves to slacken the rope that was round my body, that my feet might rest on something. This they did at the risk of being cruelly used by their master, who beat some of them severely at first for not tying me when he commanded them.

VIII.

Whilst I remained in this condition, till between five and six o'clock in the morning, I trust I prayed to God to forgive this blasphemer, who cared not what he did, but, when he got up out of his sleep in the morning, was of the very same temper and disposition as when he left me at night. When they got up the anchor, and the vessel was getting under way I once more cried and begged to be released; and now, being fortunately in the way of their hoisting the sails, they released me. When I was let down I spoke to one Mr. Cox, a carpenter, whom I knew on board, on the impropriety of this conduct. He also knew the Doctor, and the good opinion he ever had of me. This man went to the Captain, and told him not to carry me away in that manner; that I was the Doctor's steward, who regarded me very highly, and would resent this usage when he should come to know it. On which he desired a young man to put me ashore in a small canoe I brought with me. This sound gladdened my heart, and I got hastily into the canoe, and set off whilst my tyrant was down in the cabin; but he soon spied me out, when I was not above thirty or forty yards from the vessel, and, running upon the deck with a loaded musket in his hand, he presented it at me, and swore heavily and dreadfully that he would shoot me that instant, if I did not come back on board. As I knew the wretch would have done as he said, without hesitation, I put back to the vessel again; but, as the good Lord would have it, just as I was alongside, he was abusing the Captain for letting me go from the vessel; which the Captain returned, and both of them soon got into a very great heat.

The young man, that was with me, now got out of the canoe; the vessel was sailing on fast with a smooth sea: and I then thought it was neck or nothing, so at that instant I set off again for my life, in the canoe, towards the shore; and fortunately the confusion was so great amongst them on board, that I got out of the reach of the musket shot, unnoticed, while the vessel sailed on with a fair wind a different way: so that they could not overtake me without tacking: but, even before that could be done, I should have been on shore, which I soon reached, with many thanks to God for this unexpected deliverance.

I then went and told the other owner, who lived near the shore (with whom I had agreed for my passage) of the usage I had met with. He was very much astonished, and appeared very sorry for it. After treating me with kindness, he gave me some refreshment, and three heads of roasted Indian corn, for a voyage of about eighteen miles south, to look for another vessel.—He then directed me to an Indian chief of a district, who was also the Musquito admiral, and had once been at our dwelling; after which I set off with the canoe across a large lagoon alone (for I could not get any one to assist me) though I was much jaded, and had pains in my bowels, by means of the rope I hung by the night before. I was therefore at different times unable to manage the canoe, for the paddling was very laborious. However, a little before dark, I got to my destined place, where some of the Indians knew me, and received me kindly. I asked for the admiral; and they conducted me to his dwelling. He was glad to see me, and refreshed me with such things as the place afforded: and I had a hammock to sleep in. They acted towards me more like Christians than those whites I was among the last night, though they had been baptized. I told the admiral I wanted to go to the next port to get a vessel to carry me to Jamaica, and requested him to send the canoe back which I then had, for which I was to pay him. He agreed with me, and sent five able Indians with a large canoe to carry my things to my intended place, about fifty miles; and we set off the next morning. When we got out of the lagoon and went along shore, the sea was so high that the canoe was oftentimes very near being filled with water. We were obliged to go ashore and drag her across different necks of land; we were also two nights in the swamps, which swarmed with musquito flies, and they proved troublesome to us. This tiresome journey of land and water ended, however, on the third day, to my great joy; and I got on board of a sloop commanded by one Captain Jenning. She was then partly loaded, and he told me he was expecting daily to sail for Jamaica; and having agreed with me to work my passage, I went to work accordingly.

I was not many days on board before we sailed; but, to my sorrow and disappointment, though used to such tricks, we went to the south-ward along the Musquito shore, instead of steering for Jamaica. I was compelled to assist in cutting a great deal of mahogany wood on the shore as we coasted along it, and load the vessel with it, before she sailed. This fretted me much; but, as I did not know how to help myself among these deceivers, I thought patience was the only remedy I had left, and even that was forced. There was much hard work and little victuals on board, except by good luck we happened to catch turtles. On this coast there was also a particular kind of fish called manatee, which is most excellent eating, and the flesh is more like

beef than fish; the scales are as large as a shilling, and the skin thicker than I ever saw that of any other fish. Within the brackish waters along shore there were likewise vast numbers of alligators, which made the fish scarce. I was on board this sloop sixteen days, during which, in our coasting, we came to another place, where there was a smaller sloop called the Indian Queen, commanded by one John Baker. He also was an Englishman, and had been a long time along the shore trading for turtle-shells and silver, and had got a good quantity of each on board. He wanted some hands very much; and, understanding I was a free-man, and wanted to go to Jamaica, he told me if he could get one or two, that he would sail immediately for that island; he also pretended to shew me some marks of attention and respect, and promised to give me forty-five shillings sterling a month if I would go with him. I thought this much better than cutting wood for nothing. I therefore told the other Captain that I wanted to go to Jamaica in the other vessel, but he would not listen to me, and, seeing me resolved to go in a day or two, he got the vessel under sail, intending to carry me away against my will. This treatment mortified me exceedingly. I immediately, according to an agreement I had made with the Captain of the Indian Queen, called for her boat which was lying near us, and it came alongside; and, by the means of a north-pole shipmate whom I met with in the sloop I was in, I got my things into the boat, and went on board of the Indian Queen, July the 10th. A few days after I was there, we got all things ready and sailed; but again, to my great mortification, this vessel still went to the south, nearly as far as Carthagena, trading along the coast, instead of going to Jamaica, as the Captain had promised me: and what was worst of all, he was a very cruel and bloody-minded man, and was a horrid blasphemer. Among others, he had a white pilot, one Stoker, whom he beat often as severely as he did some negroes he had on board. One night in particular, after he had beaten this man most cruelly, he put him into the boat, and made two negroes row him to a desolate key, or small island; and he loaded two pistols, and swore bitterly that he would shoot the negroes if they brought Stoker on board again. There was not the least doubt but that he would do as he said, and the two poor fellows were obliged to obey the cruel mandate; but when the Captain was asleep, the two negroes took a blanket and carried it to the unfortunate Stoker, which I believe was the means of saving his life from the annoyance of insects. A great deal of entreaty was used with the Captain the next day, before he would consent to let Stoker come on board; and when the poor man was brought on board, he was very ill, from his situation during the night, and he remained so till he was drowned a little time after.

IX.

As we sailed southward we came to many uninhabited islands, overgrown with fine large cocoa-nut trees. As I was very much in want of provisions, I brought a boat-load of the nuts on board, which lasted me and others for several weeks, and afforded us many a delicious repast in our scarcity.

One day, before this, I could not help observing the providential hand of God, that ever supplies all our wants, though in the ways and manner we know not. I had been a whole day without food, and made signals for boats to come off, but in vain. I therefore earnestly prayed to God for relief in my need; and at the close of the evening I went off the deck. Just as I had laid down, I heard a noise on the deck; and not knowing what it meant, I went directly on the deck again, when what should I see, but a fine large fish about seven or eight pounds, which had jumped on board! I took it, and admired, with thanks, the good hand of God; and, what I considered as not less extraordinary, the Captain, who was very avaricious, did not attempt to take it from me, there being only he and I on board; for the rest were all gone ashore trading.

Sometimes the people did not come off for some days: this used to fret the Captain, and then he would vent his fury on me by beating me, or making me feel in other cruel ways. One day especially, in his wild, wicked, and mad career, after striking me several times with different things, and once across my mouth, even with a red burning stick out of the fire, he got a barrel of gunpowder on the deck, and swore that he would blow up the vessel. I was then at my wit's end, and earnestly prayed to God to direct me. The head was out of the barrel; and the Captain took a lighted stick out of the fire to blow himself and me up, because there was a vessel, then in sight, coming in, which he supposed was a Spaniard, and he was afraid of falling into their hands. Seeing this, I got an axe, unnoticed by him, and placed myself between him and the powder, having resolved in myself, as soon as he attempted to put the fire in the barrel, to chop him down at that instant. I was more than an hour in this situation; during which he struck me often, still keeping the fire in his hand for this wicked purpose. I really should have thought myself justifiable, in any other part of the world, if I had killed him, and prayed to God, who gave me a mind that rested solely on himself. I prayed for resignation, that his will might be done: and the following two portions of his holy word, which occurred to my mind, buoyed up my hope, and kept me from taking the life of this wicked man. "He hath determined the times before appointed, and set bounds to our habitations." (Acts xvii. 26.) And, "Who is there among you that

feareth the Lord, that obeyeth the voice of his servant, that walketh in darkness, and hath no light? Let him trust in the name of the Lord, and stay upon his God." (Isaiah 1. 10.) And this, by the grace of God, I was enabled to do. I found Him a present help in the time of need, and the Captain's fury began to subside as the night approached; but I found

> That he, who cannot stem his anger's tide,
> Doth a wild horse, without a bridle, ride.

The next morning we discovered that the vessel, which had caused such a fury in the Captain, was an English sloop. They soon came to an anchor where we were, and, to my no small surprise, I learned that Dr. Irving was on board of her, on his way from the Musquito shore to Jamaica. I was for going immediately to see this old master and friend, but the Captain would not suffer me to leave the vessel. I then informed the Doctor, by letter, how I was treated, and begged that he would take me out of the sloop: but he informed me that it was not in his power, as he was a passenger himself; but he sent me some rum and sugar for my own use. I now learned that after I had left the estate which I managed for this gentleman on the Musquito shore, during which the slaves were well fed and comfortable, a white overseer had supplied my place: this man, through inhumanity and ill-judged avarice, beat and cut the poor slaves most unmercifully; and the consequence was, that every one got into a large Puriogua canoe, and endeavoured to escape; but, not knowing where to go, or how to manage the canoe, they were all drowned: in consequence of which the Doctor's plantation was left uncultivated, and he was now returning to Jamaica to purchase more slaves and stock it again.

On the 14th of October, the Indian Queen arrived at Kingston in Jamaica. When we were unloaded I demanded my wages, which amounted to eight pounds five shillings sterling; but Captain Baker refused to give me one farthing, although it was the hardest earned money I have worked for in my life. I found out Dr. Irving on this, and acquainted him with the Captain's knavery. He did all he could to help me to get my money; and we went to every magistrate in Kingston (and there were nine), but they all refused to do any thing for me, and said my oath could not be admitted against a white man. Nor was this all; for Baker threatened that he would beat me severely if he could catch me, for attempting to demand my money; and this he would have done but I got, by means of Dr. Irving, under the protection of Captain Douglas, of the Squirrel man of war. I thought this exceedingly hard usage; though indeed I found it to be too much the practice there to pay free negro men for their labour in this manner.

One day I went with a free negro tailer, named Joe Diamond, to one Mr. Cochran, who was indebted to him some trifling sum; and the man, not being able to get his money, began to murmur. The other immediately took a horse-whip to pay him with it: but by the help of a good pair of heels, the tailor got off. Such oppressions as these made me seek for a vessel to get off the islands as fast as I could: and by the mercy of God, I found a ship in November bound for England, when I embarked with a convoy, after having taken a last farewell of Dr. Irving.— When I left Jamaica he was employed in refining sugars; and offered me a place, but I refused. And some months after my arrival in England I learned, with much sorrow, that this my amiable friend was dead, owing to his having eaten some poisoned fish.

We had many heavy gales of wind in our passage: in the course of which no material accident occurred, except that an American privateer, falling in with the fleet, was captured and set fire to by his Majesty's ship the Squirrel.

On January the seventh 1777, we arrived at Plymouth. I was happy once more to tread upon English ground: and, after passing some little time at Plymouth and Exeter, among some pious friends, whom I was happy to see, I went to London, with a heart replete with thanks to God for past mercies.

CHAPTER XII.

Different transactions of the author's life till the present time — His application to the late Bishop of London to be appointed a Missionary to Africa — Some account of his share in the conduct of the late expedition to Sierra Leona — Petition to the Queen — Conclusion.

I.

SUCH WERE the various scenes to which I was a witness, and the fortune I experienced until the year 1777. Since that period my life has been more uniform, and the incidents of it fewer, than in any other equal number of years preceding; I therefore hasten to the conclusion of a narrative, which I fear the reader may think already sufficiently tedious.

I had suffered so many impositions in my commercial transactions, in different parts of the world, that I became heartily disgusted with the seafaring life, and was determined not to return to it, at least for some time. I therefore once more engaged in service shortly after my return, and continued, for the most part, in this situation until 1784.

Soon after my arrival in London, I saw a remarkable circumstance relative to African complexion, which I thought so extraordinary that I shall beg leave just to mention it:—A white negro woman, that I had formerly seen in London and other parts, had married a white man, by whom she had three boys, and they were every one mulattoes, and yet they had fine light hair.

In 1779, I served Governor Macnamara, who had been a considerable time on the coast of Africa. In the time of my service I used to ask frequently other servants to join me in family prayer; but this only excited their mockery. However, the Governor, understanding that I was of a religious turn, wished to know what religion I was of; I told him I was a protestant of the church of England, agreeable to the thirty-nine articles of that church; and that whomsoever I found to preach according

to that doctrine, those I would hear. A few days after this, we had some more discourse on the same subject; when he said he would, if I chose, as he thought I might be of service in converting my countrymen to the Gospel-faith, get me sent out as a missionary to Africa. I at first refused going, and told him how I had been served on a like occasion by some white people, the last voyage I went to Jamaica, when I attempted (if it were the will of God), to be the means of converting the Indian prince; and said I supposed they would serve me worse than Alexander the coppersmith did St. Paul, if I should attempt to go amongst them in Africa. He told me not to fear, for he would apply to the Bishop of London to get me ordained. On these terms I consented to the Governor's proposal to go to Africa, in hope of doing good, if possible, amongst my countrymen; so, in order to have me sent out properly, we immediately wrote the following letters to the late Bishop of London:

To The Right Reverend Father in God, ROBERT, *Lord Bishop of London*.
THE MEMORIAL OF GUSTAVUS VASSA

SHEWETH,

THAT your memorialist is a native of Africa, and has a knowledge of the manners and customs of the inhabitants of that country.

That your memorialist has resided in different parts of Europe for twenty-two years last past, and embraced the Christian faith in the year 1759.

That your memorialist is desirous of returning to Africa as a missionary, if encouraged by your Lordship, in hopes of being able to prevail upon his countrymen to become Christians; and your memorialist is the more induced to undertake the same, from the success that has attended the like undertakings when encouraged by the Portuguese through their different settlements on the coast of Africa, and also by the Dutch; both governments encouraged the blacks, who by their education are qualified to undertake the same, and are found more proper than European clergymen, unacquainted with the language and customs of the country.

Your memorialist's only motive for soliciting the office of a missionary is, that he may be a means, under God, of reforming his countrymen and persuading them to embrace the Christian religion. Therefore your memorialist humbly prays your Lordship's encouragement and support in the undertaking.

 GUSTAVUS VASSA.

At Mr. Guthrie's, Taylor,
 No. 17, Hedge-lane.
 MY LORD,

I HAVE resided near seven years on the coast of Africa, for most part of the time as commanding officer. From the knowledge I have of the country and its inhabitants, I am inclined to think that the within plan will be attended with great success, if countenanced by your Lordship. I beg further to represent to

your Lordship, that the like attempts, when encouraged by other governments, have met with uncommon success; and at this very time I know a very respectable character, a black priest, at Cape Coast Castle. I know the within named GUSTAVUS VASSA, and believe him a moral good man.

I have the honour to be,
My Lord,
Your Lordship's
Humble and obedient Servant,
MATT. MACNAMARA.

Grove, 11th March, 1779.

This letter was also accompanied by the following from Doctor Wallace, who had resided in Africa for many years, and whose sentiments on the subject of the African mission were the same with Governor Macnamara's.

MY LORD, March 13, 1779.
I have resided near five years on Senegambia on the coast of Africa, and have had the honour of filling very considerable employments in that province. I do approve of the within plan, and think the undertaking very laudable and proper, and that it deserves your Lordship's protection and encouragement, in which case it must be attended with the intended success.

I am, my Lord,
Your Lordship's
Humble and obedient Servant,
THOMAS WALLACE.

With these letters I waited on the Bishop, by the Governor's desire, and presented them to his Lordship. He received me with much condescension and politeness; but, from some certain scruples of delicacy, and saying the Bishops were not of opinion in sending a new missionary to Africa, he declined to ordain me.

My sole motive for thus dwelling on this transaction, or inserting these papers, is the opinion which gentlemen of sense and education, who are acquainted with Africa, entertain of the probability of converting the inhabitants of it to the faith of Jesus Christ, if the attempt were countenanced by the legislature.

II.

Shortly after this I left the Governor, and served a nobleman in the Dorsetshire militia, with whom I was encamped at Coxheath for some time; but the operations there were too minute and uninteresting to make detail of.

In the year 1783, I visited eight counties in Wales, from motives of curiosity. While I was in that part of the country I was led to go down into a coal-pit in Shropshire, but my curiosity nearly cost me my life; for while I was in the pit the coals fell in, and buried one poor man, who was not far from me: upon this I got out as fast as I could, thinking the surface of the earth the safest part of it.

In the spring of 1784, I thought of visiting old ocean again. In consequence of this I embarked as steward on board a fine new ship called the London, commanded by Martin Hopkins, and sailed for New York. I admired this city very much; it is large and well-built, and abounds with provisions of all kinds. While we lay here, a circumstance happened which I thought extremely singular:—One day a malefactor was to be executed on a gallows; but with condition that if any woman, having nothing on but her shift, married the man under the gallows, his life was to be saved. This extraordinary privilege was claimed; a woman presented herself; and the marriage ceremony was performed.

Our ship having got laden, we returned to London in January 1785. When she was again ready for another voyage, the Captain being an agreeable man, I sailed with him from hence in the spring, March 1785, for Philadelphia. On the 5th of April we took our departure from the Land's end, with a pleasant gale; and about nine that night the moon shone bright, and the sea was smooth, while our ship was going free by the wind, at the rate of about four or five miles an hour.—At this time another ship was going nearly as fast as we on the opposite point, meeting us right in the teeth, yet none on board observed either ship until we struck each other forcibly head to head, to the astonishment and consternation of both crews. She did us much damage, but I believe we did her more; for, when we passed by each other, which we did very quickly, they called to us to bring to, and hoist out our boats, but we had enough to do to mind ourselves; and in about eight minutes we saw no more of her. We refitted as well as we could the next day, and proceeded on our voyage, and in May arrived at Philadelphia.

I was very glad to see this favourite old town once more; and my pleasure was much increased in seeing the worthy Quakers, freeing and easing the burthens of many of my oppressed African brethren. It rejoiced my heart when one of these friendly people took me to see a free-school they had erected for every denomination of black people, whose minds are cultivated here, and forwarded to virtue; and thus they are made useful members of the community. Does not the success of this practice say loudly to the planters, in the language of scripture—"Go ye, and do likewise!"

In October 1785, I was accompanied by some of the Africans, and presented an address of thanks to the gentlemen called friends or

Quakers, in the Whitehart-court, Lombard-street.* These gentlemen received us very kindly, with a promise to exert themselves on behalf of the oppressed Africans, and we parted.

III.

While in town, I chanced once to be invited to a Quaker's wedding. The simple and yet expressive mode used at their solemnizations is worthy of note. The following is the true form of it:

After the company have met, they have seasonable exhortations by several of the members, the bride and bridegroom stand up, and, taking each other by the hand, in a solemn manner, the man audibly declares to this purpose:

Friends, in the fear of the Lord, and in the presence of this assembly, whom I desire to be my witnesses, I take this my friend, M. N. to be my wife; promising, through divine assistance, to be unto her a loving and faithful husband till death separate us.

And the woman makes the like declaration.—Then the two first sign their names to the record, and as many more witnesses as have a mind. I had the honour to subscribe mine to a register in Whitehart-court, Lombard-street. This mode I highly recommend.

We returned to London in August, and our ship not going immediately to sea, I shipped as a steward in an American ship called the Harmony, Captain John Willett, and left London in March 1786, bound to Philadelphia. Eleven days after sailing, we carried our foremast away. We had a nine weeks passage, which caused our trip not to succeed well, the market for our goods proving bad; and, to make it worse, my commander began to play me the like tricks as others too often practise on free negroes in the West Indies. But I thank God, I found many friends here who in some measure prevented him. On my return to London in August, I was very agreeably surprised to find, that the benevolence of government adopted the plan of some philanthropic individuals, to send the Africans from hence to their native quarter; and that some vessels were then engaged to carry them to Sierra Leona; an act which redounded to the honour of all concerned in its promotion, and filled me with prayers and much rejoicing.

*See Appendix B.

There was then in the city a select committee of gentlemen for the black poor, to some of whom I had the honour of being known; and as soon as they heard of my arrival, they sent for me to the committee. When I came there, they informed me of the intention of government; and as they seemed to think me qualified to superintend part of the undertaking, they asked me to go with the black poor to Africa. I pointed out to them many objections to my going; and particularly I expressed some difficulties on the account of the slave dealers, as I would certainly oppose their traffic in the human species by every means in my power. However, these objections were overruled by the gentlemen of the committee, who prevailed on me to consent to go; and recommended me to the honourable Commissioners of his Majesty's Navy, as a proper person to act as commissary for government in the intended expedition; and they accordingly appointed me in November 1786, to that office, and gave me sufficient power to act for the government in the capacity of commissary, having received my warrant and the following order:

By the principal Officers and Commissioners of his Majesty's Navy.

WHEREAS you are directed, by our warrant of the 4th of last month, to receive into your charge, from Mr. Joseph Irwin, the surplus provisions remaining of what was provided for the voyage, as well as the provisions for the support of the black poor, after the landing at Sierra Leona, with the cloathing, tools, and all other articles provided at government's expence; and as the provisions were laid in at the rate of two months for the voyage, and for four months after landing, but the number embarked being so much less than we expected, whereby there may be a considerable surplus of provisions, cloathing, &c. these are, in addition to former orders, to direct and require you to appropriate or dispose of such surplus to the best advantage you can for the benefit of government, keeping and rendering to us a faithful account of what you do herein. And for your guidance in preventing any white persons going, who are not intended to have the indulgence of being carried thither, we send you herewith a list of those recommended by the committee for the black poor, as proper persons to be permitted to embark, and acquaint you that you are not to suffer any others to go who do not produce a certificate from the committee for the black poor, of their having their permission for it. For which this shall be your warrant. Dated at the Navy-Office, January 16, 1787.

<div align="right">
J. HINSLOW,

GEO. MARSH,

W. PALMER.
</div>

To Mr. Gustavus Vassa, Commissary
of Provisions and Stores for the
Black Poor to Sierra Leona.

I proceeded immediately to the executing of my duty on board the vessels destined for the voyage, where I continued till the March following.

IV.

During my continuance in the employment of government I was struck with the flagrant abuses committed by the agent, and endeavoured to remedy them, but without any effect. One instance, among many which I could produce, may serve as a specimen. Government had ordered to be provided all necessaries (slops, as they are called, included) for 750 persons; however, not being able to muster more than 426, I was ordered to send the superfluous slops, &c. to the king's stores at Portsmouth; but, when I demanded them for that purpose from the agent, it appeared they had never been bought, though paid for by government. But that was not all, government were not the only objects of peculation; these poor people suffered infinitely more; their accommodations were most wretched; many of them wanted beds, and many more clothing and other necessaries.

For the truth of this, and much more, I do not seek credit from my own assertion. I appeal to the testimony of Captain Thompson, of the Nautilus, who convoyed us; to whom I applied in February 1787 for a remedy, when I had remonstrated to the agent in vain, and even brought him to be a witness of the injustice and oppression I had complained of.* I appeal also to a letter written by these wretched people, so early as the beginning of the preceding January, and published in the Morning Herald, on the fourth of that month, signed by twenty of their chiefs.

I could not silently suffer government to be thus cheated, and my countrymen plundered and oppressed, and even left destitute of the necessaries for almost their existence. I therefore informed the Commissioners of the Navy of the agent's proceeding; but my dismission was soon after procured by the means of a gentleman† in the city, whom the agent, conscious of his peculation, had deceived by letters, and who, moreover, empowered the same agent to receive on board, at

*He then told the agent before me, he was informed by Mr. Steel, M. P. that the said expedition had cost 33,000l. and he desired that the things might be had.

†Witness Thomas Steele, Esq. M. P. of the Treasury, and Sir, Charles Middleton, Bart. &c. I should have publicly exposed him (even in writing falsely of me last March), were it not out of respect to the worthy Quakers and others.

the government's expence, a number of persons as passengers, contrary to
the orders I received. By this I suffered a considerable loss in my property:
however, the commissioners were satisfied with my conduct, and wrote
to Captain Thompson, expressing their approbation of it.

Thus provided, they proceeded on their voyage; and at last, worn out
by treatment, perhaps not the most mild, and wasted by sickness,
brought on by want of medicine, clothes, bedding, &c. they reached
Sierra Leona just at the commencement of the rains. At that season of
the year it is impossible to cultivate the lands, their provisions there-
fore were exhausted before they could derive any benefit from agri-
culture; and it is not surprising that many, especially the Lascars,
whose constitutions are very tender, and who had been cooped up in
ships from October to June, and accommodated in the manner I have
mentioned, should be so wasted by their confinement as not long to
survive it.

Thus ended my part of the long-talked-of expedition to Sierra
Leona; an expedition, which, however unfortunate in the event, was
humane and politic in its design; nor was its failure owing to govern-
ment; every thing was done on their part; but there was evidently
sufficient mismanagement, attending the conduct and execution of it,
to defeat its success.

I should not have been so ample in my account of this transaction,
had not the share I bore in it been made the subject of partial animad-
version, and even my dismission from my employment thought worthy
of being made, by Hoare and others, matter of public triumph. The
motive which might influence any person to descend to a petty contest
with an obscure African, and to seek gratification by his depression, per-
haps it is not proper here to enquire into or relate, even if its detection
were necessary to my vindication;* but I thank Heaven it is not. I wish
to stand by my own integrity, and not to shelter myself under the impro-
priety of another; and I trust the behaviour of the Commissioners of the
Navy to me entitle me to make this assertion; for after I had been dis-
missed, March 24, I drew up a memorial.†

The above petition was delivered into the hands of their Lordships,
who were kind enough, in the space of some few months afterwards,
without hearing, to order me £50. sterling—that is £18. wages for the
time (upwards of four months) I acted a faithful part in their service.
Certainly the sum is more than a free negro would have had in the
western colonies!!!

*See the Public Advertiser, July 14, 1787.
†See Appendix C.

V.

From that period to the present, my life has passed in an even tenour, and great part of my study and attention has been to assist in the cause of my much injured countrymen.

March the 21st, 1788, I had the honour of presenting the Queen with a petition on behalf of my African brethren, which was received most graciously by her Majesty.*

The negro consolidated act, made by the assembly of Jamaica last year, and the new act of amendment now in agitation there, contain a proof of the existence of those charges that have been made against the planters relative to the treatment of their slaves.

I hope to have the satisfaction of seeing the renovation of liberty and justice, resting on the British government, to vindicate the honour of our common nature. These are concerns which do not, perhaps, belong to any particular office: but to speak more seriously, to every man of sentiment actions like these are the just and sure foundation of future fame; a reversion, though remote, is coveted by some noble minds as a substantial good. It is upon these grounds that I hope and expect the attention of gentlemen in power. These are designs consonant to the elevation of their rank, and the dignity of their stations; they are ends suitable to the nature of a free and generous government; and connected with views of empire and dominion, suited to the benevolence and solid merit of the legislature. It is a pursuit of substantial greatness. May the time come—at least the speculation to me is pleasing—when the sable people shall gratefully commemorate the auspicious æra of extensive freedom! Then shall those persons† particularly be named with praise and honour who generously proposed, and stood forth in the cause of humanity, liberty, and good policy, and brought to the ear of the legislature designs worthy of a royal patronage and adoption. May Heaven make the British senators the dispersers of light, liberty, and science, to the uttermost parts of the earth! Then will be *Glory to God in the highest; on earth peace and good-will to men.* —*Glory, honour, peace, &c. to every soul of man that worketh good: to the* Britons *first* (because to them the gospel is preached), *and also to the nations. Those that honour their Maker have mercy on the poor. It is righteousness exalteth a nation, but sin is a reproach to any people; destruction shall be to the workers of iniquity, and the wicked shall fall by their own*

*At the request of some of my most particular friends I take the liberty of inserting it. See Appendix D.

†Granville Sharp, Esq. the Rev. Thomas Clarkson; the Rev. James Ramsay; our approved friends, men of virtue, are an honour to their country, ornamental to human nature, happy in themselves, and benefactors to mankind!

wickedness. May the blessings of the Lord be upon the heads of all those who commiserated the cases of the oppressed negroes, and the fear of God prolong their days; and may their expectations be filled with gladness! "The liberal devise liberal things, and by liberal things shall stand." Isaiah xxxii. 8. They can say with pious Job, "Did not I weep for him that was in trouble? Was not my soul grieved for the poor?" Job xxx. 25.

VI.

As the inhuman traffic of slavery is to be taken into the consideration of the British legislature, I doubt not, if a system of commerce was established in Africa, the demand for manufactures will most rapidly augment, as the native inhabitants will insensibly adopt the British fashions, manners, customs, &c. In proportion to the civilization, so will be the consumption of British manufactures.

The wear and tear of a continent, nearly twice as large as Europe, and rich in vegetable and mineral productions, is much easier conceived than calculated.

A case in point. It cost the Aborigines of Britain little or nothing in clothing, &c. The difference between their forefathers and the present generation, in point of consumption, is literally infinite. The supposition is most obvious.—It will be equally immense in Africa.—The same cause, viz. civilization, will ever have the same effect.

It is trading upon safe grounds. A commercial intercourse with Africa opens an inexhaustible source of wealth to the manufacturing interests of Great Britain;* and to all which the slave-trade is an objection.

If I am not misinformed, the manufacturing interest is equal, if not superior, to the landed interest, as to the value, for reasons which will soon appear. The abolition of slavery, so diabolical, will give a most rapid extension of manufactures, which is totally and diametrically opposite to what some interested people assert.

*In the ship Trusty, lately for the new Settlement of Sierra Leona, in Africa, where 1,300 pair of shoes (an article hitherto scarcely known to be exported to that country) with several others equally new, as articles of export. Thus will it not become the interest, as well as the duty, of every artificer, mechanic, and tradesman, publicly to enter their protest against this traffic of the human species?—What a striking, what a beautiful contrast is here presented to view, when compared with the cargo of a slave ship! Every feeling heart, indeed, sensibly participates of the joy, and with a degree of rapture reads of barrels of *flour* instead of *gunpowder—biscuits and bread* instead of *horse beans—implements of husbandry* instead of *guns* for destruction, rapine, and murder—and various articles of *usefulness* are the pleasing substitutes for the *torturing thumbscrew,* and the *galling chain,* &c.

The manufactures of this country must and will, in the nature and reason of things, have a full and constant employ, by supplying the African markets.

Population, the bowels, and surface of Africa, abound in valuable and useful returns; the hidden treasures of centuries will be brought to light and into circulation. Industry, enterprise, and mining, will have their full scope, proportionably as they civilize. In a word, it lays open an endless field of commerce to the British manufacturers and merchant adventurers. The manufacturing interest and the general interests are synonimous. The abolition of slavery would be in reality an universal good.

Tortures, murder, and every other imaginable barbarity and iniquity, are practised upon the poor slaves with impunity. I hope the slave trade will be abolished. I pray it may be an event at hand. The great body of manufacturers, uniting in the cause, will considerably facilitate and expedite it; and as I have already stated, it is most substantially their interest and advantage, and as such the nation's at large, except those persons concerned in manufacturing neck-yokes, collars, chains, hand-cuffs, leg-bolts, drags, thumb-screws, iron muzzles, and coffins; cats, scourges, and other instruments of torture used in the slave-trade. In a short time one sentiment will alone prevail, from motives of interest as well as justice and humanity. Europe contains one hundred and twenty millions of inhabitants. Query—How many millions doth Africa contain? Supposing the Africans, collectively and individually, to expend £5. a head in raiment and furniture yearly, when civilized, &c. an immensity beyond the reach of imagination!

This I conceive to be a theory founded upon facts, and therefore an infallible one. If the blacks were permitted to remain in their own country, they would double themselves every fifteen years. In proportion to such increase will be the demand for manufactures. Cotton and indigo grow spontaneously in most parts of Africa; a consideration this of no small consequence to the manufacturing towns of Great Britain. It opens a most immense, glorious, and happy prospect; the clothing, &c. of a continent ten thousand miles in circumference, and immensely rich in productions of every denomination in return for manufactures.

VII.

Since the first publication of my narrative, I have been in a great variety of scenes* in many parts of Great-Britain, Ireland, and Scotland, an

*Viz. Some curious adventures beneath the earth, in a river in Manchester,—and a most astonishing one under the Peak of Derbyshire—and in September 1792, I went 90 fathoms down St. Anthony's Colliery, at Newcastle, under the river Tyne, some hundreds of yards on the Durham side.

account of which might well be added here; but as this would swell the volume too much, I shall only observe in general, that in May 1791, I sailed from Liverpool to Dublin, where I was very kindly received, and from thence to Cork, and then travelled over many counties in Ireland. I was every where exceedingly well treated, by persons of all ranks. I found the people extremely hospitable, particularly in Belfast, where I took my passage on board of a vessel for Clyde, on the 29th of January, and arrived at Greenock on the 30th.—Soon after I returned to London, where I found persons of note from Holland and Germany, who requested me to go there; and I was glad to hear that an edition of my Narrative had been printed in both places, also in New York. I remained in London till I heard the debate in the house of Commons on the slave-trade, April the 2d and 3d. I then went to Soham in Cambridgeshire, and was married on the 7th of April to Miss Cullen, daughter of James and Ann Cullen, late of Ely*

I have only therefore to request the reader's indulgence, and conclude. I am far from the vanity of thinking there is any merit in this narrative: I hope censure will be suspended, when it is considered that it was written by one who was as unwilling as unable to adorn the plainness of truth by the colouring of imagination. My life and fortune have been extremely chequered, and my adventures various. Even those I have related are considerably abridged. If any incident in this little work should appear uninteresting and trifling to most readers, I can only say, as my excuse for mentioning it, that almost every event of my life made an impression on my mind, and influenced my conduct. I early accustomed myself to look at the hand of God in the minutest occurrence, and to learn from it a lesson of morality and religion; and in this light every circumstance I have related was, to me, of importance. After all, what makes any event important, unless by its observation we become better and wiser, and learn *to do justly, to love mercy, and to walk humbly before God?* To those who are possessed of this spirit, there is scarcely any book or incident so trifling that does not afford some profit, while to others the experience of ages seems of no use; and even to pour out to them the treasures of wisdom is throwing the jewels of instruction away.

*See Gentleman's Magazine for April 1792, Literary and Biographical Magazine and British Review for May 1792, and the Edinburgh Historical Register or Monthly Intelligencer for April 1792.

APPENDIX.

A. Page 102.

Montserrat.—To all men unto whom these presents shall come:

I, Robert King, of the parish of St. Anthony in the said island, merchant, send greeting: Know ye, that I, the aforesaid Robert King, for, and in consideration of the sum of seventy pounds current money of the said island, to me in hand paid, and to the intent that a negro man-slave, named Gustavus Vassa, shall and may become free, have manumitted, emancipated, enfranchised, and set free, and by these presents do manumit, emancipate, enfranchise, and set free, the aforesaid negro man-slave, named Gustavus Vassa, for ever; hereby giving, granting, and releasing unto him, the said Gustavus Vassa, all right, title, dominion, sovereignty, and property, which, as lord and master over the aforesaid Gustavus Vassa, I had, or now have, or by any means whatsoever I may or can hereafter possibly have over him, the aforesaid negro, for ever. In witness whereof I, the abovesaid Robert King, have unto these presents set my hand and seal, this tenth day of the seventh month, in the year of our Lord one thousand seven hundred and sixty-six.

ROBERT KING.

Signed, sealed, and delivered in the presence of Terry Legay, Montserrat.

Registered the within manumission, at full length, this eleventh day of July, 1766, in liber D.

TERRY LEGAY, Register.

B. Page 173.

GENTLEMEN,

By reading your book intitled, "A Caution to Great Britain and her Colonies, concerning the calamitous state of the enslaved negroes," We, part of the poor, oppressed, needy, and much degraded negroes, desire to approach you, with this address of thanks, with our inmost love and warmest acknowledgment; and with the deepest sense of your benevolence, unwearied labour, and kind interposition, towards breaking the yoke of slavery, and to administer a little comfort and ease to thousands and tens of thousands of very grievously afflicted and too heavy burthened negroes.

Gentlemen, could you, by perseverance, at last be enabled, under God, to lighten in any degree the heavy burthen of the afflicted, no doubt it would, in some measure, be the possible means under God of saving the souls of many of the oppressors; and if so, sure we are that the God, whose eyes are ever upon all his creatures, and always rewards every true act of virtue, and regards the prayers of the oppressed, will give to you and yours those blessings which it is not in our power to express or conceive, but which we, as a part of those captivated, oppressed, and afflicted people, most earnestly wish and pray for.

C. Page 176.

To the Right Hon. the Lords Commissioners of his Majesty's Treasury.

The Memorial and Petition of GUSTAVUS VASSA, *a black Man, late Commissary to the black Poor, going to Africa,*

HUMBLY SHEWETH,

THAT your Lordships' memorialist was, by the hon. the commissioners of his majesty's navy, on the 4th of December last, appointed to the above employment by warrant from that board.

That he accordingly proceeded to the execution of his duty on board of the Vernon, being one of the ships appointed to proceed to Africa with the above poor.

That your memorialist, to his great grief and astonishment, received a letter of dismission, from the hon. commissioners of the navy, by your Lordships' orders.

That conscious of having acted with the most perfect fidelity and the greatest assiduity, in discharging the trust reposed in him, he is altogether

at a loss to conceive the reasons of your lordships having altered the favourable opinion you were pleased to conceive of him, sensible that your Lordships would not proceed to so severe a measure without some apparent good cause; he therefore has every reason to believe that his conduct has been grossly misrepresented to your Lordships, and he is the more confirmed in his opinion, because by opposing measures of others concerned in the same expedition, which tended to defeat your Lordships' humane intentions, and to put the government to a very considerable additional expence, he created a number of enemies, whose misrepresentations, he has too much reason to believe, laid the foundation of his dismission. Unsupported by friends, and unaided by the advantages of a liberal education, he can only hope for redress from the justice of his cause, in addition to the mortification of having been removed from his employment, and the advantage which he reasonably might have expected to have derived therefrom. He has had the misfortune to have sunk a considerable part of his little property in fitting himself, out, and in other expences arising out of his situation, an account of which he here annexes. Your memorialist will not trouble your Lordships with a vindication of any part of his conduct, because he knows not of what crimes he is accused; he, however, earnestly entreats that you will be acted in the public service; and if it be found that his dismission arose from false representations, he is confident that in your Lordships' justice he shall find redress.

Your petitioner therefore humbly prays that your Lordships will take his case into consideration, and that you will be pleased to order payment of the above-referred-to account, amounting to 321.4s. and also the wages intended, which is most humbly submitted.

London, May 12th, 1787.

D. Page 177.

To the QUEEN's most excellent Majesty:

MADAM,

YOUR Majesty's well known benevolence and humanity embolden me to approach your royal presence, trusting that the obscurity of my situation will not prevent your Majesty from attending to the sufferings for which I plead.

Yet I do not solicit your royal pity for my own distress; my sufferings, although numerous, are, in a measure, forgotten. I supplicate your

Majesty's compassion for millions of my African countrymen, who groan under the lash of tyranny in the West-Indies.

The oppression and cruelty exercised to the unhappy negroes there, have at length reached the British legislature, and they are now deliberating on its redress; even several persons of property in slaves in the West-Indies, have petitioned parliament against its continuance, sensible that it is as impolite as it is unjust—and what is inhuman must ever be unwise.

Your Majesty's reign has hitherto been distinguished by private acts of benevolence and bounty; surely the more extended the misery is, the greater claim it has to your Majesty's compassion, and the greater must be your Majesty's pleasure in administering to its relief.

I presume, therefore, gracious Queen, to implore your interposition with your royal consort, in favour of the wretched Africans; that by your Majesty's benevolent influence, a period may now be put to their misery; and that they may be raised from the condition of brutes, to which they are at present degraded, to the rights and situation of freemen, and admitted to partake of the blessings of your Majesty's happy government; so shall your Majesty enjoy the heart-felt pleasure of procuring happiness to millions, and be rewarded in the grateful prayers of themselves and of their posterity.

And may the All-bountiful Creator shower on your Majesty, and the Royal Family, every blessing that this world can afford, and every fulness of joy which divine revelation has promised us in the next.

<div style="text-align:center">I am, your Majesty's</div>

Most dutiful and devoted Servant to command,
<div style="text-align:center">GUSTAVUS VASSA,</div>

<div style="text-align:right">The Oppressed Ethiopian.</div>

Nc. 53, Baldwin's Gardens:

<div style="text-align:center">FINIS.</div>

THE
ROSARY
HANDBOOK

A Guide for Newcomers,
Old-Timers, and Those
In Between

THE
ROSARY
HANDBOOK

A Guide for Newcomers,
Old-Timers, and Those
In Between

MITCH FINLEY

The Word Among Us Press

9639 Doctor Perry Road

Ijamsville, Maryland 21754

www.wordamongus.org

11 10 09 08 07 2 3 4 5 6

ISBN: 978-1-59325-099-7

Cover design by John Hamilton Design

Made and printed in the United States of America

Library of Congress Cataloging-in-Publication Data

Finley, Mitch.

The rosary handbook / A Guide for Newcomers, Old-Timers, and Those In Between / Mitch Finley.

 p. cm.

Includes bibliographical references and index.

ISBN 978-1-59325-099-7 (alk. paper)

1. Rosary. I. Title.

BX2163.F48 2007

242'.74--dc22

 2007001544

Contents

Introduction 7
> The Rosary and You—A Perfect Match

Chapter 1 15
> What's in It for Me: Why You Should Pray the Rosary

Chapter 2 29
> Separating Fact from Myth: The Origins and History
> of the Rosary

Chapter 3 43
> More Than Just a String of Beads: The Prayers
> of the Rosary

Chapter 4 69
> Moments for Meditation: The Twenty Mysteries
> of the Rosary

Chapter 5 131
> Getting Down to Basics: How to Pray the Rosary

Appendix 139
> Putting It into Practice: Making the Rosary Your Own

For the Benedictine Sisters
of the Monastery of St. Gertrude,
Cottonwood, Idaho,
who, when I was but a lad,
first taught me to pray the Rosary.

INTRODUCTION

THE ROSARY AND YOU—
A PERFECT MATCH

My earliest memories of the Rosary go back to the school year of 1953–54, when I was in the third grade. This was the first year that I attended a Catholic school, which happened to be Saints Peter and Paul School in the small, north-central Idaho town of Grangeville. Benedictine Sisters from the Monastery of St. Gertrude, from nearby Cottonwood, Idaho, served as our teachers. Our parents enrolled my younger sister and me in this little Catholic school even though we weren't Catholic. Less than two years later, however, the four of us—Mom and Dad included—found ourselves leaning over the baptismal font in the back of Saints Peter and Paul Church, as the pastor, Father Thomas Lafey, poured the waters of baptism over our heads. For me, it was the beginning of a lifelong love affair with Catholicism—and, as I was to discover only later—with the Rosary.

A few years ago, I had occasion to return to Saints Peter and Paul School, and I could still pinpoint the place in the school's gymnasium where I stood, one May morning—May being the month of the Blessed Virgin Mary—as a non-Catholic third grader, when one of the sisters designated me, along with some sixty other fidgeting kids, to represent one of the beads of a rosary. We were going to become, Sister said, a "living rosary." (Throughout this book, I capitalize "Rosary" whenever I refer to

the prayer form that is called "*the* Rosary." When I refer to a circlet of beads or other counter called "*a* rosary," I spell "rosary" with a lowercase "r.")

The idea was that each student would begin the prayer to be said for the bead that he or she represented, and then everyone would join in to complete the prayer until we had prayed all five decades of a complete Rosary. I was designated as a "Hail Mary," but not being Catholic then, I had little clue as to how to recite one. As I recall, I represented one of the beads toward the end of the second or third decade. I listened closely as the kids before me prayed aloud, "Hail Mary, full of grace, the Lord is with thee. Blessed art thou among women, and blessed is the fruit of thy womb, Jesus." The entire assembly would then complete the prayer: "Holy Mary, mother of God, pray for us sinners, now and at the hour of our death. Amen."

I hadn't a clue what "fruit of thy womb" might mean, but it didn't seem to bother anyone else, so why should I let it bother me? When my turn came, I recited the opening words of the prayer correctly—more or less. To my relief, the Rosary continued with no major breakdown. The Rosary became part of my life from then on—it was simply a taken-for-granted part of being Catholic.

Years later, after graduating from a Catholic high school in 1964, I joined the U.S. Navy, and one of the ways I stayed in touch with my religious roots was through the Rosary. During the last of my four years in the Navy, in January 1968, I took a week's leave and flew from Norfolk, Virginia, where I was stationed at the naval air station, to Louisville, Kentucky. From there, by bus, I traveled to Bardstown, Kentucky, and got a ride out to the famous Trappist Abbey of Gethsemani monastery,

where I was scheduled to make a weekend retreat. The white snows of winter lay all around, and the first day I was there I bought a good, sturdy rosary in the monastery's gift shop—one that I still have to this day.

During my years in the navy, I had formed the habit of taking long walks most evenings, around whatever naval air station I was attached to at the time. I walked with a rosary in my jacket pocket, and I prayed as my fingers moved slowly from one bead to the next. And so I managed to keep some semblance of a spirituality alive and kicking. Indeed, without being conscious of it, I became an amateur contemplative, for the Rosary is a prayer that lends itself to meditation on many levels—some of which we may be hardly aware of. But I'm getting ahead of myself. . . .

What's your story about the Rosary in your life? If you're a lifelong Catholic, you may have grown up in a family that prayed the Rosary together regularly at home, or maybe during Advent or Lent. Perhaps you have been praying the Rosary faithfully for many years. Then again, you might be considering returning to the Rosary after not having prayed it for a long time. Or maybe you never really learned to pray the Rosary before, and now you're wondering whether it's for you. Maybe you grew up in the years right after the Catholic Church's Second Vatican Council, in the mid-1960s, when the Rosary fell into disuse among many Catholics, and now you want to try it. And if you've recently become Catholic—or even if you're just thinking about it—you might want to find out what the Rosary is all about. Whatever role the Rosary has played in your life and whatever your reason for picking up this book, this is the book for you if you'd like to learn about, rediscover, or enrich your experience with the Rosary.

Why Another Rosary Book?

If you look around for books on the Rosary, soon you'll discover that there are more than a few available. Some are primarily devotional in nature. Others are popular studies of the Rosary. Some offer adaptations of the Rosary that incorporate Scripture into the prayer more than the conventional practice does. Others adapt the Rosary to a recovery-based spirituality. There really isn't any "wrong" approach to praying the Rosary—but if you're looking for frills, you won't find them here. This book will focus on the standard, straightforward, "no-frills" prayer that has been used for generation after generation.

The Rosary Handbook isn't just another book on the Rosary, though. My first aim in writing it was to provide a fresh perspective on the Rosary by looking at this age-old prayer through a thoroughly contemporary lens. I didn't want to simply pass along an understanding of the Rosary that was taken for granted by earlier generations. A great deal has happened in the Catholic Church in the last half century. Significant theological discussions have taken place. In particular, Catholic understanding of the role of Mary in the church and in salvation history has significantly evolved and sheds new light on the Rosary and other Marian devotions. This book will discuss the Rosary in the light of twenty-firstst century Catholic perspectives on Mary.

I wanted, also, to write a book about the Rosary that would convey and encourage the joy of praying this beloved prayer. Here, a grim or inappropriately solemn understanding of the Rosary won't be allowed to get even its toe in the door. The Blessed Mother is a joyful part of Catholic spirituality and devotional life, and the Rosary is a joyful prayer. It is quite true

that one can be a good Catholic and have little or no devotion to the mother of Jesus. Still, it's the rare Catholic who has no warm feelings whatsoever for the Blessed Virgin Mary.

In addition, I wanted to show that the Rosary is a prayer for everyone—old and young, clergy and laity, those who pray daily, and those who have trouble finding the time. And so, this book has no trace of the overly sentimental devotionalism with which Mary and the Rosary have sometimes been viewed—and with which I, for one, am not comfortable. The Rosary and the Mary of this book will never be sticky-sweet.

Finally, I wanted to provide a practical guide for prayer, not a recipe for a desired outcome. Some resources convey a kind of magical view of the Rosary. For example, there are narratives of the "true story" genre that imply that you can guarantee a loved one's safety by praying the Rosary for him or her every day. You may have read stories about parents who prayed the Rosary daily while a child was fighting in the Korean War or the Vietnam War or Afghanistan or Iraq—and he or she returned home unharmed. I dare say, though, that there are also parents who prayed the Rosary each day whose sons and daughters did not come home safe and sound. God answers our prayers in his own way and in his own time, which may or may not conform to our desires—whether we pray the Rosary or any other prayer. There are certainly benefits for us in praying the Rosary, but only God can determine the answers to our prayers.

Who Should Pray the Rosary?

Although there are many different reasons why people have a fondness for particular prayers, I believe that there are several reasons why nearly everyone will find something they like in the Rosary. First, the Rosary that this book encourages and celebrates is a devotional prayer suited to many situations and circumstances. When I say that the Rosary is devotional, I mean that it is what all prayer is—an intentional turning to the Divine Presence, to the loving God, Creator, Source, and Goal of all life, who—to paraphrase St. Augustine (A.D. 354–430)—is closer to us than we are to ourselves. Like all methods of prayer, the Rosary is a way to be with the God who Scripture tells us "is love" (1 John 4:16).

The Rosary is a simple, uncomplicated, nonliturgical way to pray when conscious thoughts and words may fail you, no matter what your feelings or emotions may be at the moment. If you are depressed, the Rosary works. If you are happy or sad, the Rosary works. If you are bored, the Rosary works. If you are anxious or worried, the Rosary works. If you are sick or just plain sick and tired, the Rosary works. No matter how you're feeling, the Rosary is a way to be physically and intentionally in the presence of the triune God—Father, Son, and Holy Spirit—in the company of the Blessed Virgin Mary, the mother of the risen Christ and, therefore—through the Sacrament of Baptism in Christ—our mother too.

Another reason that the Rosary has something to offer just about everyone is that, at the same time, the Rosary is simple and the Rosary is deep. It is so simple that the humblest believers love the Rosary. It is so deep that many of the great-

est thinkers and mystics down through the centuries have loved the Rosary. Indeed, the simplicity and depth of the Rosary are the simplicity and depth of the gospel itself, the good news of God's love and forgiveness for all in Christ. The combination of traditional prayers and meditation on sacred events makes the Rosary a particularly personal prayer that can be as uncomplicated or as complicated as you want to make it. Thus, it suits just about anyone's spirituality. In other words, chances are that the Rosary is a perfect match for you, no matter the shape or characteristics of your personal piety.

At the same time, we must admit that the Rosary doesn't suit everyone. Even the occasional saint has declared that he or she just couldn't pray the Rosary. Such saints and ordinary believers tend to be the exception, however, so give the Rosary a fair try before you decide one way or the other.

I hope that by this point I have your attention, and I hope that I have aroused your curiosity. A wonderful pilgrimage of discovery is ahead of us, one that I pray will lead us all closer to the risen Lord and to his—and our—Blessed Mother. Let us begin with joy and with hope.

CHAPTER 1

WHAT'S IN IT FOR ME?

Why You Should Pray the Rosary

I remember well the years immediately after the Second Vatican Council. The second half of the 1960s was an interesting time to be a Catholic—to say the least. One never knew what to expect next. Practically overnight the Mass became, in its appearance at least, remarkably different from what it had been for as long as anyone alive—not to mention the grandparents and great-grandparents of anyone alive—could remember. The baccalaureate Mass for my 1964 Catholic high school graduation was the standard, pre-Vatican II Mass, in which priest and congregation faced in the same direction, and all the prayers were said in Latin. Within a few short years, however, priest and assembly faced each other, and the prayers of the Mass were being said in the language of the people. Most important, the emphasis of the activity of the Mass shifted, so that the people in the pews were no longer mere spectators or observers of what the presider was doing at the altar, but were now full and conscious participants in the liturgy.

During the decades prior to Vatican II, it was not uncommon for people to pray the Rosary during Mass. Everyone was encouraged to follow the prayers that were being said in the Mass in a personal missal, and many did so. But it wasn't unusual to see someone with beads in hand, silently praying the

Rosary as the priest said Mass in Latin and the altar boys (never girls!) responded in Latin on behalf of the congregation. Once the "aftershocks" of Vatican II hit, however, Catholics got the message—either directly or indirectly—that praying the Rosary during Mass was definitely not okay. And for a good many years after Vatican II, the idea of praying the Rosary at any time at all fell into disfavor among many Catholics. Thinking back, I doubt that I held a rosary in my hands from about 1970 until 1985. That excellent old rosary I bought at the Abbey of Gethsemani lay neglected in the back of a drawer for all those years. Then, for mysterious reasons of the heart and the movement of divine grace, I returned to the Rosary.

The Rosary Is a Balanced Prayer

During the fifteen years that I wasn't praying the Rosary, I was active in my faith—studying theology and writing books and articles on popular theological topics. But I began to sense that my faith, although intellectually vibrant, was lacking an affective, devotional component. Believing that it was time for me to reintegrate my feelings into my spirituality and include a devotional component in my prayer, I returned to the Rosary. And as it turned out, I couldn't have been happier with the results. A faith with an active affective component is a balanced, healthy faith. Without it, faith may become little more than a "head trip."

The last thing I would want to do here is to denigrate the place of the intellect in faith. There are far too many great saints who were intellectuals to do that. Authentic faith should never lead us to stop thinking or to neglect the critical intellectual faculties

God gave us. At the same time, faith includes an affective, or feeling, dimension. Our emotions belong in our faith and spirituality, too. That's why devotional practices belong in the everyday life of faith—and one of the best and most time-honored of these, for Catholics especially, is the Rosary.

The Rosary Is a Comprehensive Prayer

Not only is the Rosary an excellent way to give faith a healthy affective component, it is also a theologically comprehensive prayer. Apart from the Mass, the Rosary is the most fully Christian devotional prayer available to us. In a very real sense, it has everything that is most basic to a Christian outlook on life and the world: a prayerful gesture invoking and placing ourselves in the presence of the triune God (Sign of the Cross); the most ancient creed, or statement of Christian faith, that we have (Apostles' Creed); the prayer that Jesus himself gives us in the gospels of Matthew and Luke (Our Father); prayerful reminders of the key events in the life, death, and resurrection of Jesus (mysteries); petitionary prayers to Mary (Hail Mary); prayers of praise to the God who is Father, Son, and Holy Spirit (Glory Be/Doxology); and a prayer invoking, praising, and petitioning the prayers of the Blessed Virgin Mary (Hail, Holy Queen/Salve Regina).

The Rosary is also particularly Catholic—and not just because it's mostly Catholics who pray it. (The occasional Protestant Christian prays the Rosary, it's true, but this is a relatively rare occurrence. If anything is likely to identify you to others as a Catholic it will be to have a rosary in your possession.) The Rosary is especially Catholic because it draws upon what Catholics consider the

two inseparable sources of divine revelation, Scripture and sacred Tradition—another sign of the Rosary's theological balance. All but two of the twenty mysteries, or sacred events, on which the prayers of the Rosary focus come directly from the gospels, and the other two (the fourth and fifth glorious mysteries) come from sacred Tradition.

In order to better understand the interdependence of Scripture and Tradition, we first need to grasp the nature and importance of the latter. Sacred Tradition is the term we use to refer to the living transmission of all the beliefs, doctrines, rituals, Scriptures, and life of the church. The *Catechism of the Catholic Church* (CCC) writes that "through Tradition, 'the Church, in her doctrine, life, and worship, perpetuates and transmits to every generation all that she herself is, all that she believes'" (78). We usually distinguish between sacred Tradition (capital "T") and individual traditions (lowercase "t"), which are the various customary practices "adapted to different places and times, in which the great Tradition is expressed" (CCC 83).

Sacred Tradition is the life of the church—meaning all of us—from the beginning right down to the present day. It is the Christian community's ongoing experience and understanding of the risen Christ throughout the centuries. More, it is all the true and authentic consequences of that experience. As our definition above notes, one of the first and most basic expressions of Tradition is Scripture itself. For it was the early church's experience of and reflection on the church's foundational events—in particular, the conception, birth, life, teachings, death, and resurrection of Jesus—that resulted in or gave birth to the New Testament. Indeed, it is part of sacred Tradition that the Bible as we know it includes the documents that it does, and no others.

Hence, all who accept the Christian Bible, whether they realize it or not, accept sacred Tradition, too.

In a weekly general audience in April 2006, Pope Benedict XVI explained,

> Tradition is the communion of the faithful gathered round the legitimate shepherds throughout history, a communion which the Holy Spirit nourishes, guaranteeing a connection between the experience of apostolic faith lived by the original community of disciples and the present experience of Christ in his church. (Catholic News Service, April 26, 2006)

Beautifully illustrating that connection, the pope went on to say that "Tradition is a living river" connecting the faithful to Christ.

In other words, sacred Tradition did not cease once the canon of Scripture had been established, roughly speaking, in the late fourth century. The "communion of the faithful" with the risen Lord, "gathered around the legitimate shepherds," continued and continues today, and development of the church's understanding of that experience has gone hand-in-hand with it. Through its basis in Scripture and Tradition, the Rosary is a living prayer that nourishes our intimacy with the living, risen Christ, who is continually revealed to us through Scripture, the Mass, and the sacraments.

The Rosary Is a Christ-centered Prayer in the Context of the Communion of Saints

Part of the church's ongoing reflection on its faith experience relates to the place of Mary, the mother of Jesus, in the life of the church. The Rosary is sometimes used as evidence that Catholics are guilty of giving to a mere human being the adoration appropriate to God alone. Of course, most Catholics know better. Authentic Catholicism venerates Mary; we do not worship or adore her. God alone is worthy of worship and adoration. Moreover, the Rosary—although it is set in a Marian context—is actually a Christ-centered prayer. The Rosary focuses on what theologians call "the Christ event," that is, the life, ministry, death, and resurrection of Jesus. It is a devotional prayer designed to bring these events to our attention, time and again, because they are key moments in the history of salvation and, for Christians, the foundational events in the history of the Christian community. What better form of prayer for anyone who calls himself or herself a disciple of the risen Lord?

As the mother of our Lord and, in fact, his first disciple, Mary has played an important part in the development of the church, and veneration of her has been part of the sacred Tradition of the church that has been handed down to us from the apostles. Essentially, the veneration of Mary belongs in the context of the Catholic doctrine of the communion of saints. In a nutshell, this doctrine simply says that the community of faith that is the church transcends space and time. Therefore, we belong to a community that exists in both this world and the next, a community made up of all those who strive, by God's grace, to live as disciples of Christ in this world plus the countless imperfect

but faithful disciples of Christ who have gone before us into eternity. Some hold a special place of honor in the public life of the church, beginning with the Blessed Virgin Mary, the mother of Jesus.

Just as we ask for one another's prayers in this world, so we can and should petition the saints in heaven to pray for us, as well—and logically enough, the first among the saints, the Blessed Virgin Mary, holds a special place among those whose prayers we request. Thus, our prayer for Mother Mary's intercesssion is, in its nature, no different from our requests for one another's prayers. The only unique characteristic of prayer to Mary, or to any of the saints, is who we are asking to pray for us. Just as we place a special value on the prayers of an especially holy person in this life, so we place an even greater value on the prayers of the saints—and first among them is the mother of the risen Lord.

When we pray the Rosary, we explicitly locate ourselves in the midst of this vast eternal community, and we petition our Blessed Mother for her prayers on our behalf and on behalf of all those we pray for. In this sense, to pray the Rosary is to pray with and in the whole church, the church in this world and in eternity, the earthly church and the heavenly church. Theologically, one of the activities we engage in when we pray the Rosary is to celebrate the reality to which the church's doctrine of the communion of saints refers.

The context of the Rosary, therefore, is the community of the church existing in time and space and eternity. But the focus and center of the Rosary is Christ Jesus, the Lord of time and space and the Lord of eternity. It is to him that the Rosary directs us, and in his presence that the Rosary places us—in the company of his, and our, Blessed Mother.

The Rosary Is a Spiritually Nourishing Prayer

The fact that the Rosary directs our prayer to Christ in the company of his mother is healthy for the spirituality of men and the spirituality of women—for different but complementary reasons. The Rosary nourishes in the spirituality of both men and women a healthy feminine dimension, because it is a Christ-centered prayer in a Marian, and thus feminine, context. That is, the focus of the Rosary is on Christ, but the primary prayer of the Rosary—the Hail Mary—praises the Blessed Virgin and petitions her for prayers on our behalf.

For men, praying the Rosary cultivates a deeper appreciation and respect for all things feminine. Through each Hail Mary, the Rosary places a man in the spiritual and very real presence of the woman who became, and remains, the mother of Christ—in the original Greek of the fourth-century Nicene Creed, the *theotokos* or mother of God. A particular young woman became critically important in the working out of our salvation precisely because she was and remains a woman. Thus, all women—because they are women—share in the honor and dignity of that one young woman. It was a young woman that the Creator of the universe chose, and upon whose word he waited, before the course of salvation could continue.

For a man to pray the Rosary is to expose himself, body and soul, to the woman Mary. And because all women share in the dignity of Mary's womanhood, the man who prays the Rosary—if he truly understands what he is doing, and remains open to the truth of what he is doing—cannot help but grow in sensitivity to the dignity of all women, in particular the women with whom he lives and works. Such a man gradually deep-

ens his ability to love and respect his wife, if he is married; his sisters, if he has any; and the women with whom he works—indeed all women who cross his path each day. They express the same feminine qualities as the mother of the Son of God himself. Thus, for a man who prays the Rosary and truly understands what he is doing, it would be impossible to disrespect or denigrate women in any way or to think of them as in any way inferior to himself.

If the Rosary leads the male heart to honor, welcome, and respect women as equal and complementary beings, the Rosary leads women—for the same reasons—to respect and honor themselves precisely because they are women. For a woman to pray the Rosary is to place herself in the spiritual and very real presence of the woman whose profoundly simple—yet far from simpleminded—faith made possible God's plan for the salvation of the world. The God of Israel beckoned her but left her free to choose as she would. Her yes to God is a model for all of us—women and men—to say yes to whatever God's plan is for our lives. When a woman consciously places herself in the presence of this strong, gentle, no-nonsense, delightfully surprising woman, she opens herself to the influence and guidance of this woman who so bravely cooperated with the will and plan of God.

A woman who prays the Rosary is a woman who sees no reason to think of herself as inferior to anyone, regardless of gender. At the same time, she treasures the gift of her feminine nature as equal in dignity and complementary to the masculine nature of men. The last thing a woman who prays the Rosary is likely to do—if she understands fully what she is doing—is to become a doormat for any man, no matter what assumptions some men carry around in their heads about women.

In an era when violence against women—physical and otherwise—is not uncommon, the Rosary can and should be for women a source of strength and of the power to embrace and nourish their God-given dignity. Women can pray the Rosary knowing that the woman interceding for them understands precisely what it means to be a woman. In other words—astonishing as it may be to some—the Rosary is a feminist prayer, and women and men who pray and live it are feminists in the best and truest sense of the word.

"Feminism" means taking for granted that woman and man are meant to complement each other while sharing equal dignity, equal rights, and equal humanity—nothing more and nothing less. And "feminists" are men and women who are ready to stand up and work in practical, adult, no-nonsense ways to bring about acknowledgment of this equality in places and situations where it is ignored, denied, or overlooked, no matter by whom. Of course, "feminist" does not refer here to anyone who thinks of women as superior to men, any more than one should think of men as superior to women.

To say that the Rosary is a feminist prayer means that those who pray the Rosary acknowledge the equality and complementarity of women and men and are prepared to live out and work with that equality and complementarity. It does not mean, however, that those who pray the Rosary know the solutions or answers to the practical theological questions and issues that relate to gender roles in a given society and culture, or even in the church.

Indeed, those who pray the Rosary are perhaps more likely than others to be willing to eschew dogmatism, whether from the left or from the right, because to pray the Rosary is to open

oneself to the ultimate mystery of the incarnation—the entering into human nature and human history of the divine mystery that we call God, and that the First Letter of John (4:8) identifies as love itself. To open oneself to this mystery is to know a love that fills the deepest recesses of the human heart precisely because it far transcends the human intellect. Therefore, dogmatism—in effect, an implicit, arrogant claim to personal infallibility—is no longer an option. Only humble adoration and a silent tongue constitute an appropriate response to this love and this mystery.

Praying the Rosary, therefore, is spiritually and psychologically healthy for both men and women. It is so for men because the Rosary steeps a man's heart and soul in the feminine dignity and presence of the woman Mary. It is so for women because the Rosary steeps a woman's heart and soul in the feminine dignity and presence of the woman Mary. Thus, men who pray the Rosary with understanding grow to respect and honor all women more. And thus, women who pray the Rosary with understanding grow to respect and honor themselves more.

The Rosary Is a Human, Sensual Prayer

But there is still more to be said about the value of praying the Rosary. Another important reason to pray the Rosary is its incarnational nature. Because by custom the Rosary almost always includes the use of rosary beads, or some substitute for rosary beads, the Rosary is a remarkably sensual way to pray. To pray with a rosary is to have something to grab on to. Thus, prayer becomes more than a matter of thought, words, and bodily posture; it becomes a physical activity. You hold the cir-

clet of beads, you feel the beads with your fingers, and you move the beads through your hands, from one to the next. Your hands pray as much as your mind, your words, and the rest of your body. So the Rosary is an embodied form of prayer because it involves your sense of touch.

At times of particular sadness or anxiety, or moments of special happiness or rejoicing, it can be comforting to have the prayer beads of a rosary to cling to, to hang on to, to help you focus. That's one reason, no doubt, that the Rosary remains so popular after so many centuries, with so many people of faith.

It's also true that the Rosary falls into the rhythmic, repetitive kind of prayer that eastern religions refer to as "mantric." That is, it utilizes the repetition of a single prayer in order to help the person praying to both focus his or her attention and go deeper. The "over-and-overness" of the Hail Mary, especially, gives the mind—and when prayed aloud, the tongue—something to do. Our mind tends to be like a popcorn popper: pop-pop-pop-pop, thoughts, ideas, and nonsense going off randomly in all directions, often uncontrollably, when the intention is to pray. While the conscious mind is occupying itself with the repetition of the Hail Mary, the heart, one's deeper center, can slip into the presence of our source and ultimate goal: the triune God, Father, Son, and Holy Spirit, who is love, compassion, mercy, forgiveness, and healing peace.

But, you might ask, in using repetitive prayer aren't we guilty of violating the words of Jesus in the Gospel of Matthew: "When you are praying, do not heap up empty phrases as the Gentiles do; for they think that they will be heard because of their many words" (6:7)? Fortunately, because of the teachings of the church as well as the insights of Scripture scholarship, we

know that the answer to that question is no. The point of Jesus' words in the gospel is to remind us that we don't need to repeat our requests to God over and over again out of a concern that God might not hear us. That is not the purpose of the repetitive prayers of the Rosary. The repetition is for our sake, not God's. We repeat the Hail Mary simply as a way to maintain some focus during our prayer and to nourish what we might call a "state of prayerfulness." It has nothing to do with thinking that if we repeat the prayers of the Rosary, God will hear us because of our "many words."

Finally, some may remind us that we should pray the Rosary because the Blessed Virgin Mary herself, in various apparitions, instructed us to do so. This is a reason not without value and importance, to be sure. At the same time, we must remember that the Catholic Church has never required that we accept or believe in apparitions validated by church authorities. For those of us who accept with gratitude and joy the authenticity of the Marian apparitions at, for example, Fatima and Lourdes, the Blessed Mother's admonitions to pray the Rosary are welcome. But we must keep in mind that, even based on these apparitions, we never have a right to get pushy about the Rosary with anyone, not even Catholics.

Pray the Rosary for any or all of the reasons discussed in this chapter. To put it simply, we can say that praying the Rosary is a good idea because it is such a balanced, comprehensive, Christ-centered, spiritually nourishing, thoroughly human way to pray. In a nutshell, that's pretty much it!

CHAPTER 2

SEPARATING FACT FROM MYTH

The Origins and History of the Rosary

Nothing can take the place of a good grasp of history. That goes for being a good Catholic, and it goes for being a good citizen—both of a given country and of the world—and it applies equally to being a good devotee of the Rosary. The better we understand where the Rosary came from, and the better the grasp we have of the centuries-long story of the Rosary, the greater our appreciation will be for the Rosary and for what it can do for our intimacy with Christ and for our everyday spirituality.

The origin of the Rosary is usually linked with St. Dominic de Guzmán. He lived during the twelfth and thirteenth centuries when the Albigensian heresy was spreading across Western Europe. It taught, among other things, that the soul is good and the body evil, and that suicide is virtuous. A lesson in the Roman Breviary—the official collection of prayers in Latin used for daily prayer by the clergy prior to Vatican II—is relevant. According to the breviary lesson for the feast of the Holy Rosary, St. Dominic de Guzmán prayed earnestly to the Blessed Virgin Mary for her assistance in combatting Albigensianism.

Mary's response, according to the legend, was to instruct St. Dominic to preach and promote the use of the Rosary as an antidote to heresy and sin. As the story goes, the Blessed Virgin gave Dominic the Rosary and told him that if he promoted the devotion,

his religious order would flourish. According to the breviary, from then on the Rosary was "most wonderfully published abroad and developed by St. Dominic whom different Supreme Pontiffs have in various past ages in their apostolic letters declared to be the institutor and author of the same devotion."

Many popes have indeed encouraged and promoted the Rosary, and for many decades the popes took for granted that the story about St. Dominic was historically accurate. Later research has, however, led the overwhelming majority of historians and theologians to conclude that St. Dominic had nothing to do with the origins of the Rosary.

In fact, in its history of the Rosary, the *Catholic Encyclopedia* notes that many religious traditions have used a string of beads or some similar method to count prayers. For instance, archaeologists excavating ancient Nineveh found a sculpture of two winged female figures before a sacred tree, in a posture of prayer; each figure holds her right hand up, while in her left hand each holds a circular string of beads.

In addition, for many centuries Islam has had a tradition of using the Tasbith, or bead-string, consisting of thirty-three, sixty-six, or ninety-nine beads for counting the names of Allah. And Marco Polo, in the thirteenth century, visited a region of southern India called Malabar and reported that, to his surprise, the king there used a rosary of more than a hundred precious stones to count his prayers. In the mid-sixteenth century, St. Francis Xavier and his companions were equally astonished to find that strings of prayer beads were common among the Buddhists of Japan.

In eastern Christianity, too, rosaries have been employed for many centuries as aids to prayer. The *Catholic Encyclopedia*

reports that the monks of the Greek Orthodox Church used the *kombologion* or *komboschoinion,* a cord with a hundred knots in it, to count the making of genuflections and signs of the cross. In a similar vein, buried with the mummy of a Christian ascetic named Thaias who lived during the fourth century, archaeologists found a cribbage-board-like device, which they concluded—from accounts left by ancient authorities—was used to count prayers.

Other ancient sources report that a fourth-century hermit named, appropriately enough, Paul the Hermit, took upon himself the discipline of repeating three hundred prayers every day. To keep count, he gathered up three hundred pebbles and set one aside as each prayer was completed. In the eighth century, as an act of thanksgiving for the generosity of Pope Hadrian I, the monks of St. Apollinaris were required by the pope to say *Kyrie eleison* (Lord, have mercy) three hundred times twice a day, and scholars believe that the monks must have had some way to count these prayers, perhaps using pebbles in the style of Paul the Hermit.

Scholars have discovered that as early as A.D. 800, all the priests in a monastery were required to say one Mass and fifty psalms for each deceased monk. Other ancient sources reveal that each monk was to sing two sets of fifty psalms for the souls of certain generous benefactors, that each priest was to sing two Masses, and that each deacon was to read two passion narratives from the gospels.

As time went by, however, since most of the lay brothers in monasteries were illiterate and became distinct from the choir monks, they were allowed to substitute simple prayers in place of psalms. Thus, from a source dated A.D. 1096, we learn that

when the death of a monk in another monastery was announced, every priest was to offer Mass, and every non-priest was to either say fifty psalms or repeat the Our Father fifty times. In a similar vein, members of the Knights Templar, who followed a rule that originated in 1128, were instructed that if they could not attend choir, they were to say the Our Father fifty-seven times. And when a brother died, each one was required to say the Our Father a hundred times a day for a week.

Obviously, with all these prayers of specific numbers being prayed, it was necessary to have some way to accurately count them. By the eleventh and twelfth centuries, it had become common practice to use pebbles, berries, or discs of bone threaded on a string. About the year 1075, the Countess Godiva of Coventry bequeathed in her will to a statue of the Blessed Virgin a circlet of precious stones that she had threaded on a string in order to keep accurate count of her prayers.

In another case, researchers found in the tomb of St. Rosalia, who died in 1160, a string of beads similar to the one mentioned by the Countess Godiva. Indeed, the evidence is overwhelming that such strings of beads were common as prayer aids throughout the Middle Ages. In some European languages these strings of beads were known as "paternosters," since *pater noster* is Latin for "our father." The people who made paternosterers belonged to a widely recognized, prominent craft guild. A street in London called Paternoster Row traces its name to the street where members of this guild gathered.

It's reasonable to assume that the original purpose of these strings of beads was to count the numbers of times one recited the Our Father. This is likely not only because of their name, "paternosters," but also because the prayer we know now as

the Hail Mary wasn't used as a devotional prayer until the middle of the twelfth century.

When the Hail Mary did come into popular use, it included only the first two lines of the prayer as we know it: "Hail Mary, full of grace, the Lord is with thee. Blessed art thou among women, and blessed is the fruit of thy womb, Jesus." Evidently, people considered this a salutation, or greeting, to Mary rather than a prayer, per se, and this inspired the custom of repeating it many times in succession, often accompanied by genuflections, bows, or some other bodily act of devotion. Generically, we might compare this practice to secular customs such as the firing of twenty-one-gun salutes by the military; applause (which is actually the *repetitive* clapping together of the hands) given to a performer or speaker; or a series of cheers—"three cheers," for example—given to honor someone. Similarly, the degree of honor given by the repetition of a prayer was measured by the number of times it was recited.

In the twelfth century, prior to the birth of St. Dominic in 1170, the custom had already become widespread of reciting 50 or 150 Hail Marys (the same number as the number of psalms in the Bible). There were many different versions of the Rosary, some using as few as five mysteries, others as many as two hundred mysteries. Only in 1569 did a Rosary utilizing fifteen mysteries—joyful, sorrowful, and glorious—become the standard, with the publication of an encyclical by Pope Pius V in which he declared that this would henceforth be the official, church-authorized version. It would be more than four hundred years later that another pope, John Paul II, would add the five "luminous" mysteries to the Rosary.

Scholars have deciphered the historical development of the

Rosary from evidence present in many devotional works that date to this era. In particular, one mid-twelfth-century manuscript includes instructions for how to pray fifty Hail Marys, divided into sets of ten. Similar instructions occur in a document written for a community of English hermits that is dated some twenty years prior to the first Dominican foundations in that country. In other words, the custom of praying 50 or 150 Hail Marys developed apart from and prior to the preaching of St. Dominic.

Similarly remarkable is the historically verified fact that the practice of meditating on mysteries from the gospels—in truth, the very essence of the Rosary as we know it—became customary only long after the death of St. Dominic in 1221. In fact, the introduction of this practice into the Rosary was the work of a Carthusian monk, Dominic the Prussian, in the early fifteenth century. By the end of the fifteenth century, a wide variety of methods existed for praying the Rosary. The fifteen joyful, sorrowful, and glorious, mysteries, which came into popular use later on, were not used even by the Dominicans.

In its article "The Rosary Since Vatican II," the *Marian Library Newsletter* points out that the form of the Rosary most familiar today developed in Carthusian monasteries during the fourteenth and fifteenth centuries. As the Carthusians prayed it, the Rosary consisted of the scriptural words of the Hail Mary, with 50 and then 150 *clausulae,* or brief phrases, added after the name of Jesus: "and blessed is the fruit of thy womb, Jesus." The *clausulae* evolved into the fifteen joyful, sorrowful, and glorious mysteries mentioned at the beginning of each set of ten Hail Marys.

During the middle ages, the second part of the Hail Mary took

different forms. The wording that is so familiar today ("Holy Mary, mother of God, pray for us sinners, now and at the hour of our death. Amen.") seems to have appeared in print for the first time in the Roman Breviary published in 1568. Nothing connected this wording with the Rosary specifically, however.

The newsletter continues to say that from this time on, because various indulgences were attached to the Rosary, its basic form remained unchanged for more than four centuries. That's because any prayer that could earn indulgences was to be said only according to a clearly prescribed form. Even perfectly admirable customs, such as the use of the *clausulae,* were forbidden—unless, of course, an exception was granted, as was in fact done for areas where German was spoken and where the *clausulae* were usually added.

We have definite historical evidence that St. Dominic had nothing to do with originating the use of a string of beads as a counting device; nor did he think up the custom of repeating 50 or 150 Hail Marys. Both practices were in use long before Dominic was born. There is firm evidence that the practice of meditating on the mysteries came into vogue only after Dominic had been dead for two hundred years. Not even the earliest biographies of St. Dominic make any connection between the saint and the Rosary. Nor do any of the early constitutions written for the provinces of the Dominican order say anything about the Rosary.

Finally, historians have located hundreds, probably thousands, of devotional writings, sermons, and other documents written by Dominican friars between 1220 and 1450—roughly the two hundred fifty years following the death of St. Dominic—and not a single mention of the Rosary is made in any of them. No con-

nection appears in paintings and sculptures of the saint from these two and a half centuries. Even the tomb of St. Dominic in Bologna, Italy, and, without exception, the countless frescoes by Fra Angelico with images of Dominican friars ignore the Rosary completely.

Given all this evidence, then, where did the tradition that connected the origins of the Rosary to St. Dominic come from? The *Catholic Encyclopedia* reports that all the clues historians have discovered point to one source—namely, the preaching of a Dominican friar named Alanus de Rupe in the fifteenth century. He was the first to suggest that the devotion of Our Lady's Psalter, that is, the praying of 150 Hail Marys, came from or was rediscovered by St. Dominic.

Born about 1428 in Brittany, Alanus de Rupe died at Zwolle, in Holland, in 1475. Early in life he entered the Dominican order, and while pursuing his studies at St. Jacques, Paris, he distinguished himself in philosophy and theology. From 1459 to 1475 he taught almost uninterruptedly at Paris, Lille, Douai, Ghent, and then Rostock, Germany, where in 1473 he was made master of sacred theology. During his sixteen years of teaching, he became a renowned and popular preacher.

Alanus de Rupe seems to have been a devout, devoted, and sincere man, but evidently, as the *Catholic Encyclopedia* suggests, he was also somewhat deluded. He based his claims about the Rosary and St. Dominic upon the testimony of writers who never existed. All the same, the Rosary confraternities organized by de Rupe and his confreres in cities such as Douai and Cologne attracted a great many enthusiastic participants. Following his death, numerous books were published that were filled with the ideas of Alanus de Rupe. This, then, is the source

of the legend that St. Dominic received the Rosary from the Blessed Virgin Mary.

Pope Leo X was the first pope to write approvingly of this legend as though it might be factual, in 1520, and he did so with some reserve. Many later popes, however, accepted the legend as historical, with few if any reservations at all.

There is no doubt, of course, that the widespread popularity of the Rosary in the modern era and the immeasurable good that has come from it is due in large part to the efforts and prayers of Dominican friars and women religious. But the historical evidence leaves no doubt that Dominican interest in the Rosary emerged only during the last years of the fifteenth century, long after the death of St. Dominic.

As far as the name "Rosary" is concerned, it comes from the Latin *rosarius*, meaning a garland or bouquet of roses. The earliest use of the term was figurative, as for example, in the title of a book to refer to a collection of short writings or selections from longer works. A widely popular medieval European legend told a story in which the Blessed Virgin Mary took rosebuds from the lips of a young monk as he recited Hail Marys. She then wove the rosebuds into a garland, which she placed upon her own head.

The name Our Lady's Psalter, perhaps the first name given to what we know as the Rosary, dates to about the same era. In the fourteenth-century works of Chaucer, the old English name was a "pair of beads," the word "bead" originally meaning "prayers."

The Rosary, in various forms, has been a popular part of Catholic devotional spirituality for nearly seven hundred years. The *Marian Library Newsletter* reports that Pope Leo XIII (1878–1903) wrote no less than thirteen encyclicals on the

Rosary, and in the twentieth century, popes have time and again encouraged its use. Pope John Paul II, whose papacy linked the twentieth and twenty-first centuries, promoted the Rosary as much as anyone.

During the twentieth century, countless ordinary Catholics, priests, bishops, men and women religious, and notable Catholic intellectuals—the great German Jesuit theologian Karl Rahner, the American Trappist monk and author Thomas Merton, and Dorothy Day, the cofounder of the Catholic Worker movement, among them—prayed the Rosary. In the 1940s and 1950s, Rosary devotions, crusades, and football-stadium-size rallies were a popular part of Catholic life. Messages from the Marian apparitions at Fatima and Lourdes included calls to pray the Rosary. The popular American "television priest" Bishop Fulton J. Sheen explained the use of the Rosary to huge audiences, both Catholic and non-Catholic. Fr. Patrick Peyton, of the Congregation of Holy Cross, the famous "Rosary priest," worked unceasingly to promote the Rosary through crusades and rallies in all parts of the world.

In the mid-1960s, the Second Vatican Council recommended devotion to Mary but said nothing about the Rosary. The council rightly placed considerable emphasis on the centrality of the Mass in Catholic life. Following Vatican II, evening Masses replaced evening Marian devotions in some places, and the assumption became widespread that participation in the Mass ought to take the place of all communal and private devotions. However, there is no evidence that Vatican II meant to do away with popular devotions such as the Rosary. All the council did was to teach that popular devotions should not compete with the Eucharist, but should support and lead to it.

All the same, during the decades following the Second Vatican Council, the Rosary was far less in evidence than it had been during the first half of the twentieth century. During the 1970s, what some perceived to be a crisis in Marian devotion was well under way. Some charged that both Vatican II and the liturgical reforms sparked by the council were deeply anti-Marian. In May 1971, Fr. Patrick Peyton, who was director of the Family Rosary Crusade, wrote a strongly worded letter to Pope Paul VI, in which he urged the pope to declare the Rosary a liturgical prayer. This would have placed it on the same level as, for example, the Liturgy of the Hours, formerly known as the Roman Breviary.

Pope Paul VI asked the Vatican Congregation for Divine Worship to prepare a draft of a document that would encourage families to pray the Rosary. The members of the congregation asked Father Ignacio Calabuig, OSM, and the faculty of the Pontifical Theological Faculty Marianum, in Rome, to study the matter and come up with a draft for an encyclical. Three years and four revisions later, they sent a draft to the pope including three forms of the Rosary that might be recommended for use. Pope Paul VI responded with disapproval, noting that it would be confusing and discouraging to people to appear to alter the traditional form of the Rosary.

Marialis Cultus (For the Right Ordering and Development of Devotion to the Blessed Virgin Mary), the apostolic exhortation by Pope Paul VI on devotion to Mary originally inspired by Father Peyton's 1971 letter, was published in February 1974. The document discussed the place of Marian devotion in the liturgy of the church, provided directives for developing that devotion, and encouraged the restoration and a better understanding of

the Rosary among the people. It also included a section outlining the characteristics of the Rosary, which the *Marian Library Newsletter* summarizes succinctly in these words:

a) Contemplative—"By its nature the Rosary calls for a quiet rhythm and a lingering pace, helping the individual to meditate on the mysteries of the Lord's life as seen through the eyes of her who was closest to the Lord." Without the contemplative element, the Rosary becomes a "mechanical repetition of formulas, . . . a body without a soul."

b) Christ-centered and Marian—"The Rosary is a 'compendium of the entire Gospel' centered on the mystery of the redemptive Incarnation." It is directed toward the events of Christ's life as seen by Mary.

c) In Harmony with the Liturgy—Since the Rosary is centered on the same mysteries celebrated in the liturgy, it is "excellent preparation" for and a "continuing echo" of the liturgy. ("The Rosary Since Vatican II," *Marian Library Newsletter,* Spring 1995)

The newsletter goes on to say that *Marialis cultus* also called for adaptations to the Rosary so that its "spiritual richness" might be appreciated more. This had several results. One of the most remarkable, which has not, in fact, gained widespread acceptance, is called the Fiat Rosary. It was developed by Cardinal Leon Suenens, of the Netherlands, and approved by both Pope Paul VI and Pope John Paul II. In this form of the Rosary, the first prayer said is one to the Holy Spirit. The purpose of this prayer is to place the one praying, in union with Mary,

consciously into the very center of the joyful, sorrowful, and glorious mysteries of Christ. In the Fiat Rosary, there are nine mysteries, three taken from each of the joyful, sorrowful, and glorious mysteries. For each mystery, the one praying says three, rather than ten, Hail Marys, followed by a Glory Be. The Fiat Rosary can be prayed on traditional rosary beads by using only the first three decades.

The huge popularity of the Rosary down through the centuries should not be taken to mean, however, that it has suited everyone equally. The *Marian Library Newsletter* notes that in her writings, the great nineteenth-century French mystic and saint Thérèse of Lisieux wrote words that, in the first editions of the manuscript that later became her autobiography, were deleted by well-meaning editors. Thérèse wrote: "What difficulties I have had throughout my life with saying the Rosary. I am ashamed to say that the recitation of the Rosary was at times more painful than an instrument of torture."

The newsletter went on to point out that in a similar vein, Fr. Vincent Dwyer, a twentieth-century American Trappist monk and author, wrote that the Rosary is "one of the great vehicles that helped people enter the quiet space with the Master"; yet, he continued, "I myself find it impossible to say the Rosary, but it is always with me in my pocket."

While the Rosary experienced some decline during the last thirty or forty years of the twentieth century, the first few years of this century are witnessing an increase in interest in this traditional prayer form. There is something about the Rosary that makes it attractive and rewarding. St. Thérèse and Fr. Dwyer will always have their sympathizers, and for some the Rosary may never be suitable. But most people who give the Rosary a

chance find themselves basking in its spiritual riches and in the calm that it tends to engender. The Rosary is a prayer of quiet, of listening, and of active acceptance of God's will in all things, and this kind of prayer will never be out of fashion.

The Rosary as we know it today is the result of a centuries-long development. Still, the heart of the matter has always been basically the same. Praying the Rosary is a way for devout, faith-filled Catholics to remind themselves that "this is the day that the LORD has made" (Psalm 118:24). Above all, the Rosary is a way to bring to mind the life and gospel of Christ, in companionship with his—and our—Blessed Mother, Mary.

CHAPTER 3

MORE THAN JUST
A STRING OF BEADS

The Prayers of the Rosary

Each of the prayers that make up the Rosary contributes something essential to a balanced, mature Christian faith and to adult ways of living that faith. We can say, indeed, that the Rosary reflects the most basic aspects of the Christian faith. Let's take a look, now, at these prayers and see what we can gain toward a deeper understanding of each one.

The Sign of the Cross

In the name of the Father, and of the Son, and of the Holy Spirit. Amen.

We begin by praying the Sign of the Cross, which gives the entire Rosary trinitarian character, invoking the triune God: Father, Son, and Holy Spirit. With this prayer and its accompanying sacred gesture—touching forehead, then chest, then left and right shoulders—we also declare our commitment to the Catholic faith and the one, holy, catholic, and apostolic church—meaning all of us—whose mission it is to live, nourish,

and preserve that faith in this world. We do not pray only in the name of the Father, or only in the name of the Son, or only in the name of the Holy Spirit, but in the name of the triune God.

By this prayer-gesture, we remind ourselves, too, that we do all things in the name of the cross of Christ. We remind ourselves of the cross not merely as the instrument of the death of Jesus more than two thousand years ago, but also as the means of our salvation. By virtue of our baptism, all the dark, painful, troubled, and anguished times in our lives become a share in the cross of Christ, through which we will also share in his resurrection. We affirm our acceptance of this reality when we bless ourselves with the Sign of the Cross.

At the same time, by making the Sign of the Cross, we affirm our identity as Catholics, for one of the ancient traditions that the Protestant Reformation abandoned was this one. Indeed, we have written testimony from the early second century that Christians practiced the custom of tracing the Sign of the Cross on their foreheads. So, for many generations up to the present day, to bless oneself with the Sign of the Cross has been to identify oneself as Catholic. The Eastern Orthodox churches retain this tradition, too, but in a slightly different form, touching the right shoulder first and then the left.

Making the Sign of the Cross, we pray, saying, "In the name of the Father, and of the Son, and of the Holy Spirit." But what, we may ask, does it mean to pray "in the name of" someone? In ordinary human parlance, to speak in someone else's name means to speak for him or her, to represent his or her thoughts and, indeed, his or her person. An attorney speaks "in the name of" the client, for example. A diplomatic envoy speaks "in the name of" the president or government of his or her country.

In other words, to speak "in the name of" someone else is to present oneself as a genuinely designated representative of that other person and one appointed to speak for him or her.

It may seem presumptuous, therefore, to pray "in the name of" the Father, the Son, and the Holy Spirit. By what right do we address our prayers to the triune God "in the name of" the Trinity's own self? But that is the great joy and dignity of our baptism. For when we were baptized, we were baptized into Christ, and we were baptized "in the name of the Father, and of the Son, and of the Holy Spirit." Through baptism we became members of the mystical body of Christ. As St. Paul explains, "Now you are the body of Christ and individually members of it" (1 Corinthians 12:27). So, to prayerfully make the Sign of the Cross and speak the words "In the name of the Father, and of the Son, and of the Holy Spirit" is to speak from our membership in the body of Christ that St. Paul talks about. Because we are "in Christ," we can pray to God in his own name, since there is no distance between God and ourselves. When the Father looks at his Son, we might say, he cannot help but see us, too.

The Apostles' Creed

I believe in God, the Father almighty, Creator of heaven and earth, and in Jesus Christ, his only Son, our Lord, who was conceived by the Holy Spirit, born of the Virgin Mary, suffered under Pontius Pilate, was crucified, died, and was buried. He descended into hell. The third day he rose again from the dead. He ascended into heaven and is seated at the right hand of the Father. From thence he shall come to judge the living and the dead. I believe in the Holy Spirit,

the holy Catholic Church, the communion of saints, the forgiveness of sins, the resurrection of the body, and life everlasting. Amen.

Although the Apostles' Creed didn't become part of the Rosary until sometime in the seventeenth century, it is the oldest extant prayer of its kind in the Christian tradition, dating back to the early decades of the church. It was not, however, as the title suggests, composed by the twelve apostles of Jesus. Rather, the point of this title is that the prayer conveys the "mind" of the apostles—the content of their belief, if you will.

When we pray the Apostles' Creed, we consciously unite ourselves to the earliest followers of the risen Christ and to the countless ordinary believers—saints and sinners—who preceded us down through history, endless numbers of whom prayed the very prayer we are praying and held in their hands rosaries very much like the rosaries we hold in our hands today as we say this prayer.

The words of this creed, this prayerful, concise expression of the content of our belief, carry considerable meaning in every phrase, so we will benefit from taking a closer look at each part of the prayer.

"I believe in God, the Father almighty, . . ." With these words, we embrace the metaphor for God clearly preferred by Jesus in the gospels and, indeed, by the New Testament as a whole— namely, "Father." The Aramaic word that Jesus used is *Abba,* which is perhaps more accurately translated as "Papa," or even "loving Papa." This, at any rate, is how we should understand the metaphor "Father" when applied to God. In other words,

God has the same warm, strong, welcoming, and always-forgiving love for us that a human "loving papa" has for his children. More about the term "Father" below. . . .

To "Father," the creed immediately adds the modifier "almighty." A dictionary defines "almighty" as "having absolute power; all-powerful." Sometimes we wonder why, if God is almighty, doesn't he do something to stop the wars, innocent suffering, and cruelty in the world. Why doesn't God simply rid the world of evil? Why doesn't God cure people who have terminal illnesses? Why doesn't he punish people who hurt innocent children? To ask such questions, however, is to misunderstand who God is and in what sense he is almighty. God's all-powerfulness is absolute, but so also is his wisdom, which leaves all human beings free—free even to choose evil and act maliciously. And while terminal illnesses, natural disasters, and the like wreak havoc and spread pain and sorrow, all these things provide us with opportunities to practice charity and act in "godlike" ways, if we will, to one another. Our belief in an all-powerful God leaves both the mystery of God's love and the reality of evil and suffering intact.

The almightyness of God is best understood in his action as Creator as the source of all things in creation; hence, the words that immediately follow "almighty." Also, it is no accident that the Apostles' Creed calls God both "almighty" and "Father"—that is, "loving Papa"—at the same time. The two images are meant to condition and qualify each other. It makes perfect sense, then, that this prayer is followed immediately by the prayer that addresses God as "our Father."

". . . *Creator of heaven and earth*, . . ." So, the God who is both "almighty" and "Father" (loving Papa) is precisely the

God who created or brought into existence everything that is. He created the world "according to his wisdom" not because he needed to, or by chance, but because he "wanted to make his creatures share in his being, wisdom, and goodness" (*Catechism of the Catholic Church,* 295). God had no other reason for creating us other than his love and goodness, and he wants to share his life with us, his creatures.

"*. . . and [I believe] in Jesus Christ, his only Son, our Lord, . . .*" These words make the point that Jesus of Nazareth, who became the risen Christ, is the "only" Son of God. Here is the second real crunch point of the Apostles' Creed. The first one is belief in God. Given belief in God, however, once you believe that Jesus is and was God's "only Son," then you have no choice but to be a Christian, because no other major religious founder, leader, or prophet has ever claimed to be who Jesus and the Christian tradition claim that he is—namely God's "only Son." If you believe this, then the only choice you can make is to be a Christian.

"*. . . who was conceived by the Holy Spirit, born of the Virgin Mary, suffered under Pontius Pilate, was crucified, died, and was buried.*" The main point of these words is to declare Jesus' divine and human nature and the truth that he really and truly lived and died in a specific time in actual human history. Why mention Pontius Pilate, one might ask. The point of mentioning the name of the Roman figure most directly responsible for Jesus' crucifixion is to emphasize the historicity of Jesus' life and death, to fix it at a precise time in human history—namely, during the years when the Roman procurator of Judea was one Pontius Pilate, from about the years A.D. 25 to 35. The main point of these words is to declare that Jesus, in both his humanity and his divinity, endured the pain of being nailed to a cross

and died a real death, and that his really and truly dead body was placed in a tomb.

"He descended into hell." Probably the most perplexing words in the Apostles' Creed, this phrase may well leave even many Catholics wondering what it means. However, a few minutes doing a little research does clear things up considerably. In his still-excellent work *Dictionary of the Bible* (Milwaukee: Bruce, 1965), the late Father John L. McKenzie is about as helpful as anyone has ever been or is ever likely to be when it comes to explaining the point of this phrase. Father McKenzie writes,

> The phrase "descended into hell" rests upon the language of the O[ld] T[estament]. "Hell" here represents the H[e]b[rew] Sheol, the abode of the dead. The concept of Sheol in the O[ld] T[estament] implies no reward or punishment and no distinction between the state of the good and the wicked. In the O[ld] T[estament] "to die" is "to descend into Sheol" and one who rises from the dead rises from Sheol.

In other words, the Apostles' Creed is being redundant here. It says something like, "He died, and he really and truly died." Interpretations of this phrase that rely upon legendary traditions—suggesting, for example, that when Jesus died, he went to release from hell the great figures from the Old Testament era—are best ignored. As Father McKenzie comments, such interpretations "have no basis in the New Testament."

"The third day he rose again from the dead." With the statement that Jesus' resurrection happened on "the third day," once again the Apostles' Creed insists on the temporal and historical

nature of events that are foundational to the Christian faith and to the church. Then, with no attempt to interpret or explain, the creed simply states the resurrection of Jesus as a historical fact. Those who have experienced the presence of the risen Lord need no proof, and for those who have not, no proof is possible. Empirical, scientific data are not the only valid and acceptable kinds of data upon which to base one's life, choices, and behavior. In other words, even atheism is as much of a belief system as any religion, requiring a similar "leap of faith."

These words do not attempt to explain Jesus' resurrection; they leave the mystery intact. Theologians may ponder and hypothesize, and they may do so to our benefit. Indeed, some suggest, for example, that Jesus' resurrection was an event that happened in, but also transcended, time and space. Such attempts to aid the modern imagination can be helpful, but none will ever clear up the ultimate mystery of the Christian faith. The believing "heart" relates better to the resurrection than does the intellect, but it can never be divorced from the intellect.

"He ascended into heaven and is seated at the right hand of the Father." These words simply clarify metaphorically that through his resurrection, Jesus entered, fully human and fully divine, into complete intimacy with the same Father first named in the beginning of the creed.

"From thence he shall come to judge the living and the dead." This phrase echoes the words of Jesus in Matthew 25:31-46. In Matthew's gospel, Jesus tells the familiar story of the sheep and goats at the last judgment. The inclination may be to place the emphasis on the judgment, but the clear intention of Jesus in telling this story is to teach his disciples the importance of feeding the hungry, clothing the naked, and so forth. So fundamen-

tal are these works of mercy, that our eternal destiny depends on whether we act in merciful ways toward others or not. That's probably the best idea to keep in mind with regard to the words in the Apostles' Creed regarding the final judgment, too. The intention is not to scare the living daylights out of us, but to inspire us to live and act in compassionate ways.

"*I believe in the Holy Spirit, . . .*" With the first two Persons of the holy Trinity already covered earlier in the prayer, the creed now makes clear that Christians do believe in a triune God, the third Person of whom is the Holy Spirit. The creed declares belief in the Spirit without attempting to provide a theological explanation of the Holy Spirit's identity. That was left to later theological reflection. All that matters here is that Christian faith includes belief in Father, Son, and Holy Spirit. One must look elsewhere to clarify the nature of belief in the Trinity.

"*. . . the holy Catholic Church, . . .*" The Nicene Creed, approved by the Council of Nicea in A.D. 325, uses a lowercase "c" for the word "catholic," meaning "universal" in the generic sense of the word, when it declares belief in "one, holy, catholic and apostolic church." Not so the Apostles' Creed. Belief here is in the Catholic Church and no other Christian community or tradition. Hence, the rare attempt to adapt the Rosary for Protestant use typically substitutes the Nicene Creed for the Apostles' Creed, primarily because the Nicene Creed speaks of the "catholic church" rather than the "Catholic Church."

"*. . . the communion of saints, . . .*" This is one of the least-appreciated aspects of Catholic belief. In truth, this belief encompasses so much as to boggle the mind. In a nutshell, "the communion of saints" refers to the entire community that is the church in time and space and eternity. Everyone who belongs to the church

now present in the world and in history, and everyone who ever belonged to the church who has "passed on" to the mystery that is eternity/heaven belongs to the communion of saints.

In the creed, we express our belief that we belong to a community that is in, and transcends, the everyday world we experienced yesterday, are experiencing today, and will probably experience tomorrow. The mind-boggling part happens when we begin to ponder the implications of our membership in this community. If all this is true, what does it mean here and now? This isn't the appropriate place to go into all the possibilities—that could take another book. But think it over. What does it mean to you that you have a real and intimate personal relationship with all other believers in the world and with all those who have already passed through the thin veil that separates this world from the next?

"... *the forgiveness of sins, ...*" Well, you may think, this isn't so difficult to understand. We believe that God forgives sins, of course. Nothing complicated about that. Ah, but believing in the forgiveness of sins in the abstract is one thing, and believing in the forgiveness of sins for, say, yourself, is quite another. You there—you with all your mostly pitiful little sins, and your mean, selfish, little sinfulness, and your huge tendency to not really trust in God's love—you there, do you really and truly believe in the forgiveness of your sins? Do you have any sins that you just can't forget about, even if you have already confessed them in the Sacrament of Reconciliation? If so, chances are that you have a tough time believing in the forgiveness of sins. Psychological insights into spirituality insist that sometimes the most difficult part of believing in God's forgiveness is being able to forgive yourself. So this isn't as simple as it looks, is it?

"... *the resurrection of the body*, ..." We rattle this phrase off easily; how smoothly it rolls off the tongue. Here it is, what we might call the ultimate mystery of the Christian life, and with a blithe spirit we claim it for ourselves. It is a "mystery," we admit that. But do we realize that for Christian faith, a mystery isn't the same thing as a nut to crack or a puzzle to solve? Theologians try at length to explain the meaning of Christian mysteries. Certainly, the kind of mystery that faith speaks of isn't the same as the kinds of mysteries you find in a "whodunit" novel. A Christian mystery isn't merely something that we'll never completely understand, although it is that, too. Also, a Christian mystery isn't just a truth that we can only know because it is revealed by God.

Perhaps the best and most concise way to explain what we mean by "mystery" here is that it is a human experience of the divine; we can experience it but we can't fully grasp it intellectually. The heart can know it better than the intellect can know it, although the intellect can know something about it. We need to be able to trust both brain and heart. Authentic Christian faith includes both the mind and the heart, and we have a tendency to trust one more than the other, when we need to trust both. Well might we reflect on the admonition of the seventh-century French Catholic mathematician and philosopher Blaise Pascal, who understood the need to balance both intellect and heart. "If we submit everything to reason," he wrote, "our religion will be left with nothing mysterious or supernatural. If we offend the principles of reason, our religion will be absurd and ridiculous" (*Pensées,* § IV, 273).

The point here is that the resurrection is the ultimate mystery for any of us, because when we pray the Apostles' Creed, we claim that we accept that our ultimate destiny is "the resurrec-

tion of the body." The best, indeed the only, information we have about what this means comes from the resurrection narratives in the gospels, especially the accounts of the disciples' encounters with the risen Jesus. From these narratives, we gather more about what resurrection does not mean than what it does mean. Resurrection does not mean the resuscitation of a corpse, for it's clear that the risen Christ's body is not the same as your run-of-the-mill, everyday body. He enters rooms without using the door, for example. Yet, he shares a meal of cooked fish, and he invites Thomas to touch his wounds, so we're not talking about a totally spiritualized, nonmaterial body either.

The long and the short of it is that, first, we believe that our ultimate destiny includes "the resurrection of the body." And second, we sure look forward to experiencing that, whatever it is!

". . . and life everlasting. Amen." This final phrase from the Apostles' Creed can be misleading, because "everlasting" is a concept that relies on categories of time and space. "Everlasting" sounds like endless time, but that's not what the creed means here. It means "eternal" life, and "eternal" is not the same as "everlasting." The reference here is to what we might call another way or mode of being—and even that doesn't do it justice. The point is that we pass through ordinary death to Something Else and We're Really Going to Like It. And we'll find out what it is only on the other side of death.

The final word, "amen," means, of course, that we totally do agree with and embrace everything we just said in praying the Apostles' Creed—or, at least, we want to totally embrace it, and we're trying to totally embrace it. "Lord, I do believe. Help my unbelief." It's a sort of religious term for "Right on!" or "Ain't no doubt about it!"

The Our Father

The Our Father is based upon the prayer Jesus teaches to his disciples in the Gospels of Matthew (6:9-13) and Luke (11:2-4), more the former than the latter. This is the one prayer that all Christians share, for precisely this reason, although Protestants add an ancient but nonscriptural doxology, "For thine is the kingdom, and the power, and the glory, forever." Because this doxology is not without historical merit today, Catholics add a version of it—in the context of the Mass only—separated from the Our Father itself by a prayer said by the priest.

It is not without significance that Jesus teaches his disciples to address God as *Abba,* meaning "Father" or "loving Papa." Christian feminists sometimes suggest that we should, at the very least, sometimes also use the metaphor "Mother" to refer to God. They base this suggestion on the assertion—which can neither be proven nor disproven—that to use the metaphor "Father" for God, or to use masculine pronouns to refer to God, supports and fosters authoritarian paternalism and anti-female biases in the church.

Nevertheless, regardless of the cultural or theological ideology of our particular historical era, there are compelling historical, scriptural, and practical reasons to continue the use of the appellation "Father" and the masculine pronouns consistent with it.

It's true that in a few instances in the gospels, Jesus uses a female character as a metaphor for God, such as the woman who lights a candle and sweeps her house searching for a lost silver coin, in Luke 15:8-10. In Matthew 23:37, Jesus compares himself to the hen who gathers her brood under her wings. But Jesus

never calls God his or our "mother," and he never uses feminine pronouns to refer directly to God. Rather, the only mother Jesus has when he is incarnated is his human mother, Mary. By extension, in virtue of our baptism, we must say the same. In Christ, God is our Father and Mary is our mother—God in divine, loving, papa-like ways, Mary in heavenly, yet human, mother-like ways, always keeping in mind the special nature of her relationship with her fully divine and fully human Son.

In his excellent book *Calling God "Father": Essays on the Bible, Fatherhood & Culture,* Canadian Protestant Scripture scholar John W. Miller writes,

> Not once in biblical tradition is God ever spoken of as "she" or "her" or regarded as genderless. On the other hand, God is not portrayed there simply as male either, but as a father whose tenderness and compassion are often mother-like. In no instance does this imply that God has become a mother-figure to his worshipers. The uniformity of the canonical representation of God as father is one of its most notable features. (New York: Paulist Press, 1999, p. 5)

That said, we must nevertheless note that gender is a human characteristic and not necessarily a divine characteristic. But for Jesus to become human, he had to be born of a woman. From a human perspective, then, and consistent with the way that we as human beings understand procreation, Mary is Jesus' mother, and God, then, is Jesus' father. In calling God his, and our, Father—a relationship with which we, as human beings, are intimately familiar—Jesus tells us a great deal not only about how we should relate to God, but about how God feels about

us. That's not to say that God isn't mother-like as well as father-like, but that from a human standpoint it wouldn't make sense to call God "Mother." (In fact, many men could benefit from more of a "feminine" perspective, which is another benefit of saying the Rosary!)

Some Catholic feminists, in liturgical references and elsewhere, change references to God as "Father" to "God," thus preferring an impersonal, genderless God to a personal, fatherly God. Sometimes they change "Father" to "Mother." In other instances they change "Father" to "loving God," "compassionate God." Such changes, though, while well-intentioned, are inconsistent with scriptural tradition and with our understanding of familial relationships.

At the same time, however, we must admit that the version of the Our Father used most commonly includes words and phrases that are either archaic, misleading, or both. This familiar version is beloved by the countless people who use it, and it is highly unlikely that it will be changed in the foreseeable future. Still, for the sake of a better understanding of the Our Father, it can only be helpful to look at the meanings most likely first intended both by Jesus and by Matthew and Luke, who record the Lord's Prayer in their gospels.

At first glance, the text of the Lord's Prayer in Matthew's gospel (below, left) seems rather similar to the Our Father (below, right). As we go line by line through the text, though, we will notice places at which Matthew's gospel seems to better convey Jesus' meaning, particularly toward the end of each prayer:

Matthew 6:9-13	Our Father
Our Father in heaven,	Our Father, who art in heaven,
hallowed be your name.	hallowed be thy name.
Your kingdom come.	Thy kingdom come.
Your will be done,	Thy will be done,
on earth as it	on earth as it
is in heaven.	is in heaven.
Give us this day	Give us this day
our daily bread.	our daily bread.
And forgive us our debts,	And forgive us our trespasses
as we also have forgiven	as we forgive those who
our debtors.	trespass against us.
And do not bring us to	And lead us not into
the time of trial,	temptation
but rescue us from	but deliver us from evil.
the evil one.	Amen.

"*Our Father, who art in heaven, hallowed be thy name.*" Jesus taught his apostles and us that God is our father as well as his, and we acknowledge that relationship when we pray this first line. We don't talk about many things as being "hallowed" these days, and in fact, "hallowed" is a rather old-fashioned if not archaic word for "holy" or "sanctified." So, when we begin to say the Our Father, we are telling God that we think of him as a father and that we know that he is worthy of our devotion.

"*Thy kingdom come.*" In this line we express our desire to bring about the kingdom of God on earth—as he originally intended it at the creation of the world. The Greek term *basileia*,

which is translated as "kingdom" here, is sometimes also translated as "reign," which suggests even more the active or dynamic nature of what Jesus is talking about. The Greek word refers, in essence, to the glory of God, or God's very presence itself, permeating all of creation. The late Fr. Raymond Brown, SS, in his pioneering essay "The Pater Noster as an Eschatological Prayer," suggested that if we were to paraphrase, we might say that "Thy kingdom come" means something like "May your divine presence permeate all of creation right now" (*New Testament Essays,* New York: Paulist Press, 1965).

"Thy will be done, on earth as it is in heaven." Jesus, as well as the early Jewish Christian community for which the Gospel of Matthew was written, took for granted that God's "will" refers to God's ultimate plan for all creation, that is, the redemption and subjecting of all things to the Father's will, specifically in the person of his Son, Jesus (see Ephesians 1:5-12). When the early Christians prayed these words, they knew full well that they were asking their Father/loving Papa to bring about, immediately, the final completion of all things in Christ and the end of time. Think about that the next time you pray these words!

"Give us this day our daily bread . . ." Who does not pray these words and assume that this is a prayer for three square meals a day? While this is a perfectly understandable prayer to pray, it's not at all what these words in the Our Father mean. Fr. Brown suggests that Jesus is referring here is to the "living" bread of the Eucharist. It makes perfect sense, then, that the Our Father begins the Liturgy of the Eucharist in the Mass. Other scholars have suggested still a different interpretation, which also has its basis in Scripture. In this interpretation, when we ask God to "give us this day our daily bread," we are giving

control of our lives completely to him and agreeing to follow his will for us. In the same chapter of Matthew's gospel, Jesus says, " Do not worry, saying 'What will we eat?' or 'What will we drink?' or 'What will we wear?' . . . [I]ndeed your heavenly Father knows that you need all these things. But strive first for the kingdom of God and his righteousness, and all these things will be given to you as well" (6:31-33).

"And forgive us our trespasses as we forgive those who trespass against us." The key word here is "forgive." We ask for our Father's forgiveness in light of our forgiveness of others. The Greek word translated in the familiar version of the prayer as "trespasses" is, however, more accurately translated as "debts," as in the above translation of Matthew's gospel: "And forgive us our debts, as we also have forgiven our debtors" (6:12). The implication seems to be that sin results in being indebted. If we presume that sin damages our relationships with both God and neighbor, then through sin we become spiritually indebted to both God and neighbor. The second part of this phrase makes a direct correlation between God's forgiveness of us and our forgiveness of those whose sins leave them indebted to us. God's forgiveness of us depends on our forgiveness of one another.

"And lead us not into temptation . . ." If any part of the familiar version of the Our Father begs to be changed, it's probably this one, because it so clearly misrepresents the meaning intended by Jesus and by the Gospel of Matthew. The trouble with this phrase is that it clearly implies that God is responsible for temptation. There are some very ancient texts in the Old Testament that speak of God's tempting people, but usually the reference is more to a testing, not to God's actually trying to trip people up. The New Testament's Letter of James says, "No

one, when tempted, should say, 'I am being tempted by God'; for God cannot be tempted by evil and he himself tempts no one" (1:13). We can avoid this conundrum, however, if, with Fr. Brown, we realize that the intended meaning of this phrase is a reference to the final conflict, at the end of time, between God and Satan. A better translation might be "and lead us not into trial" (See the text of the Our Father in Matthew's gospel), which is actually, in the original Greek, a prayer asking God to spare us from any need to even show our faces to Satan at the final coming of the kingdom of God.

"*. . . but deliver us from evil.*" Some Scripture scholars opt for translating this "but deliver us from the Evil One," as in the translation of the Our Father in Matthew's gospel, instead of "from evil." Regardless, the meaning is clear that we are petitioning our Father to save us from all kinds of bad news and bad experiences—all that is bad, wrong, or wicked in any way.

"*Amen.*" Catholics sometimes forget to conclude the Our Father with an "amen" because they have learned not to say it at Mass until after the priest's prayer and the doxology. But, as in our other prayers, it is an important sign that we believe and intend to live by the words that we have just prayed.

It seems more than fitting that the Our Father should have a prominent place in the Rosary as a Christian devotional prayer, because it is the prayer that Jesus taught us to pray. It is the indispensable prayer for Christians that, in a very real way, sums up and crowns all of our prayers by affirming our relationship with God as well as the way we are to live our lives.

The Hail Mary

Hail, Mary, full of grace,
 the Lord is with thee (you).
Blessed art thou (are you) among women,
 and blessed is the fruit of thy (your) womb, Jesus.
Holy Mary, mother of God, pray for us sinners,
 now and at the hour of our death. Amen.

The Hail Mary is recited more times than any other prayer in the Rosary and is the prayer that we most commonly associate with the Rosary. As we know it today, the Hail Mary consists of three sentences, two of which are scriptural greetings, and the last of which is a petition. Like the Our Father, the familiar version of the Hail Mary uses the archaic words "thee," "thy," and "art thou" rather than the more contemporary if also more pedestrian terms "you," "your," and "are." The older version of the prayer may suggest more of a sense of holiness and mystery, but you should feel free to use whichever version is more comfortable for you.

"Hail Mary, full of grace, the Lord is with thee (you)." When we say the first part of the Hail Mary, we echo the greeting of the angel Gabriel to Mary in the infancy narrative recorded in the Gospel of Luke. When the angel appeared to Mary, he said, "Greetings, favored one! The Lord is with you. . . . [Y]ou have found favor with God" (1:28, 30). When we greet Mary in this way, we acknowledge the special grace that God bestowed upon Mary in asking her to be the mother of his Son.

"Blessed art thou (are you) among women, and blessed is the fruit of thy (your) womb, Jesus." Up until the name "Jesus," these are the very words that Mary's cousin Elizabeth spoke to her upon her arrival (see Luke 1:42). In using this greeting and adding Jesus' name, we share Elizabeth's excitement that God's plan of salvation is unfolding through Mary, and we recognize—along with Elizabeth—that Mary is indeed the mother of our Lord.

"Holy Mary, mother of God, pray for us sinners, now and at the hour of our death. Amen." This last line is the actual prayer, or petition, of the Hail Mary, which didn't officially become part of the prayer until sometime in the sixteenth century. Individuals occasionally added their own similar supplications, such as this one from the fourteenth century, which the *Catholic Encyclopedia* notes has been incorrectly attributed to Dante: "Oh blessed Virgin, pray to God for us always, that he may pardon us and give us grace, so to live here below that he may reward us with paradise at our death." The form of the prayer that we use today was included in the Roman Breviary in 1568. The Catechism of the Council of Trent attributed the addition of that final line to the church itself, writing,

Most rightly has the Holy Church of God added to this thanksgiving, petition also, and the invocation of the most holy Mother of God, thereby implying that we should piously and suppliantly have recourse to her in order that by her intercession she may reconcile God with us sinners and obtain for us the blessing we need both for this present life and for the life which has no end.

And that is what we do in this prayer, whatever the precise origins of the words themselves may be. Just as we instinctively turn to our earthly mothers for help when we make mistakes, we as sinners ask Mary, our heavenly mother, to intercede for us with God, our Father.

The Glory Be/Doxology

Glory be to the Father,
 and to the Son,
 and to the Holy Spirit.
As it was in the beginning,
 it is now and ever shall be,
 world without end. (now and forever.) Amen.

A "doxology" is any short prayer of praise to God. The Glory Be, or doxology, that Catholics are most familiar with, and that is used in the Rosary, gives praise to the triune God.

We recall that from "the beginning," God's divine presence, or "glory," has permeated all of creation and will do so always and everywhere. The version of this prayer that many Catholics remember and continue to use ends with the phrase "world without end," whereas a more recent version found in some collections of prayers uses the phrase "now and forever" (in parentheses above). While the latter phrase probably says more clearly what the prayer means to say, the former is undeniably more poetic and carries more of the mystery to which the words refer.

Some who pray the Rosary add another short prayer following each Glory Be, which goes like this:

O my Jesus, forgive us our sins, save us from the fires of hell, and lead all souls to heaven, especially those in most need of thy (your) mercy. Amen."

The Hail, Holy Queen/Salve Regina

Hail, Holy Queen, Mother of Mercy,
 our life, our sweetness, and our hope!
To thee (you) do we cry,
 poor banished children of Eve; (the children of Eve;)
to thee (you) do we send up our sighs,
 mourning and weeping
 in this vale (valley) of tears. (in this land of exile.)

Turn then, most gracious advocate,
 thine (your) eyes of mercy toward us;
and after this our exile, (lead us home at last and)
show unto us the blessed fruit
 of thy (your) womb, Jesus.
O clement, O loving, O sweet Virgin Mary.

Customarily, the Rosary concludes with the recitation of the Salve Regina, the title of which, in Latin, means "hail, Holy Queen." This classic prayer for Mary's intercession is striking for its imagery and for its poetic cadence. An updated version of the prayer uses modern pronouns and substitutes slightly different wording (above, in parentheses).

"Hail, Holy Queen, Mother of Mercy, our life, our sweetness,

and our hope." In this prayer, we first call upon Mary as "Holy Queen" and "Mother of Mercy." Mary is Mother of Mercy in a double sense—both because she is merciful, and because Jesus, her son, is the fullest expression possible of God's mercy. We can turn to Mary in times of need, because she is "our life, our sweetness, and our hope."

"To thee (you) do we cry, poor banished children of Eve; to thee (you) do we send up our sighs, mourning and weeping in this vale (valley) of tears." The second sentence of the prayer states the central motive in calling upon Mary for help, namely, the experience of human anguish and sorrow. We refer to ourselves as pitiful "banished children of Eve." A later line in the original version (and the same line in the updated version) refers to our condition as "exile." As "children of Eve," we recognize that we are sinners. But to call ourselves "banished" may seem incongruous in the light of the incarnation and redemption of Christ, for in him, we are in fact no longer banished. (The updated version of the prayer actually deletes that phrase.) However, because we are still on a pilgrimage and because our salvation is incomplete on this side of eternity, the words of the prayer do describe a real dimension of our experience in this life. A constant, underlying theme of our experience is of incompleteness in this world, and that is what this part of the prayer expresses. The prayer dates back to Europe in the Middle Ages, when many people experienced lives of great physical hardship. And so, for many, the "vale of tears" in which they found themselves was their earthly condition—from which heaven would release them "after this our exile."

"Turn then, most gracious advocate, thine (your) eyes of mercy toward us; . . ." The prayer acknowledges that Mary is

our advocate with Jesus and asks for her mercy, her assistance in our earthly life.

"*. . . and after this our exile, show unto us the blessed fruit of thy (your) womb, Jesus.*" Finally, the prayer asks Mary for the ultimate gift of union with Christ following our death. The updated version is more active in tone, substituting "lead us home at last" for "after this our exile."

"*O clement, O loving, O sweet Virgin Mary.*" The prayer concludes with another expression of praise for Mary. The archaic adjective "clement" means "inclined to be lenient or merciful."

When the Rosary is prayed in a group, the leader then says, "*Pray for us, O Holy Mother of God, . . .*" which the congregation concludes by responding, "*that we may be made worthy of the promises of Christ.*"

The Hail, Holy Queen is often given beautiful musical expression in its Latin original, as a Gregorian chant. If you have never heard this chanted version of the prayer in Latin, be sure to track down a recording of it.

MOMENTS FOR MEDITATION

The Twenty Mysteries of the Rosary

I don't know about you, but I've always loved a good mystery—especially the part when the detective assembles all the clues and cleverly identifies the murderer, etc., etc. Clever detective that I fancied myself to be in my youth, however, I couldn't figure out what the word "mystery" had to do with the events that we meditate upon in the Rosary. The problem, I soon learned, wasn't in the Rosary, but rather in my understanding of the meaning of "mystery." Upon consulting Webster's, I learned that circumstances that require ingenuity for a solution are not properly called "mysteries" at all but rather puzzles, and that the term "mystery" is correctly defined as "a religious truth that one can know only by revelation and cannot fully understand." Thus, the term "mystery" is often applied to events whereby God's self-revelation in human history took place.

Each of the mysteries of the Rosary is an event whereby God revealed both himself and his love for humankind, particularly in the context of his entrance into creation and human history in the person of Jesus of Nazareth. Each event has its unique characteristics, and each reveals something special about God's love, but each also reveals a reality that far transcends the grasp of the human mind. In this sense, each is and remains a revelation of the mystery of God's love.

The mysteries as we know them today emerged in roughly three stages. First, during the twelfth century it became the custom among Christians, when praying, to recite a phrase referring to a significant event in the life of Jesus or Mary, prior to reciting one of the psalms. Eventually the psalms were dropped, and this way of praying consisted only of reflecting on the events in the life of Jesus or Mary.

Second, during the thirteenth and fourteenth centuries the custom developed of focusing on various joyful events in the life of Mary from the gospels. Often, the recitation of this "joy" was accompanied by saying a Hail Mary. One might, for example, recite fifty joyful meditations from the life of Mary, joined by fifty Hail Marys. During the fourteenth century, this devotion expanded to include the "sorrows" from the life of Mary, as well as her "joys" in heaven. Eventually it became standard practice to recite fifty earthly joys of Mary, fifty earthly sorrows, and fifty heavenly joys (glorious mysteries), each one paired with a Hail Mary.

The final stage in the development of the Rosary mysteries took place in the fifteenth century. Up until this point, meditation on the events in Mary's life was useful only to those who could read, because it was impossible to remember 150 meditations. Each meditation had to be written down, and that excluded those who were illiterate (which, at the time, was almost everybody). So that the meditations could be accessible to everyone, the list was cut to fifteen—five for each set of meditations, paired with 150 Hail Marys (ten Hail Marys per "mystery"). At this point, the meditations, or mysteries, became focal points for recitation of the Hail Marys, and, combined with the Our Fathers and the Glory Be, became the Rosary more or less as we know it today.

This way of organizing the Rosary first appeared in print in a book published in 1483 titled *Our Dear Lady's Psalter.*

A major change took place in 2002, when Pope John Paul II proposed the addition of five luminous mysteries to the fifteen joyful, sorrowful, and glorious mysteries. The pope also suggested the practice, which many people have found helpful, of concluding each mystery "with *a prayer for the fruits specific to that particular mystery.*" "In this way," he went on to say, "the Rosary would better express its connection with the Christian life" (*Rosarium Virginis Mariae,* 35). Thus, the Rosary continues to be a living, active part of our faith. Although all of the mysteries can be prayed at any time you like, they have typically been associated with certain days of the week or with particular liturgical seasons.

The Joyful Mysteries

Traditionally prayed on Mondays and Saturdays

Like all the mysteries of the Rosary, the joyful mysteries describe events that are central to what theologians call "the Christ event." The joyful mysteries are events related to the incarnation, that is, the coming into history, of Jesus the Christ. If anything is particularly mysterious about these events, it is how deeply ordinary and human each one is. Nothing is more common than the conception and birth of a baby; and yet, nothing is more miraculous. If the joyful mysteries share something in common, it is the presence of the holy in the ordinary. On the surface, each one is as ordinary as the day is long: a young

woman becomes pregnant; she visits her pregnant cousin; she gives birth to a baby; she and her husband take their infant son to fulfill the traditions of their religion. Yet, each event is also utterly unique, carrying the presence of God into time and space in a once and for all, unrepeatable way that changes everything forever.

1. The Annunciation: Authentic Faith Is Open to the Unexpected

Fruit of the Mystery: Humility

In the sixth month the angel Gabriel was sent by God to a town in Galilee called Nazareth, to a virgin engaged to a man whose name was Joseph, of the house of David. The virgin's name was Mary. And he came to her and said, "Greetings, favored one! The Lord is with you." But she was much perplexed by his words and pondered what sort of greeting this might be. The angel said to her, "Do not be afraid, Mary, for you have found favor with God. And now, you will conceive in your womb and bear a son, and you will name him Jesus. He will be great, and will be called the Son of the Most High, and the Lord God will give to him the throne of his ancestor David. He will reign over the house of Jacob forever, and of his kingdom there will be no end." Mary said to the angel, "How can this be, since I am a virgin?" The angel said to her, "The Holy Spirit will come upon you, and the power of the Most High will overshadow you; therefore the child to be born will be holy; he will be called Son of God. And now,

> your relative Elizabeth in her old age has also conceived a son; and this is the sixth month for her who was said to be barren. For nothing will be impossible with God." Then Mary said, "Here am I, the servant of the Lord; let it be with me according to your word." Then the angel departed from her.
>
> —Luke 1:26-38

The annunciation is one of the most dramatic events in all of the gospels. We are so familiar with the narrative, however, that we tend to read it, or hear it read, in a rather blasé frame of mind. We know all about it, we think. We know the characters—Mary and the angel Gabriel. We already know who says what and when. And we know how the story ends. Ho, hum. We've heard it so many times before! We are well advised, however, to give ourselves a mental wake-up call so that we will read with our eyes really open and our minds truly alert. This narrative, like countless narratives throughout Scripture, is packed with astonishing details that we routinely miss. Also, it is not without its humorous aspects.

Pay close attention to what happens here. The first character we are introduced to is "the angel Gabriel." The first hearers, and later the first readers, of this account were Jewish. They knew perfectly well from the Hebrew Scriptures who the angel Gabriel was. Gabriel was the heavenly messenger who interpreted King Nebuchadnezzar's dream for Daniel (Daniel 8:15-27). In that narrative, Gabriel was God's instrument to reveal the superiority of the wisdom of Israel's God over the worldly wisdom of the pagans. The fact that Gabriel is the angel who

visits Mary suggests the superiority of the revelation Gabriel is about to speak to Mary. This fact is also a direct inference that the birth of Jesus will fulfill the prophecy spoken by Gabriel to Daniel in Daniel 9:20-26.

Luke introduces his narrative by stating simply that everything he is about to tell us took place in "a town in Galilee called Nazareth." This sentence sets the stage, and what it told Luke's first audience was that the following event took place in the most obscure and least important of places—in a word, Hicksville. Nazareth was Nowhere. Nothing important had ever happened there, and nobody important lived there or was even from there. It was the least likely place for the Son of God to be conceived. To say that Jesus had "humble" beginnings doesn't even come close!

Gabriel went to Nazareth, the story goes, to see a virgin whose "name was Mary." Apart from the fact that she was engaged to Joseph, that's all we are told about her. In his article "The Historical Mary" (*America*, Dec. 19–26, 2005), Fr. Robert P. Maloney, CM, gives us some insight into this obscure young woman. Given the name "Miriam," after the sister of Moses, Mary was a poor peasant girl of about thirteen or fourteen years old, who spoke Aramaic with a Galilean accent. But she also may have had a passing familiarity with the Latin spoken by the soldiers of the Roman occupation; with Greek, which was the language of the marketplace; and, of course, with Hebrew, which was spoken in synagogue.

As familiar as we are with this story, the Gospel of Luke goes to some lengths to show us that the events that take place are anything but predictable. First, an angel appears to Mary (hardly an everyday occurrence, we imagine) and greets her. Yet all Luke

tells us is that Mary is "much perplexed" by Gabriel's *words* to her, when all he has said so far is "Greetings, favored one! The Lord is with you." It's clear, though, that Gabriel's words give young Mary pause. At first, she says nothing in response to the angel and bides her time, pondering "what sort of greeting this might be." So Gabriel speaks again, reassuring her by saying, "Do not be afraid," and explaining why she has nothing to fear. Nothing we have been told so far tells us that Mary was afraid, but apparently that's how the angel has interpreted her silence. The reason that Mary shouldn't be afraid, Gabriel goes on to explain, is that she has "found favor with God," but once again, Mary doesn't say a word.

Gabriel keeps right on delivering his message all the same, informing young Mary that "now" she "will conceive in [her] womb and bear a son. . . ." And if that isn't enough, Gabriel forges right ahead—still no pause for a reaction—and informs Mary that she "will name him Jesus." And still no response from Mary!

Then comes the second part of Gabriel's verbal one-two punch. He instructs Mary, telling her that the infant she will give birth to "will be called Son of the Most High, and the Lord God will give him the throne of his ancestor David." These words are loaded. The Hebrew Scriptures refer to God as "the Most High" a total of 109 times, so there is no question of who Gabriel is talking about here. He is telling Mary, point-blank, that the baby she is going to conceive and give birth to is God's own Son. By this time in the narrative, you would think that Mary would be at least stammering, "but . . . but . . . but. . . ." Not so, however; still she remains silent. But if she was "pondering" on Gabriel's words when all he had done was to greet

her, by now she has got to be doing some *major* pondering. Things just keep getting "curiouser and curiouser."

Gabriel finishes dropping his verbal bomb with remarks about how God will give the son Mary will bear "the throne of his ancestor David," and how he will "reign over the house of Jacob forever," and how his "kingdom" will "have no end." Luke doesn't tell us whether Mary was standing or sitting when Gabriel arrived, but if she was standing in the beginning, you'd think that she would definitely be sitting down by now. . . .

Regardless, however, Mary finally speaks. Given all the talking Gabriel has been doing, it's almost as if this is the first time Mary can get a word in edgewise, and her question is a perfectly sensible one. She bypasses all the talk of thrones and kingdoms, for the moment, and gets right down to practicalities. Mary knows a thing or two about where babies come from, and so she asks, "How can this be, since I am a virgin?" This question makes sense, but remember the situation. An *angel*, for crying out loud, shows up and lays a rather long, impressive message on young Mary, but it's as if she's not all that impressed! She doesn't let loose with the first-century Palestinian equivalent of "No way!" or "Yeah, right!" She doesn't ask, "Who the heck are you, anyway?" No, she seems to take the angel at his word. But she also has her questions. Even from an angel, she wants some answers, thank you very much—no disrespect intended.

For his part, Gabriel doesn't stand on formalities. He doesn't fall back on his credentials and say, "Hey, I'm an angel—I know what I'm talking about, okay? Don't you worry your little head about how this is going to happen. Just keep quiet and do as you're told." No, Mary asks a sensible, understandable question, and Gabriel is happy to give a straightforward reply: "The

Holy Spirit will come upon you, and the power of the Most High will overshadow you; therefore, the child to be born will be holy; he will be called Son of God."

Again, Mary remains silent! Scripture scholars tell us that it's indisputable that the theological point Luke wants to make here is that Mary became pregnant as a virgin. Theologically, this says more about Jesus, though, than it does about Mary. The main reason for making this point isn't to glorify virginity or denigrate sex, especially sexual intimacy in marriage. The main reason for emphasizing that Jesus had no biological human father is to make clear that he is the Son of God. At the same time, this point makes clear how fully human Jesus' entrance into space and time is. He gets his humanity from a fully human mother. He is, in other words, fully divine and fully human, and neither fact may be downplayed at the expense of the other.

But Gabriel isn't done yet. Here comes bombshell number two. Mary's elderly cousin Elizabeth, whom everyone thought was unable to have a baby, is already six months pregnant. "For nothing," Gabriel explains, "will be impossible with God"—the implication being that if God can do this for Elizabeth, then he can darn well do what Gabriel has just told Mary is going to happen to her.

Mary's final response to the angel is to express complete openness to God's will for her life: "Here am I, the servant of the Lord; let it be with me according to your word." She might as well have said, "If God wants me to be of service to him in some way, I'm fine with that, no matter what it is."

Luke concludes his narrative by simply telling us that the angel took his leave.

Reflecting on this narrative—this first joyful mystery—in the context of the Rosary, we can learn much about the nature of Christian faith, and it all comes down to a fairly simple idea: ultimately, faith means openness to God's will and trusting acceptance of his call, no matter what demands it makes upon us, no matter what risks it brings with it.

We can look at it this way. We will never experience anything even remotely as dramatic as what happened to Mary, it's true. But all the same, angels bearing God's will for us come into our lives each and every day, if only we are prepared to recognize them. They speak to us in the everyday events of our ordinary lives. They whisper to us words like "Be patient with that child" or "that teenager" or "your spouse" or "your fellow employee." Angels also whisper words such as "Love your young adult offspring by telling him that it's time to get a job and move out."

Angels beckon us in all kinds of ordinary ways every day to act on God's will so that we, too, may become instruments of God's loving presence in our little corner of the world. Young Mary also sets an example of what authentic adult faith looks like. She listens closely to the angel, but she also shows no signs of "blind faith." She does show signs of doubt, however. She doubts that it's possible for her to conceive a child except by the usual method. Therefore, she asks her question. This is because faith and doubt are by no means mutually exclusive. Having doubts and asking questions go hand-in-hand with adult faith.

The angel's response to Mary's question does nothing to clear things up, however—especially as far as a modern, scientific mind-set is concerned. But even for Mary, in her time and place, the angel's reply to her question simply says that God will take

care of it, which is good enough for Mary. From this we can learn that even when we don't get clear, scientific answers to our questions, and when we still have our doubts, we can still trust in God's wisdom and love. The bottom line is that we need to believe, with Mary as our model of faith, that "nothing will be impossible with God."

No matter what happens to us, and no matter what happens in our life, we can always make Mary's final words to the angel our words, too: "Here am I, the servant of the Lord; let it be with me according to your word."

2. The Visitation: Authentic Faith Inspires Us to Make Sacrifices for Others

Fruit of the Mystery: Love of Neighbor

> In those days Mary set out and went with haste to a Judean town in the hill country, where she entered the house of Zechariah and greeted Elizabeth. When Elizabeth heard Mary's greeting, the child leaped in her womb. And Elizabeth was filled with the Holy Spirit and exclaimed with a loud cry, "Blessed are you among women, and blessed is the fruit of your womb." . . .
> And Mary remained with [Elizabeth] about three months and then returned to her home.
>
> —Luke 1:39-42, 56

The next thing we know, Mary takes off for the home of her elderly cousin Elizabeth. Luke is vague—"in those days,"

he writes—about how soon after Gabriel's visit Mary hits the road, but we may presume that it was only a matter of days. Our curiosity may run a little wild at this point. Did Mary tell her parents what had happened to her? Did she wonder how she would explain this to the neighbors or her friends? Did Mary get an anxiety attack after the angel left, and start wondering what she was going to do now? It would seem only natural, even if she was now involved with the supernatural up to her eyeballs. We're left with our curiosity, however, since the Gospel of Luke only wrote about what God did and is doing. Perhaps that was all that Luke thought his audience needed or wanted to know.

Apparently, if "in those days" Mary did any spiritual or emotional wrestling with herself—and it would be perfectly human if she did—before long she sets aside any preoccupation with herself and thinks of Elizabeth, who no doubt could use the company and help of her younger cousin. Luke tells us nothing about the journey itself, only that when Mary arrived, the infant John (the Baptist) in Elizabeth did a little in utero flip. Then, Elizabeth gives voice to what became the next part of the Hail Mary, after the angel's greeting: "Blessed are you among women, and blessed is the fruit of your womb."

So, not only does Mary know about Elizabeth's remarkable pregnancy, but somehow Elizabeth has also learned about Mary's miraculous pregnancy. The Gospel of Luke's theological purpose, of course, is to relate the two blessed events and to link Jesus and John the Baptist, even before they are born. Elizabeth speaks for the entire Christian community down through history when she adds, "And blessed is she [Mary] who believed that there would be a fulfillment of what was spoken to her by the Lord" (1:45).

Following Mary's Magnificat ("My soul magnifies the Lord"), which runs from verses 46 to 55—one of the greatest and most beautiful canticles in the entire Bible, but not immediately relevant to our focus here—Luke concludes by informing us that Mary's visit with Elizabeth lasted "about three months." Since we learned from Gabriel that Elizabeth was already six months into her pregnancy, we may conclude from this that Mary remained with Elizabeth either until just prior to John's birth, or until just after John was born. The following verses say nothing about Mary's being present for the birth, however, so again we are left guessing. Theologically, it would be interesting if Mary were present to assist with the delivery of John the Baptist, but any suggestion that this was the case will always remain pure speculation.

As we pray the Rosary, this mystery is a terrific reminder of the humanity of Mary and of the importance to her of extended family relationships. Even when she has had the most amazing experience herself, she is thinking not of herself but of the needs of her elderly cousin. Clearly, the central focus in young Mary's life is already the message that her son will proclaim—that the purpose of life is love of God and neighbor.

3. The Nativity: Authentic Faith Discovers the Glorious in the Ordinary

Fruit of the Mystery: Poverty

In those days a decree went out from Emperor Augustus that all the world should be registered. This was the first registration and was taken while Quirinius was governor

of Syria. All went to their own towns to be registered. Joseph also went from the town of Nazareth in Galilee to Judea, to the city of David called Bethlehem, because he was descended from the house and family of David. He went to be registered with Mary, to whom he was engaged and who was expecting a child. While they were there, the time came for her to deliver her child. And she gave birth to her firstborn son and wrapped him in bands of cloth, and laid him in a manger, because there was no place for them in the inn.

—Luke 2:1-7

The infancy narrative in the Gospel of Luke—from which this short selection is taken—is familiar to anyone who has ever attended church services on Christmas, even if that's the only day in the year he or she went anywhere near a church. For that matter, it's familiar to anyone who ever saw the late cartoonist Charles Shulz's half-hour animated television feature "A Charlie Brown Christmas." It's common, however, for people to take this narrative as nothing more than charming Christmas nostalgia, and to miss the meanings that were intended by the gospel and that would have easily been understood by those who first heard it.

Luke makes sure to situate his account of the birth of Jesus historically. That's why he informs us that it was a very particular Roman emperor, Augustus, who demanded that a census be taken for the first time. Not only that, but it was the governor named Quirinius who was in office, not some other governor at some other time. This is Luke's way of saying, "I didn't make this up, it really happened, and this is when and where it happened."

Next, we get a genealogical note. Luke writes that Joseph took Mary to Bethlehem to register for the census because that was the hometown for everyone in the family line that traced its origins back to the prominent Jewish king David. Thus, even though Jesus' Father is the God of Israel, even through his human foster father Jesus comes from a royal lineage.

From Luke's observation that the newborn Messiah ended up in a feed box for animals, we may conclude that the birth took place in a shack or cave, a shelter for cattle, or something along those lines. The couple was unable to find a room in an inn, which makes sense given the huge influx of people into Bethlehem for the census. Miriam, "Mary" to us, gives birth to a male child and wraps the infant in "swaddling clothes" or "bands of cloth"—depending on the translation you're reading—and places him in "a manger." Luke doesn't mention it, but we can assume that before wrapping the baby up and putting him to bed, the new mother would first have cuddled and breastfed him, all the while gazing at him with wonder and praising God for the miracle of her baby.

So far, the theological purpose at hand is, first, to declare that Jesus' birth was an actual, historical event, and second, to illustrate the poverty and anonymity of Jesus' birth. The Son of the King of the universe arrives in the usual, thoroughly ordinary human manner. Jesus doesn't fly in on a cloud bank with angels blowing trumpets in order to stun the whole world with his power and majesty. Obscure, poor, and gloriously ordinary—that's how the Messiah and Son of God arrived.

Reflecting on this mystery in the context of the Rosary, we could find ourselves rethinking any romantic notions we may have had about the meaning of Christmas. For, the true joy of

Christmas has nothing to do with most of what goes on in the name of the annual "holiday shopping season." Indeed, the contemporary tendency in the marketplace to replace the greeting "Merry Christmas" with "Happy Holidays" should encourage us to treasure, even more, the church-related situations where we may use the former greeting as a true expression of faith.

4. The Presentation: Authentic Faith Is Open to the Prophetic Word

Fruit of the Mystery: Obedience

> When the time came for their purification according to the law of Moses, they brought him up to Jerusalem to present him to the Lord.
>
> —Luke 2:22

According to Jewish custom, Mary was required to present herself in the Temple to be "purified" following Jesus' birth because, under Jewish law, she was ritually impure after giving birth. Bible scholars remain puzzled by the reference here to "their" purification. The way the original Greek is constructed, it must refer to both Mary and Joseph, but this makes no sense, because Jewish law made no provision for the purification of the husband, only that of the wife.

In addition to requiring Mary's purification, Jewish law required that a firstborn son be consecrated to the Lord with a sacrifice. Underscoring the poverty of Mary and Joseph, Luke's gospel tells us that they brought one of the sacrifices that was

offered by poor couples, namely, "a pair of turtledoves or two young pigeons" (2:24).

When they arrive at the Temple, the little family encounters old Simeon, whom Luke describes as "righteous and devout, looking forward to the consolation of Israel, and the Holy Spirit rested on him" (2:25). Not only that, but, Luke says, "It had been revealed to him by the Holy Spirit that he would not see death before he had seen the Lord's Messiah" (2:26). All this, and everything that follows, restates for us that the birth of Jesus was a major manifestation of the holy in an ordinary, everyday event.

Simeon goes on at some length about the impact Jesus will have and the consequences for Mary, herself. Then along comes the devout, elderly Anna, who adds her prophetic comments to those of Simeon. Luke comments that Anna began to "speak about the child to all who were looking for the redemption of Jerusalem" (Luke 2:38). One may wonder whether this kind of talk in Jerusalem, where people from all around came to the Temple, may have spread to Mary and Joseph's close-knit hometown of Nazareth. One might think that the gossip mill would shift into overdrive.

According to Luke, Mary and Joseph are startled by the words of Simeon and Anna. They "were amazed," Luke says. But given everything that Luke has already told us about events prior to and at the time of Jesus' birth, we may justifiably be puzzled by Mary's and Joseph's amazement in the Temple. What with the angel Gabriel announcing Jesus' conception, and angels and shepherds showing up when Jesus is born, one would think that by now Mary and Joseph would be a little less likely to be amazed by anything where Jesus is concerned. But, not so, evidently.

Of course, we do well to keep in mind that the main concern of the Gospel of Luke is to make theological rather than historical points, and so the reason for the gospel's remarks about Mary's and Joseph's continued amazement may have more to do with Luke's ongoing desire to point out who Jesus is than to provide us with a literal description of how Mary and Joseph reacted to what Simeon and Anna said. At the same time, if the human author of Luke's gospel got his information from Mary, herself—which may or may not be the case—years after the events described by the gospel, years after the death and resurrection of Jesus, she might understandably recall being more amazed at the time than she actually was.

No matter what the facts may be, however, the overall meaning of the presentation of the infant Jesus in the Temple is clear from the words of Simeon, which all believers can make their own: "My eyes have seen your salvation, which you have prepared in the presence of all the peoples, a light for revelation to the Gentiles and for glory to your people Israel" (Luke 2:30-32).

As a mystery of the Rosary, the presentation is an inspiration to cherish our own relationship with Mary as her children in Christ. Just as she and Joseph presented the infant Christ in the Temple, so Mary constantly presents us to Jesus with her love for us all.

5. The Finding of Jesus in the Temple: Authentic Faith Doesn't Cling to Preconceived Notions

Fruit of the Mystery: Joy in Finding Jesus

Now every year his parents went to Jerusalem for the festival of the Passover. And when he was twelve years old, they went up as usual for the festival. When the festival was ended and they started to return, the boy Jesus stayed behind in Jerusalem, but his parents did not know it. Assuming that he was in the group of travelers, they went a day's journey. Then they started to look for him among their relatives and friends. When they did not find him, they returned to Jerusalem to search for him. After three days they found him in the temple, sitting among the teachers, listening to them and asking them questions. And all who heard him were amazed at his understanding and his answers. When his parents saw him they were astonished; and his mother said to him, "Child, why have you treated us like this? Look, your father and I have been searching for you in great anxiety." He said to them, "Why were you searching for me? Did you not know that I must be in my Father's house?" But they did not understand what he said to them. Then he went down with them and came to Nazareth, and was obedient to them. His mother treasured all these things in her heart.

And Jesus increased in wisdom and in years, and in divine and human favor.

—Luke 2:41-52

The last of the five joyful mysteries comes from a familiar event that only the Gospel of Luke describes. Again, many commentators on Luke, down through the centuries, see this as evidence that the author of Luke may have had direct testimony from Mary herself. Whether or not this is the case, Luke's account of the loss and finding of the boy Jesus in the Temple in Jerusalem is filled with a wealth of insights.

First, we learn from Luke that it was a yearly custom for Mary, Joseph, and Jesus to journey to Jerusalem for the Passover festival. Then he tells us that, at this particular time, Jesus was twelve years old. Keep in mind that twelve was considered a more mature age in that period and culture than it is in our day and culture. Twelve was on the verge of adulthood. Indeed, it's no accident that even in our own era it is at the age of twelve that Jewish boys and girls celebrate Judaism's coming-of-age rituals, bar mitzvah (for boys) and bat mitzvah (for girls).

Luke tells us nothing about what Mary, Joseph, and Jesus did at the festival itself, only that when it was time to make the return trek to Nazareth, Mary and Joseph took it for granted that Jesus was "in the group of travelers." Based on past experience, apparently, they had no reason to think otherwise for an entire day. It was that long before it dawned on Mary and Joseph that Jesus wasn't in the "group of travelers" at all.

So there they are, a day's travel from Jerusalem, and they discover that they need to turn around and go back. That's two days that Jesus is missing by the time they get back to Jerusalem. Think about it. How would any parent feel if a child was missing for two days? Then, when they do get back to Jerusalem, Luke tells us that they look for Jesus for three more days before they finally

find him. So that's five days all together that Jesus is missing. Put yourself in their place. How would any parent feel if a child was missing for five days? Are we talking frantic here, or what?

Finally, Mary and Joseph happen upon the twelve-year-old Jesus in, of all places, the Temple. Notice that the Temple was far from being the first place they looked for Jesus. They searched high and low for three days before they even thought to look in the Temple. Perhaps Mary and Joseph didn't think of Jesus as the kind of boy who was likely to be hanging out in the Temple. First, they looked in the marketplaces, in the homes, perhaps, of friends and relatives, maybe in whatever was the ancient equivalent of today's video arcades. Maybe Mary and Joseph didn't check the Temple because they didn't think of their son as an overly pious lad. Maybe they just didn't expect him to be hanging out in the Temple chewing the fat with the rabbis.

Mary and Joseph find their wayward sheep "sitting among the teachers, listening to them, and asking them questions." Luke reports that Jesus was basically knocking everyone's socks off with "his understanding and his answers." A gifted child! Luke says that Jesus' "parents . . . were astonished." A dictionary defines "astonished" as "being filled with sudden wonder or amazement." Note that being astonished is not incompatible with being "fit to be tied," which would only be natural for Mary and Joseph at this particular moment. In fact, the first words out of Mary's mouth express just such feelings.

"Child, why have you treated us like this?" Mary asks, with admirable restraint, we might say. In other words, Mary asks her twelve-year-old son how he could have been so thoughtless and insensitive. Didn't he care that she and Joseph had been worried sick? Why didn't he at the very least get a message to

them through someone else in their traveling group so they would know where he was and what he was up to? It would be perfectly understandable if Mary and Joseph had said at this moment, "You get yourself out of this Temple right now, young man! Now we have to walk all the way back to Nazareth by ourselves. You're grounded for a month, and at that you should consider yourself fortunate! Don't you ever pull a stunt like this again, do you hear me?"

Luke doesn't report that Mary and Joseph said anything along those lines, though. Instead, Mary tells Jesus what should have been obvious to him, that they had been looking everywhere "in great anxiety." Instead of apologizing, however, Jesus calmly replies that Mary and Joseph should have known that he had to be in his "Father's house," or as other translations would have it, "about [his] Father's interests."

Whatever Mary and Joseph thought about Jesus' response— perhaps that it was thoughtless or insensitive or both—Luke remarks that they had no idea what their son was talking about. In other words, they were clueless. Mary and Joseph may have said something like, "Come on, we're going home, now," but whether they did or not, Jesus evidently knew that his little adventure was over.

Luke's concluding words about this event simply tell us that young Jesus went back to Nazareth with Mary and Joseph and (from then on, anyway) "was obedient to them." Apparently, even if at that particular moment in the Temple Jesus was a smart-mouth kid, he seems to have learned from his mistake. What a deeply insightful and human observation Luke makes, too—and how easy it is to believe that his words come from conversations he might have had with Mary herself in later

years—when he remarks that she "treasured all these things in her heart." What mother wouldn't?

Luke's final words, telling us all we know about Jesus' so-called "hidden years," are filled with both poetry and theological insight: "And Jesus increased in wisdom and in years, and in divine and human favor" (2:52).

The Sorrowful Mysteries

Traditionally prayed on Tuesdays and Fridays

This group of mysteries of the Rosary all come from the passion narratives in the gospels, that is, the gospels' accounts of the suffering and execution of Jesus by crucifixion. Once again, they are all concerned with a key event in the redemption and salvation of the world, and once again each one looks, on the surface, as ordinary as can be. A man agonizes over his impending torture and death. He is tortured and mocked by his executioners. His executioners force him to drag the cross upon which he will be crucified to the place where his execution will take place. Finally, nails driven through his feet and wrists pin him to the cross, and he dies a long and agonizing death. Especially for the era in which it occurred, it all looked so ordinary. But who the man was who suffered and died—that's what makes all the difference.

Each mystery carries an infinitely holy meaning and purpose that changes everything for all time. By his incarnation, suffering, death, and resurrection, Jesus accomplishes the redemption of the world. These mysteries tell us of the suffering and death phase, if you will, of the events that brought about our salvation.

1. The Agony in the Garden: Authentic Faith Abandons Self to God, No Matter What

Fruit of the Mystery: Sorrow for Sin

> They went to a place called Gethsemane; and he said to his disciples, "Sit here while I pray." He took with him Peter and James and John, and began to be distressed and agitated. And he said to them, "I am deeply grieved, even to death; remain here, and keep awake." And going a little farther, he threw himself on the ground and prayed that, if it were possible, the hour might pass from him. He said, "Abba, Father, for you all things are possible; remove this cup from me; yet, not what I want, but what you want."
> —Mark 14:32-36

The Gospels of Matthew, Mark, and Luke all describe Jesus' agony in the garden of Gethsemane. The Gospel of John— unique in many ways—mentions only that Jesus "went out with his disciples across the Kidron valley to a place where there was a garden, which he and his disciples entered" (18:1).

The Gospel of Mark, which is quoted here, is the oldest, and linguistically the most primitive, of the four gospels. It uses strong, graphic language to describe Jesus' experience in the garden. Mark says that Jesus was "distressed and agitated." The older Revised Standard Version translates these words as "greatly distressed and troubled." The point, however, is that Mark has no doubt about how human Jesus' anguish was as he anticipated the hours ahead of him.

The Gospel of Matthew, not as old as Mark's gospel and probably a little older than the Gospel of Luke, says that, in the garden of Gethsemane, Jesus "began to be grieved and agitated." Then Jesus speaks for himself, saying, "I am deeply grieved, even to death."

Luke's passion narrative parallels those of Mark and Matthew and also includes elements that are both divine and uniquely human:

Then he withdrew from them about a stone's throw, knelt down, and prayed, "Father, if you are willing, remove this cup from me; yet, not my will but yours be done." Then an angel from heaven appeared to him and gave him strength. In his anguish he prayed more earnestly, and his sweat became like great drops of blood falling down on the ground. (Luke 22:41-44)

For his own theological reasons, Luke remarks that Jesus was strengthened by an angel—perhaps to make more graphic for his readers the divine presence at this terrible hour. Then, Luke describes Jesus' suffering in a unique and particularly graphic way, saying that Jesus' "sweat became like great drops of blood." There is no question, then, that in the opinion of these three gospel writers, Jesus' experience in the garden was one of intense, painful anguish.

For those who pray the Rosary using the sorrowful mysteries, the model provided by Jesus here illustrates the need, in the midst of anxiety, stress, and fear, to abandon oneself to God, our loving Father. We do well in such circumstances to tell him clearly what we want, as Jesus did, and then abandon ourselves

to his care, making the words of Jesus our own: "Not what I want, but what you want."

2. The Scourging at the Pillar: Authentic Faith Embraces Jesus' Humanity and Divinity

Fruit of the Mystery: Purity

> Then Pilate took Jesus and had him flogged.
>
> —John 19:1

Only the fourth gospel says that Jesus was scourged or flogged, and it says nothing about a pillar. Perhaps we can attribute the inclusion of a pillar in the name of this mystery to the influence of artistic depictions down through the centuries that show Jesus tied to a pillar while being flogged. Or perhaps there was an assumption that a person being flogged would have had to be tied to something in order to be kept standing.

This second sorrowful mystery—particularly since it appears in only one short sentence in only one of the gospels—can't really be separated from the event that follows it in all four gospels, namely, the third sorrowful mystery, "the crowning with thorns." Down through the centuries, however, it has served the purpose of helping those who pray the Rosary to focus on the very real physical nature of Jesus' suffering at the hands of those who tortured him. It is noteworthy, in fact, that the scourging of Jesus appears only in the fourth gospel. This is one of the ways that John emphasizes Jesus' humanity. This is remarkable, however, since John also inclines heavily toward presenting Jesus in the

light of his divinity, in ways that the other three gospels do not.

For example, instead of giving us a fourth infancy narrative, John's gospel begins with a unique prologue that calls Jesus "the Word" who "was with God . . . and was God" (1:1). Yet the Gospel of John never goes so far as to ignore or even downplay Jesus' humanity. This mention of Jesus' flogging is but one example of how the fourth gospel regularly shines a light on how fully human Jesus was, even as it places a unique emphasis on his divinity.

3. The Crowning with Thorns: Authentic Faith Shares in the Physical and Mental Suffering of Christ

Fruit of the Mystery: Courage

> And they clothed him in a purple cloak; and after twisting some thorns into a crown, they put it on him. And they began saluting him, "Hail, King of the Jews!" They struck his head with a reed, spat upon him, and knelt down in homage to him. After mocking him, they stripped him of the purple cloak and put his own clothes on him. Then they led him out to crucify him.
>
> **—Mark 15:17-20**

This event, which all four of the gospels include, is both a detailed description of how Jesus was tortured before being crucified and an ironic presentation of Jesus' deepest identity and meaning. For, in terms of his ultimate identity, he is King of the universe.

As one of the mysteries of the Rosary, however, this event in the passion of Jesus continues the Rosary's reminder to us of the extent to which Jesus went in order to fully embrace the experience of being human. If every human life includes anguish and suffering, darkness and pain; if being human means being misunderstood and rejected; if it means being on the receiving end of injustice, then Jesus felt what we all feel—only to a far greater extent than most of us will ever feel it.

Jesus didn't just come into the world of time and space and live a more or less ordinary, average human life. No. He knew great joy, to be sure, but his life included the deepest darkness and pain that any human life could ever know. This is how deep his love for us is—so deep that he accepted the worst that could happen. The crown of thorns that humans, in their ignorance and cruelty, pushed down onto his head and into his scalp, tortured him with an intense physical pain, no doubt. But how often do we reflect on the psychic pain that Jesus must also have known? It's only human to want to be accepted, appreciated, and loved by others. So, along with his physical suffering, Jesus must have experienced the most intense psychic and spiritual pain, as well.

As we ponder Jesus' crowning with thorns, we might well reflect on the psychic pain he undoubtedly knew but that so rarely receives any attention. The crown of thorns might be understood, in fact, as a symbol for the psychic suffering of Jesus. Reflecting on this, then, we may come to a deeper appreciation of ways that our own psychic pain and mental anguish can, through our intimacy with Christ, be as much a sharing in his suffering as any physical suffering we may have to endure. And because our psychic suffering can be a sharing in the psychic pain of Jesus, it can also be a sharing in his redemptive suffering, too.

96

4. The Carrying of the Cross: Authentic Faith Moves Us Forward, Even During Trials and Tribulations

Fruit of the Mystery: Patience

> So they took Jesus; and carrying the cross by himself, he went out to what is called The Place of the Skull, which in Hebrew is called Golgotha.
>
> —John 19:16b-17

Of the four gospel writers, only John—for his own theological purposes—says that Jesus carried his cross himself. Matthew, Mark, and Luke all say that after Jesus stumbled, Simon of Cyrene carried Jesus' cross for him to Golgotha—and not altogether willingly, either. Carrying his cross himself, or trudging along with Simon of Cyrene, the point is that Jesus' suffering continued—there was no letup. Carrying his cross or stumbling along with Simon of Cyrene, Jesus continued his pilgrimage to crucifixion and death, and all the way he had nothing to go on but faith.

Sometimes, we forget that Jesus' divinity did not override his humanity. As he went to his execution, he had no "inside information," no special reassurance that his life and death would not be for nothing. He had to rely on faith, which meant for him—just as it does for us—his trusting relationship with his Father in heaven. As he walked his path of suffering to Golgotha, Jesus had to trust in his Father's loving care. He had to abandon himself to his unavoidable fate and trust that God's love was trustworthy. And that's exactly what we must do, as well.

OK, final answer below.

Final:

<document content>

There may be something rather sad, in fact, about the simple statement, "It was nine o'clock in the morning when they crucified him." Here it is a new day, and it begins with the barbaric act, resulting from human brutality, ignorance, and fear, of nailing of the Son of God to a cross. Mark's account of Jesus' crucifixion is simple and straightforward, yet each sentence is worthy of our attention.

Mark sets the scene by explaining to his gentile Christian audience that "Golgotha" means "the place of a skull." The skull is a symbol of death, even in our own culture. How appropriate the setting, he might have added, for here is the place where the most significant death in all of human history will occur.

We learn that before the soldiers crucified Jesus, they tried to make him drink a mixture of wine and myrrh, the latter of which was a mild painkiller. Could this have been motivated by some passing shadow of compassion on the part of the soldiers? Regardless, Mark tells us that Jesus refused to drink. Could it be possible that the reason Jesus refused the drugged wine is that his love for humankind is so deep that he wanted to accept the fullness of human suffering and death without having it dulled even slightly?

With almost brutal simplicity, Mark tells us that "they crucified him," and there was no need to explain what that meant, since it would have been so perfectly obvious to Mark's first audience. Everyone knew about crucifixion: the nails through the wrists—New Testament Greek has no word for "wrist," and authorities on human physiology agree that only nails through the bones of the wrist could bear the full weight of the human body on a cross; the nails through the feet; and the hanging for hours until death occurred, not from loss of blood but by sheer,

vivid pain and slow suffocation as the lungs collapsed under the weight of the body.

Finally, Mark includes the observation that, crass to the end, the soldiers "cast lots"—shoot craps, in fact—to see who will keep Jesus' "clothes." This is how total Jesus' poverty is. He goes to his death without even clothes on his back. Again scholars agree that Jesus was undoubtedly crucified naked; the addition of a loincloth to the corpus on crucifixes was the result of a concern for modesty in later centuries.

Jesus dies in the depths of the most horrible and degrading human suffering and the most complete human poverty. And he does so without complaint, out of love for his Father and obedience to his Father's will, but ultimately, out of love for all humanity. No one can say it better than the Gospel of John: "No one has greater love than this, to lay down one's life for one's friends" (15:13).

The Glorious Mysteries

Traditionally prayed on Wednesdays and Sundays, although Sundays during Lent are traditionally sorrowful mystery days, and Sundays during Advent are joyful mystery days

The first three glorious mysteries all come from the postcrucifixion narratives in the gospels and the Acts of the Apostles. The fourth and fifth glorious mysteries are unique because they come not from New Testament events but from sacred Tradition. As such, they illustrate the intimate, interdependent connection that has existed since the very earliest days of Christianity between

Scripture and Tradition, a connection that Roman Catholicism has honored and preserved down through the centuries to the present day.

The fourth and fifth glorious mysteries, the assumption and coronation of Mary, come from sacred Tradition, the same Tradition from which the Christian Scriptures came. Devotion to Mary has been part of the Christian tradition from its earliest days following the resurrection of Jesus. Indeed, there can be no doubt that Mary had a special place of honor among the apostles of Jesus for as long as she remained on this earth. It is impossible to believe otherwise. That is how far back our devotion to Mary goes. So, the fact that Scripture doesn't speak of the mysteries about Mary explicitly is incidental. They are a perfect reminder of the continuing importance and value of Tradition and an illustration of the theological balance that characterizes the Rosary. The Rosary is obviously heavily scriptural; but, these two mysteries call to our attention the constant blessings that sacred Tradition makes possible in the life of Christian faith. They also remind us of the unbreakable union that exists between Scripture and Tradition.

1. The Resurrection: Authentic Faith Experiences the Risen Christ

Fruit of the Mystery: Faith

When the sabbath was over, Mary Magdalene, and Mary the mother of James, and Salome bought spices, so that they might go and anoint him. And very early on the first day of the week, when the sun had risen, they went to

the tomb. They had been saying to one another, "Who will roll away the stone for us from the entrance to the tomb?" When they looked up, they saw that the stone, which was very large, had already been rolled back. As they entered the tomb, they saw a young man, dressed in a white robe, sitting on the right side; and they were alarmed. But he said to them, "Do not be alarmed; you are looking for Jesus of Nazareth, who was crucified. He has been raised; he is not here. Look, there is the place they laid him. But go, tell his disciples and Peter that he is going ahead of you to Galilee; there you will see him, just as he told you."

—**Mark 16:1-7**

The resurrection of Christ is, without question, the event upon which the entire Christian faith depends. If the resurrection didn't happen, all of Christian history and the faith of countless Christians for more than two thousand years would fall like a house of cards. In the familiar words of St. Paul, "If Christ has not been raised, your faith is futile . . ." (1 Corinthians 15:17). To accept this assertion is one thing, however, and to even begin to understand it is quite another.

The first glorious mystery leads us to the resurrection narratives of all four gospels, of course, and each has its own audience in mind and its own theological perspective. It is worth your while to read slowly through each one, taking note of the similarities and differences. For our purposes, however, the words of the angel to "Mary Magdalene and the other Mary" (Matthew 28:1) are enough to start our reflections: "Do not be

afraid; I know that you are looking for Jesus who was crucified. He is not here; for he has been raised . . ." (Matthew 28:5-6).

Scripture scholars and theologians discuss and debate the meaning of "resurrection" *ad infinitum,* and better minds than ours have been boggled by it. There are those who tend to turn the resurrection into a holy magic show, while at the other extreme, there are those who would deny that anything unique at all happened to Jesus after he died. In the end, we must turn to the gospel narratives, to the church's ongoing experience of the risen Lord in its midst for more than two millennia, and finally, to common sense.

We don't know what a hypothetical eyewitness to the resurrection of Jesus would have seen, and we never will. If anything is a mystery, it is the resurrection. And yet, if anything is available for us to experience in all kinds of ordinary and unpredictable ways, it is the risen Christ. Sometimes I think that when it comes to the resurrection, we do better to listen to poets than to theologians. Native American Catholic poet Sherman Alexie's poem "Drum as Love, Fear, Prayer," in his book *The Summer of Black Widows* (New York: Hanging Loose Press, 1996), includes a description of the meaning of the resurrection in words that are not pious but still breathe new life into our understanding of the resurrection:

> Then she tells me that Jesus is
> still here
> because Jesus was
> once here.
> and parts of Jesus are
> still floating in the air.

She tells me Jesus' DNA is
part of the collective DNA.
She tells me we are all part
of Jesus, we are all Jesus in part.
She tells me to breathe deep
during all of our storms
because you can sometimes taste Jesus
in a good, hard rain.

The knack we need to develop is that of clinging simultaneously to both the mystery and the electricity—metaphorically speaking, of course—of the resurrection. Our best bet is to open ourselves to the mystery of the resurrection, open ourselves prayerfully to its power, and cling to it with all our might. Let the theologians ponder and debate. Their work is important; but, in the everyday world, we need to "taste Jesus in a good, hard rain"—as well as in our neighbors and in all things ordinary and everyday. The resurrection isn't a nut to be cracked, it's an experience to be had. It isn't a problem to solve, it's a reality to love and embrace.

When we pray the first glorious mystery, we quietly celebrate not only the mystery at the heart of our faith, but the mystery at the heart of the universe. The essence of the resurrection is that it is profound to the point of absolute simplicity. And so, one of the best responses we can make to the mystery of the resurrection of Christ and the mystery of our own resurrection—our share in his resurrection—is to pray from a faith-filled heart an Our Father, ten Hail Marys, and a Glory Be. In other words, we pray from the heart, not from the head—which is why the Rosary is so perfect.

2. The Ascension: Authentic Faith Keeps Us Focused on the Here and Now

Fruit of the Mystery: Hope

> After his suffering [Jesus] presented himself alive to [the apostles] by many convincing proofs, appearing to them during forty days and speaking about the kingdom of God. While staying with them, he ordered them not to leave Jerusalem, but to wait there for the promise of the Father. "This," he said, "is what you have heard from me; for John baptized with water, but you will be baptized with the Holy Spirit not many days from now."
>
> So when they had come together, they asked him, "Lord, is this the time when you will restore the kingdom to Israel?" He replied, "It is not for you to know the times or periods that the Father has set by his own authority. But you will receive power when the Holy Spirit has come upon you; and you will be my witnesses in Jerusalem, in all Judea and Samaria, and to the ends of the earth." When he had said this, as they were watching, he was lifted up, and a cloud took him out of their sight. While he was going and they were gazing up toward heaven, suddenly two men in white robes stood by them. They said, "Men of Galilee, why do you stand looking up toward heaven? This Jesus, who has been taken up from you into heaven, will come in the same way as you saw him go into heaven."
>
> —**Acts 1:3-11**

The second glorious mystery refers to the only account that exists for it, in the beginning of the Acts of the Apostles. We live, of course, in the era of space exploration, and we need to recognize that the traditional presentation of the ascension of Jesus into heaven relies on an archaic cosmology, or understanding, of the universe, where heaven was literally "up." The ascension narrative is not to be taken without an interpretation that fits with our modern understanding of how the universe is structured.

The point is not that Jesus "ascended" into heaven, literally, as much as that he made the transition from earth into the mystery of God's loving presence to which the word "heaven" refers. When the Acts of the Apostles states that Jesus "was lifted up, and a cloud took him out of their sight," we need to be open to the likelihood that we're reading metaphors meant to communicate the truth that Jesus truly did "go," as it were, from this world to the mystery called "heaven." Also, we need to understand that heaven isn't a place; rather, heaven is, more accurately, a state of being.

The other truth communicated by this account is that Jesus made the transition from earth to heaven under his own power, so to speak. Whereas Mary (as we shall see) was "assumed" by God into heaven, Jesus "ascended," himself, with no need of his Father's assistance.

Some theologians suggest that the resurrection and ascension of Jesus are actually two facets of the same event, with some passage of time between the two. Be this as it may, the author of the Gospel of Luke and the Acts of the Apostles—scholarly consensus attributes both documents to the same source—clearly believed that it was important to describe the two events separately.

One lesson we can learn from this mystery of the Rosary is

that our destiny, like that of Jesus, is not of this world. Rather, we are destined, from the moment of our creation, for bigger things that are beyond space and time. Just as Jesus "ascended" from this world, so we will pass from this world into heaven—again, whatever that may mean. In the meantime, however, we are called to focus on this world. We are not to stand around looking "up" to heaven. We are to live a life dedicated, day in and day out, to the loving service of God and neighbor.

3. The Descent of the Holy Spirit: Authentic Faith Is Open to the Holy Spirit in All Times and Places

Fruit of the Mystery: Love of God

> When the day of Pentecost had come, they were all together in one place. And suddenly from heaven there came a sound like the rush of a violent wind, and it filled the entire house where they were sitting. Divided tongues, as of fire, appeared among them, and a tongue rested on each of them. All of them were filled with the Holy Spirit and began to speak in other languages, as the Spirit gave them ability.
>
> **—Acts 2:1-4**

Once again, we rely for this mystery entirely upon a single account in the Acts of the Apostles. Acts 1:14 includes "Mary the mother of Jesus" among those who, after the ascension of Jesus, "were constantly devoting themselves to prayer." Christians naturally assume, therefore, that Mary was among those

who "were all together in one place" for the descent of the Holy Spirit on the first Pentecost.

Whether this narrative is meant to be taken as a literal account of events witnessed everyone present, or whether the author of the Acts of the Apostles used symbolic and metaphorical language to express the truth of a shared faith experience, is largely unimportant. Either way, the point is that a profound transformation took place among the first followers of Jesus that could only be attributed to the activity and grace of God.

From this point on, the disciples have the courage and authority to proclaim the gospel and call others into loving intimacy with the risen Lord and with the community of his followers, the church. Chapter 2 of Acts concludes with a description of a life of shared faith that Christian communities have held as an ideal ever since:

> All who believed were together and had all things in common; they would sell their possessions and goods and distribute the proceeds to all, as any had need. Day by day, as they spent much time together in the temple, they broke bread at home and ate their food with glad and generous hearts, praising God and having the goodwill of all the people. And day by day the Lord added to their number those who were being saved. (2:44-47)

Again, whether this is a literal historical description is unimportant. What matters is that it is a clear statement of the belief of the author of Luke and Acts—and, presumably, the faith community he wrote for—that faith needs to be much more than a private, personal matter.

Authentic Christian faith can't help but have an impact on a believer's lifestyle choices. Also, any who request membership in the community of faith do so in response to the presence and beckoning of Christ. Therefore, we who welcome them had better be careful about taking any credit for ourselves.

4. The Assumption of Mary: Authentic Faith Looks Forward to Having a Glorified Body

Fruit of the Mystery: Grace of a Happy Death

> We pronounce, declare, and define it to be a divinely revealed dogma: that the Immaculate Mother of God, the ever Virgin Mary, having completed the course of her earthly life, was assumed body and soul into heavenly glory.
> —**Pope Pius XII,** *Munificentissimus Deus,* **44**

Pope Pius XII promulgated his declaration on the assumption of Mary, "body and soul," into heaven, on November 1, 1950. He chose to say nothing one way or the other about whether Mary first experienced natural death or not. Regardless, the first thing we need to understand about this doctrine is that it was not a recent development. Belief among Christians in the assumption of the Blessed Virgin Mary goes back to at least the third century, and while none of the New Testament documents mention this event explicitly—or even mention belief in this event—it is by no means inconsistent with Scripture, and is even consistent with deep scriptural themes.

The first known analysis of the assumption was written by

Theoteknos, a sixth-century bishop of Jericho. His argument went like this: since the Hebrew Scriptures tell us that Elijah ascended (1 Maccabees 2:58), and that a place in heaven was prepared for the apostles, so much more likely is it that Mary, the virgin mother of Jesus, must have been assumed into heaven to a place prepared for her.

Belief in this doctrine developed, for the most part, through sermons and devotional literature, which suggested that in view of her mission as the *theotokos,* or mother of God, it made sense that Mary experienced death, but not that her body would return to the earth. She gave physical life to Christ, so it was appropriate that he would give eternal life to her body. From the thirteenth century onward, theologians such as St. Thomas Aquinas and St. Bonaventure declared that belief in the assumption of Mary was a valid belief. It is also noteworthy that the Orthodox and Eastern churches, too, have always recognized the assumption of Mary.

In other words, when Pius XII declared the assumption of Mary to be a dogma of the Catholic Church, he gave the official stamp of approval to a belief that had ancient origins and had been around for many, many centuries as a part of the church's sacred Tradition. Just as Tradition gave birth to the New Testament, so Tradition gave birth to the doctrine of the assumption of Mary. This particular glorious mystery reminds us both of Mary's assumption into heaven and of the important role of Tradition in the ongoing life of the church.

It is also worth noting that the great twentieth-century German psychologist Carl Jung, although not a Christian, was delighted when he learned of Pope Pius XII's declaration. He stated publicly that the doctrine of the assumption reflected the Catholic Church's acceptance and appreciation for the physical world.

In a very real sense, the doctrine of the assumption of Mary celebrates the destiny that all the faithful will experience—that is, an existence of risen glory. Mary shared in the destiny of the risen Christ, just as we all will. But, by virtue of her special role in the history of salvation, Mary experienced the fullness of the risen life immediately upon the conclusion of her earthly existence.

5. The Coronation of Mary as Queen of Heaven: Authentic Faith Looks to Mary as a Model

Fruit of the Mystery: Trust in Mary's Intercession

> From the ancient Christian documents, from prayers of the liturgy, from the innate piety of the Christian people, from works of art, from every side we have gathered witnesses to the regal dignity of the Virgin Mother of God; We have likewise shown that the arguments deduced by Sacred Theology from the treasure store of the faith fully confirm this truth. Such a wealth of witnesses makes up a resounding chorus which changes the sublimity of the royal dignity of the Mother of God and of men, to whom every creature is subject, who is "exalted to the heavenly throne, above the choirs of angels."
>
> —Pope Pius XII, *Ad Caeli Reginam*, 46

This mystery has been a part of the Rosary since at least the twelfth century. In 1954, Pope Pius XII added to the church's calendar the feast of the Queenship of the Blessed Virgin Mary.

The original date selected for this feast was May 31, but it was later moved to August 22, a week after the feast of the assumption. This memorial celebrates the event that is highlighted by the fifth glorious mystery of the Rosary. From a devotional perspective, it is because of Jesus' close relationship with his mother and the role she played in our salvation that she also shares in his kingship.

Christians and church documents have referred to Mary as "queen" since the fourth century. Various songs, litanies, and prayers have also called Mary "queen." The church has attributed the title of "queen" to Mary in modern times through official documents such as the Second Vatican Council's document on the church, *Lumen Gentium*: "And exalted by the Lord as Queen over all things, that she might be the more fully conformed to her Son" (59), and the 1954 encyclical of Pope Pius XII quoted above, *Ad Caeli Reginam*: "She is crowned in heavenly blessedness with the glory of a Queen" (1).

Once again, the Rosary includes an insight from sacred Tradition among the mysteries upon which it invites us to meditate. While the mystery of the assumption of Mary is an official church doctrine, solemnly established as such by an infallible papal decree, the mystery of the coronation of Mary remains firmly rooted in church documents and devotional practice as another way to venerate and honor the Blessed Virgin Mary.

What can we learn from reflecting on this particular mystery? Perhaps the main purpose of this mystery is to remind us of the great dignity of Mary. Her son is King of heaven, and so, in virtue of her special and unique role as the mother of the Lord, we call her Queen of heaven. It's as simple and as profound as that.

The Luminous Mysteries

Now prayed on Thursdays

The luminous mysteries, sometimes called the mysteries of light, are the most recent mysteries to be added to the Rosary. Pope John Paul II, in his 2002 apostolic letter *Rosarium Virginis Mariae,* pointed out that these five mysteries all come from the public ministry of Jesus in the gospels. In explaining his theological rationale for adding these mysteries to the Rosary—the first time anyone had done so in many centuries—John Paul II wrote that the mystery of Christ as a whole is a mystery of light. Indeed, the Gospel of John refers to him as the "light of the world" (8:12). The pope explains,

This truth emerges in a special way during the years of his public life, when he proclaims the Gospel of the Kingdom. In proposing to the Christian community five significant moments—"luminous" mysteries—during this phase of Christ's life, I think that the following can be fittingly singled out: (1) his Baptism in the Jordan, (2) his self-manifestation at the wedding of Cana, (3) his proclamation of the Kingdom of God, with his call to conversion, (4) his Transfiguration, and finally, (5) his institution of the Eucharist, as the sacramental expression of the Paschal Mystery. Each of these mysteries is *a revelation of the Kingdom now present in the very person of Jesus.* . . . (*Rosarium Virginis Mariae,* 21)

Although the Holy Father did not point this out, it is noteworthy, too, that the events upon which the luminous mysteries focus are all major events in the gospels that had previously not beeen part of the Rosary. The addition of these "new" Rosary mysteries brings a more complete balance to the Rosary and a more complete awareness of the public ministry of Jesus to those who pray the Rosary. By drawing the luminous mysteries from events in the gospels, Pope John Paul II also reminded the world of the centrality of the gospels as a source for any form of Christian prayer or devotion.

1. The Baptism of Jesus: Authentic Faith Is Rooted in the Grace of Baptism

Fruit of the Mystery: Openness to the Holy Spirit

> Then Jesus came from Galilee to John at the Jordan, to be baptized by him. John would have prevented him, saying, "I need to be baptized by you, and do you come to me?" But Jesus answered him, "Let it be so now; for it is proper for us in this way to fulfill all righteousness." Then he consented. And when Jesus had been baptized, just as he came up from the water, suddenly the heavens were opened to him and he saw the Spirit of God descending like a dove and alighting on him. And a voice from heaven said, "This is my Son, the Beloved, with whom I am well pleased."
> —Matthew 3:13-17

In his apostolic letter *Rosarium Virginis Mariae,* Pope John Paul II reflected briefly on each of the new luminous mysteries. Although it may not seem particularly significant at first glance, in each case where the event recalled by a mystery occurs in two or more gospels, the pope explicitly referred to this fact by adding to the reference of the chapter and verse the words "and parallels." For example, his reference to this first luminous mystery reads, "cf. Matthew 3:13-17 and parallels" (21). In other words, the Holy Father knew, and acknowledged quite openly, that there are other baptism-in-the-Jordan narratives in addition to the one in Matthew. The pope acknowledged this in a matter-of-fact way, in passing, but in doing so he reflected the mature Catholic understanding of the Scriptures and the whole modern history of Catholic Scripture scholarship, including its various scientific and historical methods. Not only does he affirm the modern history of Catholic Scripture scholarship, but by his own example he reminds all Catholics that there is nothing helpful about a naive, simplistic, or overly literal approach to the Bible. The same is true for the Rosary, which—it should be clear by now—is so deeply rooted in the Scriptures through its mysteries and its prayers.

One unique characteristic of Matthew's baptism-in-the-Jordan narrative is that it alone includes the interaction and dialogue between Jesus and John the Baptist. Of particular significance for Matthew's Jewish Christian audience is John's open acknowledgment of Jesus' superiority. At the same time, it is also significant that Jesus gently rebuffs John's objection. Jesus had no objection to accepting John's baptism, for to do so was to "fulfill all righteousness." In Matthew's gospel, this phrase meant to fulfill prophecy and act according to the requirements of moral con-

duct according to God's will. In other words, in Matthew's gospel Jesus wants to act in accord with his Jewish roots.

In Mark and Luke, as well as in Matthew, the Spirit descends like a dove, and God's voice from heaven announces Jesus' divine sonship and reveals his Father's approval of him. Notice that Matthew says that "the heavens were opened to him," which suggests that only Jesus witnessed this phenomenon, and, by extension, that only he heard the voice of God speaking. Nothing would indicate that onlookers saw or heard it.

Of course, one important purpose of the baptism-in-the-Jordan narratives in all three gospels is to witness to Jesus' deepest identity, that is, that he is the Son of God, with whom God is "well pleased." That much is common to Matthew, Mark, and Luke. As we pray this mystery of the Rosary, it reminds us of Jesus' divinity in a world where many do not believe that Jesus was divine. At the same time, we may remind ourselves that, in the gospels, context is always significant. The verses that come before and after any given saying or parable of Jesus, for example, affect how we understand that saying or parable. In Matthew's gospel, the baptism of Jesus segues right into his account of the temptation of Jesus in the desert. In effect, Matthew follows up an affirmation of Jesus' divinity with an affirmation of his humanity.

Believers sometimes tend to neglect this balance in their attitude toward Jesus, overlooking or downplaying his humanity in favor of his divinity. In a secularized culture, however, the opposite is more common, where people think of Jesus as just "a good man." In such a cultural context, therefore, it's good that the first of the luminous mysteries reminds us of Jesus' divinity.

2. The Wedding at Cana: Authentic Faith Takes All Worries and Concerns to Christ

Fruit of the Mystery: To Jesus through Mary

> On the third day there was a wedding in Cana of Galilee, and the mother of Jesus was there. Jesus and his disciples had also been invited to the wedding. When the wine gave out, the mother of Jesus said to him, "They have no wine." And Jesus said to her, "Woman, what concern is that to you and to me? My hour has not yet come." His mother said to the servants, "Do whatever he tells you." Now standing there were six stone water jars for the Jewish rites of purification, each holding twenty or thirty gallons. Jesus said to them, "Fill the jars with water." And they filled them up to the brim. He said to them, "Now draw some out, and take it to the chief steward." So they took it. When the steward tasted the water that had become wine, and did not know where it came from (though the servants who had drawn the water knew), the steward called the bridegroom and said to him, "Everyone serves the good wine first, and then the inferior wine after the guests have become drunk. But you have kept the good wine until now." Jesus did this, the first of his signs, in Cana of Galilee, and revealed his glory; and his disciples believed in him.
>
> —John 2:1-11

This second luminous mystery occurs only in the Gospel of John. As we noted earlier, one of the dominant characteristics of the fourth gospel is the way that it emphasizes and highlights the divinity of Jesus—even though it also leaves no doubt about Jesus' full and complete humanity. This conviction about Jesus' divinity shows itself in this luminous mystery when Jesus causes water to become high-quality wine. But there is much more that goes on in this wonderful narrative, and if we overlook it, we deprive ourselves of many spiritual benefits.

Notice, first, that the first person mentioned in the narrative is not Jesus, but "the mother of Jesus." The gospel then adds—as if it were an afterthought—that "Jesus and his disciples had also been invited to the wedding." The reader can't help but conclude that the main character in this narrative is Mary. Can anyone read this familiar story and not feel compelled to admit that the faith community from which it came had a special place in its heart for the mother of Jesus?

It is noteworthy, of course, that the fourth gospel never refers to the mother of Jesus by her name. Any explanation for this must remain in the realm of conjecture, of course; but, it doesn't seem unreasonable to suggest that perhaps the reason for not calling Mary by her name is that she was like a mother in the community of faith in which the Gospel of John developed. Just as a woman's children in our own time and culture are not likely to refer to her by her name, so, perhaps, in the community of John's gospel, the mother of Jesus was so beloved, and her presence so respected, that no one would ever call her by her name, especially in the third person, but would always think of and refer to her in terms of her relationship with the Lord.

Only the community of the fourth gospel preserved and passed down the story of the wedding at Cana. Perhaps this was because the account of this event came from Mary herself. And perhaps the community of the fourth gospel preserved the memory of this event because—as John 19:26-27 clearly implies—Mary stayed with John, "the beloved disciple," from the day of Jesus' crucifixion until the end of her earthly life. To repeat, this is all conjecture, but it's a reasonable possibility.

To return to our narrative, the interaction between the main characters (the mother of Jesus, Jesus himself, and his disciples) and the context (a wedding) results in some delightful, and sometimes amazing, insights. At the same time, it's important to not read into the narrative romantic or pious interpretations that the text simply doesn't support.

Without giving any prelude or description of the setting, the gospel simply says, "When the wine gave out . . ." It's almost as if it was common, or at least not unusual, at weddings in Jesus' time and culture for the wine supply to run out. Regardless, however, the main character in the story—"the mother of Jesus"—evidently notices this problem and immediately informs Jesus about it: "They have no wine." Jesus' response is the first-century Palestinian equivalent of, "Mother! What do you expect me to do about it?" Then, however, Jesus adds words—"My hour has not yet come"—that have no modern equivalent, so we find it difficult to understand what Jesus meant. Perhaps he didn't feel that the time was right to begin his public ministry. And although it may strike modern ears as somewhat disrespectful for Jesus to address his mother as "Woman," this was a normal, polite custom, so we shouldn't attribute anything negative here.

Some Catholic Scripture scholars suggest that Jesus and the Gospel of John want to show by these words that Jesus didn't go around causing miracles to happen for frivolous reasons, even for friends and family, contrary to the fanciful miracle stories in many of the apocryphal gospels. These so-called "gospels" were never accepted by the Christian faith community as divinely inspired.

The narrative continues with "his mother" apparently ignoring or overlooking Jesus' response. Addressing the servants without speaking directly to Jesus at all, Mary turns the whole situation over to him. "Do whatever he tells you," she says to the servants. This is the crucial moment in the narrative. John's gospel says nothing about why "the mother of Jesus" presents Jesus with the fact that the wine supply has been exhausted. She just does so. The gospel also does not tell us why his mother ignores Jesus' initial response. Again we are left to our conjectures.

Perhaps Mary's response to Jesus' words comes from her confidence that he will act on her compassionate concern for the newlywed couple, no matter what his personal inclination might be. Indeed, that appears to be the case, for once Mary tells the servants to do whatever he tells them, Jesus acts on his mother's concerns, rather than according to his own preferences, by causing the water in six twenty-to-thirty-gallon jars to become fine wine. The gospel comments that this was "the first of his signs," for the fourth gospel never uses the word "miracle" to describe such events. Rather, they are signs, the primary purpose of which is to reveal Jesus' "glory," that is, his divine nature, and to bring those who witness these "signs" to faith.

Meditating on this event in the context of the Rosary, we come to know more about who Mary is, about who Jesus is,

and about the nature of their relationship with each other—not only then, but now, as well. The Gospel of John is clear about this: "the mother of Jesus" has influence with her son. Although he may be inclined one way, she can incline him another way. In the Cana wedding narrative, Mary actually seems to bring to her son's attention the need to act with compassion, when he was not thinking of the need to do so. None of the gospels include a narrative of the wedding of Mary and Joseph. Still, who knows what memories Mary had from her own nuptials? She could empathize with the young couple, whereas Jesus showed no sign of doing so. Sometimes a mother needs to step in and use her influence.

Traditionally, prayer to Mary for her intercession has taken this insight quite seriously. Perhaps—countless numbers of Catholics down through the centuries may have supposed—the Lord still can be influenced by his mother when he might not otherwise be inclined to help. Some might wonder about this presumption: after all, the postresurrection church must take for granted not the Jesus of first-century Palestine—who, on occasions before his public ministry began, such as this one, may have been a bit slow on the uptake—but the risen Christ. Still, the mother-son relationship is a part of the heavenly condition that both Jesus and Mary enjoy. So, praying to Mary to intercede with Jesus for us and our concerns seems natural and understandable. Indeed, this perspective is utterly fundamental to the Rosary.

3. The Proclamation of the Kingdom: Authentic Faith Experiences God's Kingdom Now and Anticipates the Kingdom to Come

Fruit of the Mystery: Repentance and Trust in God

> [Jesus said:] "The time is fulfilled, and the kingdom of God has come near; repent, and believe in the good news."
> —Mark 1:15

This third luminous mystery fills a significant gap in the echoing of the gospel that the Rosary has always meant to do. The consensus among both Catholic and mainline Protestant New Testament scholars is that these words of Jesus, from very early in the oldest of the four gospels, gather into a nutshell the heart of Jesus' message. If you want to know the foundation of all of Jesus' preaching, teaching, and actions, you get it in this one short sentence. The problem for us, however, is that this one short sentence is not so easy for us, in the twenty-first century, to comprehend. We need to make a little effort to figure out its meaning. When we do that, however, we begin to understand just how earth shaking and life changing the gospel really is.

Let's take it one phrase at a time:

"The time is fulfilled, ..." These words resonated with meaning for Mark's earliest readers, for they knew what it meant to be waiting for so long for the coming of the Messiah. Nothing could have been more exciting than the announcement that the time of waiting was over.

"*. . . and the kingdom of God has come near; . . .*" The Greek phrase for "kingdom of God" is *basileia tou theou,* and it is a far more dynamic idea than our geographical notion of a kingdom. Sometimes the phrase is translated "reign of God," an attempt to inject into the translation some of the dynamic, active meaning of the Greek phrase. To say that the *basileia tou theou* "has come near" is to say that the personal presence of God and his infinite love have begun to permeate the universe and transform all things. In Jesus, God's own personal self has come near in a completely new way. Indeed, Jesus is the most complete manifestation possible of God's own self in history and in time and space. But to speak of the *basileia tou theou* is to give the incarnation cosmic dimensions. Now the love of God is breaking into creation in a way that is beginning to transform all things.

It is important to notice, however, the phrase "has come near." Jesus does not say that the *basileia tou theou* is here totally and completely, here and now. Rather, his words must be understood to announce the beginning of the *coming* of the kingdom of God, not its final accomplishment. Thus, Scripture scholars refer to what they call the already-but-not-yet character of the kingdom of God in time and space. Yes, the kingdom or reign of God is near and beginning to transform everything. But obviously, the final consummation of all things in Christ has not yet been completed.

"*. . . repent, . . .*" Who has never seen a sign along the side of a road urging everyone to "Repent!" The "repentance" that those who post such signs have in mind is most likely fairly straightforward: you should put your evil ways behind you and start living by the Ten Commandments.

But the word in the Greek New Testament that is behind English words such as "repentance" is *metanoia,* and it means far more than merely to "give up drinkin' and cussin' and start goin' to church on Sunday." *Metanoia* refers to transforming your life by adopting a whole new way of looking at life and at the universe. If you've been going in one direction, you need to turn around and go in the opposite direction. From now on, your perspective on yourself, your lifestyle, and your relationships with others and with the earth, our home, must be that of Christ.

Repentance means changing your lifestyle from the ground up. To paraphrase words from the Gospel of John, *metanoia* means living in and on behalf of the world, but not according to the values and ideals of the world—insofar as the world rejects the most basic values, ideals, and goals of the gospel. In other words, repentance is not for the faint of heart, and it's a lifelong project. Also, true Christian faith is not merely a source of comfort and reassurance. It is that, too, of course. But the comfort of the gospel cannot be separated from the challenges and demands of the gospel. As an old saying puts it, the gospel of Christ, to be real, must comfort the afflicted and afflict the comfortable. And if you're living in just about any of the so-called "developed" western nations, believe me, you are probably among the comfortable that the gospel of Christ should afflict.

At this point, to pay close attention to where our line of thought has been going is to find oneself puzzling over the word "gospel," which we will need to sort out in order to understand the next phrase:

"*. . . and believe in the good news.*" The Greek word *evan-*

gelion, which is sometimes translated "gospel" and sometimes translated "good news," is, like so many words in the New Testament, not easy to translate into English. Old translations sometimes used "glad tidings," which is quaint, but not particularly helpful to understanding what it really means. The "gospel" or "good news" refers to a reality that frequently we don't understand at all. What exactly is this "good news"?

At its most basic level, "gospel" refers to the news about the reality of God's love for us and for all creation, which is unconditional in the sense that our Father never withholds his love as long as we are open to receiving it. The good news about God's love for us, both collectively and individually, is inseparable from the announcement of Jesus about the arrival, already-but-not-yet, of the kingdom or reign of God—for they are one and the same reality. The kingdom of God is our Father's loving presence permeating, healing, and rescuing all. This is also the message of salvation and the news about our redemption. These are all ways of talking about the same reality—namely, God's love for us and its healing and saving effects.

Moreover, understanding and accepting this gospel are what motivate the *metanoia,* the conversion or repentance that we discussed above. The only appropriate response to the gospel is to turn away from self in order to focus more on God and neighbor.

In the context of the Rosary, this mystery reminds us of God's infinite love, which arrives and is arriving in the coming of his reign or kingdom. Consequently, this mystery is meant to touch our heart and reinvigorate our dedication to living the fullness of the Christian life, a life centered not on self, but on God and others.

4. The Transfiguration: Authentic Faith Is Aware of Its Roots

Fruit of the Mystery: Desire for Holiness

> Jesus took with him Peter and James and John, and led them up a high mountain apart, by themselves. And he was transfigured before them, and his clothes became dazzling white, such as no one on earth could bleach them. And there appeared to them Elijah with Moses, who were talking with Jesus. Then Peter said to Jesus, "Rabbi, it is good for us to be here; let us make three dwellings, one for you, one for Moses, and one for Elijah." He did not know what to say, for they were terrified. Then a cloud overshadowed them, and from the cloud there came a voice, "This is my Son, the Beloved; listen to him!" Suddenly when they looked around, they saw no one with them any more, but only Jesus.
>
> —Mark 9:2-8

If any of the mysteries of the Rosary deserves to be called "luminous," the transfiguration of Christ certainly does. This event, which appears in slightly different forms in the Gospels of Matthew, Mark, and Luke, describes an astonishing experience that Jesus shared with Peter, James, and John. Some parts of the narrative have perplexed generations of gospel scholars. For example, what is the point of Peter's apparently senseless remarks about wanting to set up "three dwellings"? Endless pious suggestions and guesses have been made about the meaning of these words. Essentially, however, this narrative reveals Jesus' deepest identity as the Son of God. The apostles hear a second time the

words "This is my Son, the Beloved; listen to him!" which God proclaimed at Jesus' baptism in the Jordan. The narrative also relates Jesus to Moses and Elijah, two of the greatest figures in the Hebrew Scriptures, making Jesus the fulfillment of everything taught by these two ancient personages, and more. For a brief moment, Peter, James, and John get a glimpse of Jesus in his final glory. One wonders if they ever reflected on this moment in the difficult days following Jesus' death.

As a mystery of the Rosary, the transfiguration event may be a good reminder to us of Jesus' divinity and of our own relationship with Judaism through the Hebrew Scriptures or Old Testament. We may find ourselves wanting to learn more about the Judaism from which Christianity emerged. And in difficult times, we can try to remember that Jesus has promised us a share in his glory, too.

5. The Institution of the Eucharist: Authentic Faith Is Devoted to the Eucharist

Fruit of the Mystery: Adoration

> For I received from the Lord what I also handed on to you, that the Lord Jesus on the night when he was betrayed took a loaf of bread, and when he had given thanks, he broke it and said, "This is my body that is for you. Do this in remembrance of me." In the same way he took the cup also, after supper, saying, "This cup is the new covenant in my blood. Do this, as often as you drink it, in remembrance of me."
>
> **—1 Corinthians 11:23-25**

The last of the luminous mysteries is particularly significant for Catholics, for whom the Eucharist carries such profound meaning. There are four accounts of this mystery in the New Testament, one in each of the Gospels of Matthew, Mark, and Luke and one in St. Paul's First Letter to the Corinthians. In fact, the institution narrative in 1 Corinthians is the oldest we have, since Scripture scholars date this letter at about twenty years older than the oldest gospel, that of Mark.

This luminous mystery affords a rich opportunity for us to deepen our appreciation for the Sacrament of the Eucharist by focusing on the meaning of the words Jesus used at the Last Supper. Catholics are familiar with the traditional words of institution used in the Mass, words that come directly from the New Testament accounts of the Last Supper. Taking the bread, Jesus says that the bread is his body; and taking the cup of wine, he says that the wine is his blood. We can gain a great deal by understanding that in Jesus' time the phrase "body and blood" was a Semitic way of saying what we would say today with words such as "whole self." In essence, Jesus' words mean, "This bread and wine are my whole self."

Catholics have understood this reality for a long time. Following the Counter-Reformation Council of Trent, in the mid-sixteenth century, only the priest received Communion from the cup; everyone else was limited to consuming the consecrated bread. Still, everyone understood that the "whole person" of Christ was present in the consecrated bread. Even today, when a person is very ill and unable to swallow the consecrated host, he or she may be given a few drops of only the consecrated wine for Communion. In either case, whether receiving only the bread or only the wine, to receive either or both is to receive the

whole Christ, "body and blood, soul and divinity," to use the traditional phrase.

Another insight that we do well to keep in mind, when it comes to understanding the Eucharist today, is that the Eucharist is an opportunity to be with the Lord Jesus as he is now—that is, in his risen state. It is the risen Lord who is present in our midst when we celebrate the Eucharist, and it is the risen Lord we receive in holy Communion. The Mass is not some mysterious, sacramental "blast from the past." Rather, the risen Lord is present among us, and it is the whole person of the risen Christ that we receive when we receive Communion—nothing more and nothing less.

It is nothing short of wonderful that, with the addition of the luminous mysteries to the Rosary by Pope John Paul II, this centuries-old prayer now includes a meditation upon, and a reminder of, the tremendous grace of the Eucharist. What an unmatchable gift! Each time we pray the luminous mysteries, we are reminded of the depth, breadth, and height of the love of Christ for all of us, present in every breath we take and every beat of our heart, and present in a very special way every time we participate in the Mass and receive holy Communion. What a tremendous privilege it is to participate in the Mass!

CHAPTER 5

GETTING DOWN TO BASICS

How to Pray the Rosary

If you've never prayed the Rosary before, this chapter will give you the basics; and, if you're returning to the Rosary after a long time away, you can use this chapter as a "refresher course." Keep in mind, though, that there are no "Rosary police" checking up on you to make sure that you're doing it "the right way." In the long run, you may pray the Rosary however you prefer to pray it. The main objective of the Rosary is the same as any method of prayer—to nourish your intimacy with the triune God and with the communion of saints in this world and the next. So whatever serves that purpose is good.

If you want to pray the Rosary in the customary manner, however, there is a traditional way to go about it. The prayers of the Rosary will be provided here, in case you don't already know them.

Because praying the Rosary involves repetitive prayer, it's a good idea to have a rosary. If you don't have a religious goods store in your area, you can find several sources on the Internet—some of which even offer free rosaries.

There are two basic ways to pray the Rosary—alone or with one or more people. If you are praying the Rosary with others, the custom is for one person to lead the group, primarily by saying the first half of each prayer and announcing each of the

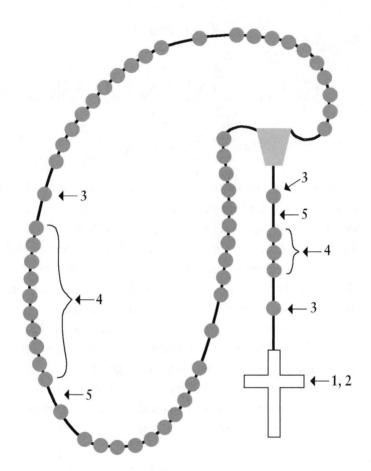

1. The Sign of the Cross
2. The Apostles' Creed
3. The Our Father
4. The Hail Mary
5. The Glory Be

mysteries. For simplicity's sake, we'll assume here that you are praying the Rosary by yourself. If you join a group, most likely many of those present will understand how to pray the Rosary as a group, so all you'll need to do is follow along. When praying the Rosary alone, you may either recite the prayers aloud or say them silently—it's up to you.

The rosary consists of six Our Father beads and five decades (sets of ten) Hail Mary Beads plus one set of three Hail Mary beads. The Apostles' Creed is said on the crucifix, and the Glory Be is said on the chain or knot after each set of Hail Marys. The Hail, Holy Queen is said at the end of the Rosary. Here's how to go about it. You may be surprised when you see how easy it really is:

Make the Sign of the Cross

You begin the Rosary by making the sign of the cross using the small crucifix on the rosary. Simply hold the crucifix on your rosary with your fingers and trace the sign of the cross on your forehead, your chest, and then your left and right shoulders while saying,

> In the name of the Father [forehead], and of the Son [chest], and of the Holy [left shoulder] Spirit [right shoulder]. Amen.

Say the Apostles' Creed

Still holding the crucifix, pray the Apostles' Creed:

I believe in God, the Father almighty, Creator of heaven and earth, and in Jesus Christ, his only Son, our Lord, who was conceived by the Holy Spirit, born of the Virgin Mary, suffered under Pontius Pilate, was crucified, died, and was buried. He descended into hell. The third day he rose again from the dead. He ascended into heaven and is seated at the right hand of the Father. From thence he shall come to judge the living and the dead. I believe in the Holy Spirit, the holy Catholic Church, the communion of saints, the forgiveness of sins, the resurrection of the body, and life everlasting. Amen.

Say the Our Father

Holding the first bead of your rosary (the bead closest to the crucifix), pray the Our Father:

Our Father, who art in heaven, hallowed be thy name. Thy kingdom come. Thy will be done, on earth as it is in heaven. Give us this day our daily bread. And forgive us our trespasses as we forgive those who trespass against us. And lead us not into temptation but deliver us from evil. Amen.

(If you came, or are coming, to Catholicism from a Protestant tradition, remember that Catholics say a doxology—"For the kingdom, and the power, and the glory are yours now and forever"—only in the context of the Mass, and then it is separated from the Our Father by a prayer said by the priest.)

Say Three Hail Marys

Next, hold each of the three beads in the next series one at a time, and pray a Hail Mary for each bead:

> Hail, Mary, full of grace,
>> the Lord is with thee (you).
>
> Blessed art thou (are you) among women,
>> and blessed is the fruit of thy (your) womb, Jesus.
>
> Holy Mary, mother of God, pray for us sinners,
>> now and at the hour of our death. Amen.

Say the Glory Be/Doxology

Holding the chain or knot that comes after the series of three Hail Mary beads, pray the Glory Be:

> Glory be to the Father,
>> and to the Son,
>> and to the Holy Spirit.
>
> As it was in the beginning,
>> it is now and ever shall be,
>> world without end. (now and forever.) Amen.

If you like, you can say the following lines at the end of each Glory Be:

O my Jesus, forgive us our sins, save us from the fires of hell, and lead all souls to heaven, especially those in most need of thy (your) mercy. Amen.

It's up to you whether you use this prayer, or not. If it appeals to you, go ahead and say it. If not, skip it.

Say the Five Decades

The next set of prayers—consisting of an Our Father, ten Hail Marys, and a Glory Be—is repeated five times, once for each mystery of the Rosary. While holding the next, single bead, announce the first mystery of the kind you are praying today—joyful, sorrowful, glorious, or luminous. For example, "The first joyful mystery, the annunciation." Theoretically, the idea is to meditate or reflect upon this mystery while praying an Our Father, ten Hail Marys, and a Glory Be. If you can do that, great. If not, don't worry about it. Personally, I suspect that the repetitive nature of the Rosary actually short-circuits conscious reflection on anything—let alone a mystery of faith—and acts something like a mantra does in the meditation methods of Zen Buddhism. The Rosary gives the fingers and tongue something to do, so that your mind and heart can "go deep," as it were, in wordless prayer.

After announcing the first mystery, and still holding the single bead, pray the Our Father. For each of the ten beads in the first

decade of the Rosary, say one Hail Mary. When you reach the chain or knot after the tenth Hail Mary bead, say one Glory Be. Then hold the next single bead, announce the next mystery, say an Our Father, say the next set of ten Hail Marys, and say another Glory Be. Do this until you finish all five decades.

Say the Hail, Holy Queen/Salve Regina

When you have completed the fifth decade of the Rosary and said the final Glory Be, say the Hail, Holy Queen:

Hail, Holy Queen, Mother of Mercy,
 our life, our sweetness, and our hope!
To thee (you) do we cry,
 poor banished children of Eve; (the children of Eve;)
to thee (you) do we send up our sighs,
 mourning and weeping
 in this vale (valley) of tears. (in this land of exile.)

Turn then, most gracious advocate,
 thine (your) eyes of mercy toward us;
and after this our exile, (lead us home at last and)
show unto us the blessed fruit
 of thy (your) womb, Jesus.
O clement, O loving, O sweet Virgin Mary.

If you wish, you may also add this final verse-and-response prayer:

V: Pray for us, O holy mother of God,
R: That we may be made worthy of the promises of Christ.

And that's it. That's all there is to praying the Rosary. After you have prayed the Rosary a few times, you'll know how easy it is. The more you pray the Rosary, however, the deeper you'll get into it and the more you'll discover its spiritual riches.

PUTTING IT INTO PRACTICE

Making the Rosary Your Own

One of the beauties of the Rosary is that no two people are going to have exactly the same experience with it: it is a personal prayer that you can adapt to the individual circumstances of your life. You may decide to pray the Rosary as it has traditionally been prayed, without any variations. Or, you may develop a fondness for a particular set of mysteries, or even substitute your own meditations for the traditional mysteries. You may decide to focus on cultivating the fruits of the mysteries while you pray; or, you may find that you can't concentrate on anything other than the prayers themselves. You may use the Rosary at particular times of the day or in particular situations, and you may even fall asleep sometimes while you're praying it. And all of that is okay! You should feel free to make the Rosary your personal prayer of devotion.

To describe all of the ways people have found to use the Rosary would take another book. But the following story by Lynn Morales should give you at least a few ideas of how the Rosary could be adapted to your life. A convert to Catholicism, Lynn started praying the Rosary only recently. For Lynn—like the rest of us—the hardest part was getting started. But once she made the effort, she found creative ways both to pray the Rosary and to fit it into her busy days. Even more, she found it

to be a source of inspiration and closeness to God. What more could any of us want?

I am a stay-at-home mom, and I've prayed the Rosary for about a year now. It has been such a blessing. I am a convert to the Catholic faith, and I used to look at the Rosary as something "too Catholic," too hard to do, and—worst of all—boring!

The blessing is that while the Rosary may seem like a rote prayer, I discovered that the more I do it, the more the Holy Spirit illuminates my faith and leads me to pray and intercede for myself, my family, and others. It has strengthened my relationship with our Lord. Every day I look forward to where the Rosary will lead me.

I try to say the Rosary after I drop my kids off at school, but the beauty of the Rosary is its flexibility. Many times I will start the Rosary in the morning and not finish it until I am in bed. Sometimes, I can just say one decade at different times of the day because I am rushing around. This calms me and reminds me to make everything a prayer.

After I drop off my children at school, I have a precious half hour for the commute home. I used to dread the ride home because I sit in traffic, but now it's my special time with the Lord and Mary. I start the Rosary right after my last child shuts the door. I always wonder if someone who sees me might think that I have rascals for children, since I always make the sign of the cross as I pull out of the school parking lot!

I dedicate the first mystery to my husband, our marriage, and my vocation as a wife. I ask the Lord to bless him as a husband and father and help me to love and serve him. After twelve years of marriage, you might think that I would have this down, but

the Rosary nudges me to love my spouse in a deeper way.

For the second mystery, I pray for my five children—especially for holiness or for a particular struggle that they are going through. If I know that they have something important happening in their lives, like a test or report due for school, I tell them that I will pray the Rosary for them. I try to remind the kids that I pray to Mary to intercede for them, so they know that I take the time to think and pray for them. Many times this leads me to new insights with my children. I hope that, in the chaos of daily life, it comforts them to know that their mom lifts them up in prayer to our Blessed Mother.

The third mystery I dedicate to my extended family and friends. I ask the Lord, Who should I pray for? I am amazed at the people who come into my thoughts as I pray. Many times I will be inspired to take action when these intentions come up.

I call the fourth mystery my "dandelion patch." Just like a lawn may have several dandelions that break up a nice landscape, I pray in the fourth mystery that the Lord will help me pull up any "dandelions" like petty grudges, judgments, or anger. I firmly believe that the Lord wants us to be "sweet soil," and that holding on to little or big grudges takes up precious room for his Holy Spirit to put down roots and grow in us. If you don't pull out the "dandelions," even if they look harmless, they will take up room and spread. For instance, I will pray for someone who has made negative comments about my children and ask the Lord to forgive my bitter feelings. Unforgiveness, anger, and bitterness take root easily—so I try to yank out these "dandelions" every day. Sometimes it seems like the same old weeds keep coming up, but with the Rosary it gets easier to spot them and remove them.

For the fifth mystery, I pray for my parish priests and for vocations. I also try to pray for our country and for wisdom for our president and his cabinet. I made a commitment that if I was praying the Rosary while I was driving, and mumbled, grumbled, or glared nastily toward other drivers, I would start the decade over. Driving in the Washington, DC, area, I have had many opportunities to start over!

There are so many different ways to pray the Rosary. On Saturdays, I do what I call a "potpourri Rosary," which means that I think about the fruit of a certain mystery and see where the Holy Spirit leads me to pray. For instance, the first joyful mystery is the annunciation, and a fruit of that mystery is "humility." I try to pray for humility for myself or for some other person who comes to mind. I love the idea that each mystery has a "fruit." When I think of fruit, I think of how nourishing it is for your body. I feel like I get nourished with fresh fruit from the Rosary every day.

The fruits of the mysteries of the Rosary are not what the world idolizes, such as intelligence, wealth, or power. For example, the fruits of the sorrowful mysteries are sorrow for sin, purity, courage, patience, and—my favorite mystery and fruit—perseverance. These fruits remind me of what is important to our Lord and his kingdom.

Another way I have started to pray the Rosary is based on the idea that there are five "p's" in the lives of mothers—prayer, person, partner, parent, and provider—as outlined in Holly Pierlot's book *A Mother's Rule of Life* (Manchester, NH: Sophia Institute Press, 2004). After I read this book, I thought I would take these five "p's" to the Rosary. So for the first mystery (*prayer*), I pray that I grow closer to our Lord in prayer, or I pray for anyone else I know, who I think needs to draw closer to him. Sometimes I ask,

Is my prayer life okay with you Lord? Am I doing too much, too little? Should I read something new?

For the second mystery (*person*), I pray that I take care of my body so I can be available for the Lord or I pray for someone else's spiritual, mental, or physical health. Sometimes my prayer is as simple as, Lord, I need a good night's sleep. Please help me get to bed early.

For the third mystery (*partner*), I pray for my spouse and that I can love and see him as our Lord does.

For the fourth mystery (*parent*), I pray for my children and for my friends' children. Many times, I will pray for my children's future spouses, especially that they will be holy and kind. Many times, I will thank the Lord just for giving me perseverance with my children, since I don't always feel successful as a parent.

For the fifth mystery (*provider*), I pray that I will fulfill my vocation as a wife and mother. With this last decade, I pray that I don't let chores around the house or other things overshadow my presence to my family. I feel so energized when I get things "done," that I sometimes neglect my family in the process. The "love-to-get-things-done" side of me sometimes would rather send out another e-mail, finish laundry, or clean the bathroom, rather than play games or read books with my children.

Like a physical workout, sometimes beginning the Rosary is the hardest part for me, but I'm always fortified when I do it. Often, I feel like I don't say the Rosary "right" because of distraction or fatigue, but I never regret praying the Rosary, even if I have to muddle through. What mother doesn't want her child to come to her? Mother Mary is always available. Discover the Rosary and see where Mary will lead you—right to Jesus, her son.

—Lynn Morales

Also from The Word Among Us Press

Item# BROSE3

The Mysteries of Christ: A Scriptural Rosary
Includes the new Mysteries of Light and reflections by Pope John Paul II

The rosary is a treasured tradition of the church, "a marvelous prayer" in the words of Pope John Paul II. *The Mysteries of Christ: A Scriptural Rosary* features pertinent Scripture verses from both the Old and New Testament for each Our Father and Hail Mary for all twenty mysteries of the rosary. Also included are excerpts from Pope John Paul II's letter *On the Rosary,* and colorful artwork illustrating each of the twenty mysteries.

112 pages, 5 x 9, softcover.